After Hours
with
P.G. Wodehouse

After Hours
with
P. G. Wodehouse

Richard Usborne

Hutchinson
LONDON SYDNEY AUCKLAND JOHANNESBURG

© Richard Usborne 1991
Preface © Sheran Hornby 1991

The right of Richard Usborne to be identified as
Author of this work has been asserted by
Richard Usborne in accordance with the Copyright,
Designs and Patents Act, 1988

This edition first published in 1991 by
Hutchinson

Random Century Group Ltd, Random Century House,
20 Vauxhall Bridge Road, London, SW1V 2SA

Random Century Australia (Pty) Ltd
20 Alfred Street, Milsons Point, Sydney NSW 2061, Australia

Random Century New Zealand Limited
PO Box 40–086, Glenfield, Auckland 10, New Zealand

Random Century South Africa (Pty) Ltd
PO Box 337, Bergvlei, 2012 South Africa

British Library Cataloguing in Publication Data
Usborne, Richard
    After hours with P.G. Wodehouse.
    1. Fiction in English. Wodehouse, P.G. (Pelham
    Grenville), 1881–1975
    I. Title
    823.912

    ISBN 0–09–174712–0

Set in Baskerville by Speedset Ltd, Ellesmere Port
Printed and bound in Great Britain by
Mackays of Chatham PLC, Chatham, Kent

Contents

Preface

Dick Usborne has asked me to write a preface to this book because Plum Wodehouse was my step-grandfather. My mother's father died when she was a baby and my grandmother later married Plum when my mother was still a young girl. They had no children of their own and Plum always regarded my mother as his daughter. He adopted her, she took his name and he adored her. He made two dedications to her. In *Leave it to Psmith* (1923) – 'To my daughter Leonora, Queen of her Species' and in *The Heart of a Goof* (1926) – perhaps having had second thoughts – 'To my daughter Leonora, without whose never failing sympathy and encouragement this book would have been finished in half the time.'

My mother died suddenly in 1944 when I was ten and my brother, Edward, was eight. On being told of her death, Plum, who had not seen her during the war years, said, 'I thought she was immortal.' So did we, her family. When I was eighteen and until they died – Plum in 1975 and Bunny in 1984 – I went regularly to New York to stay with them. We got to know each other very well, which was both fun and rewarding for me.

Plum thought that I looked like an old Chinese gangster when he saw me shortly after my birth in 1934. Eighteen years later when I first visited them, it cannot have been much fun for them to have had a well-loved but not well-known grand-daughter to stay in their New York apartment for three months. Plum had to move out of his cosy study so that I could have my own bedroom. He did this without any complaints until I decided to make up for lost time and read the Jeeves/Wooster stories in their large drawing room, where Plum was trying to write. I would scream with the uncontrolled laughter only an eighteen-year-old can produce. 'Darling, can't you be a little quieter?' 'But Plum, you wrote it, didn't you?' seemed to me at the time an unanswerable excuse.

I adored him and felt very protective towards him as the years rolled on. They moved to Remsenburg, Long Island, where Plum loved to be driven to collect the post and the newspapers from the local village. 'How well you drive!' – not exactly a compliment as my grandmother was colour blind and frequently drove through red lights.

He never carried any money and when we went out together he would check that I had some. It was my grandmother who controlled the purse strings. His relationship with her was a rare one – they were totally devoted and he depended on her to make all the decisions, down to the colour of his socks. She was a strong character with enormous charm. She was naturally gregarious yet she sacrificed her own wishes to those of Plum during the last thirty years of his life and protected him from the endless stream of visitors, who would have invaded him had she not kept them at bay. Thus he was able to continue writing without constant interruptions.

Plum was a totally lovable and kind man, he was very gentle and completely lacking in any form of worldliness: he was just like a great big cuddly teddy bear. He was not serious-minded and was invariably good-humoured, although seldom humorous in conversation. This was all the more surprising because in writing, once he had worked out his plot, he wrote his first draft pretty easily, and one might have been forgiven for thinking that he would talk humorously just as readily. Anyhow, this was not so, and furthermore, even if you were to tell or read him something which was right up his vein of humour, he still would not actually laugh but would smile and obviously enjoy it.

However, if you didn't know him, and told him something funny, he was so well-mannered that he would force himself to laugh. He would screw up his face and make a curious noise which those who knew him realised was his attempt at laughter.

Plum had a horror of meeting new people. He detested anyone who held forth at length, until he knew them well; he dreaded meeting anyone with pretensions to intellectuality or serious literary criticism. He and my grandmother hardly ever had anyone for a meal, and throughout his life it is fair to say that he hated social events. Within the family, the 'Wodehouse Glide' referred to the invariable situation which arose when

viii

some person of eminence had come to see Plum. In a matter of moments Plum, without being noticed, would have disappeared mysteriously from the room having yet again performed his famous glide. Some member of the family would then be detailed to fetch him back.

I always felt that when my brother and I went to stay with them, they loved seeing us but after a couple of days (in *Right Ho, Jeeves* considered the medium dose for an adult) of family talk, cricket, theatre, books, crosswords, dogs, etc., Plum was longing to return to his daily writing routine which he had had partially to abandon on our arrival. My grandmother once said that if you put Plum in a dog kennel with food, pen and paper he would complain if you tried to move him two days later. He was so much a creature of discipline and habit that he hated change.

One of my favourite stories about Plum concerns my great friend, the actress Elizabeth Taylor. We have known each other since childhood and in 1963 she brought Richard Burton to meet my family for the first time. The following is an extract from a letter Richard wrote to Plum, describing the scene:

'This conversation is inane,' I said. 'You all sound like characters from P. G. Wodehouse.' I pronounced 'Wodehouse' as any sensible man would, rhyming 'Wode' with 'Spode'.

'Woodhouse,' said this same Sheran, her fine face quivering with generations of good Huguenot blood, slightly perhaps inbred.

'Wode-as-in-Spode-house,' I said.

'Wood-as-in-good-house,' she said.

'What makes you so sure that it is "Wood" and not "Wode"?' I asked.

'Because he is,' she said, 'my Grandfather.'

Now there was one of those moments in time, uniquely torn from eternity, when you realize you have touched, episcopally touched, the hand that had held the hand that held the pen that hieroglyphed the page that created Beach and the Empress of Blandings and Jeeves and 'Catsmeat' Potter-Pirbright and Augustus Fink-Nottle and Wooster and 'The Great Sermon Handicap' and the only prose writer, with the exception of E. M. Forster, James Joyce,

Samuel Butler, Laurence Sterne, Robert Burton and Francis Bacon, whose prose I had committed to memory. I loved your granddaughter on the spot and pencilled her in for my third wife, should the occasion arise. The occasion hasn't arisen and isn't likely to as Sheran went off and married a Hornby (very nice, too, though a trifle tall for my 5'11").

When my husband Simon and I stayed at Remsenburg we often played bridge with my grandparents. Plum was a pretty moderate player and I have always relished the story of him, on being asked by his partner at the end of a hand why he had not played his ace earlier, replying, 'Oh, I played it as soon as I found it.' He once wrote to me that he thought it unfair that South always had the best cards in bridge columns.

As Simon and I frequently flew the Atlantic to see my grandparents, Plum often asked us about flying. 'How do I guarantee that the aeroplane will go where I want it to go, and more important still, how can I be sure that the person sitting next to me won't talk non-stop?' We replied that check-ins and boarding passes overcame the first worry and buying the seat next to him would deal with the second one. However, after the war he never travelled by aeroplane.

Dick Usborne is the acknowledged expert on Plum's work. He has written so much and so well about every aspect of this 'marvellous stuff' – one of Plum's favourite expressions about other people's work – that this collection of his articles and lectures will add enormously to our knowledge of one of our great writers. I am, of course, biased, but I am so happy to be associated with this book.

Sheran Hornby

1
At Home at Ninety

Over the years I have written, for magazines and newspapers, or for reading as talks, a number of pieces about P.G. Wodehouse and his œuvre (I promise not to use that word again). Here they are, most of them, whole or in part, brought to book. Those that I delivered as talks differ somewhat in tone from the others, but not, I hope, obtrusively enough to give you a bumpy ride.

I started to become a Wodehouse expert, not to say fanatic, not to say bore, in 1955 when Herbert Jenkins – his then English publishers – asked me to write a book about his books, to be published in 1961 at the time of his eightieth birthday. I was flattered by the request, to which I said Yes in spite of the measly terms Jenkins were offering. I was also puzzled, because I was a literary nobody and, though I hadn't then read or re-read all the Wodehouse books, I knew he was very much a Somebody. I assumed that several other somebodies had been offered the commission and had turned it down, perhaps because of the measly terms. In fact, Jenkins told me much later, Wodehouse had advised them to put me on to the job. He had been living in America since the end of the war, and he had read, and liked, my first and only book, Clubland Heroes, *a not-too-reverent study of three lesser popular writers who had enhanced my boyhood – John Buchan, 'Sapper' and Dornford Yates. It had not been Wodehouse's idea that there should now be a book assessing his place in English literature, but he had said, in effect, 'If you must, try this chap Usborne'. It would have given me confidence, and cost Jenkins nothing, if they had told me this in the first place.*

I wanted to go over to New York and talk to the man about whose books I had agreed to pontificate, but Jenkins wouldn't pay for the trip and I couldn't afford it then. So Wodehouse and I became pen- or rather typewriter-pals. He forgave and answered all the intrusive questions I fired at him: 'Did you have a lot of aunts?', 'Which do you consider your three best short stories?', 'Is there a real castle in your mind and memory when you write about Blandings?', 'Is there any connection between your fictional Jeeves and J.M. Barrie's factual mastermind manservant Thurston?' . . . and so on.

1

That fourth question was not brilliant. Wodehouse's Jeeves had appeared, though only for a few words, in a magazine story that was one of twelve in a volume titled The Man with Two Left Feet, *published by Methuen in 1917. Barrie's play,* The Admirable Crichton, *was first produced in London in 1902, but Thurston (see Cynthia Asquith's* Portrait of Barrie) *did not join Barrie till 1922, and survived him. The story-form of foolish master/clever manservant goes back at least two thousand years, to Greek and Roman comedy.*

Wodehouse was an excellent correspondent, and ultimately he was writing to me as 'Dear Dick' and signing himself 'Plum'. I never dared write to him as anything but 'Dear Mr Wodehouse', though I have come to think of him, and refer to him, as Plum.

My Wodehouse at Work *was published on time for his eightieth birthday. It was not till ten years later that, being in New York (at my own expense) on some other quest, I met Plum, for the first and last time. I had asked him if I could come to Long Island to see him, and said that, if so, I hoped he would let me write about my visit.*

He was shy, rather deaf and obstinately modest about his work. His accent was totally English, though he had lived in America for the last quarter of a century.

A longer version of this piece appeared in the Guardian *in August 1971.*

He will be ninety in October. The caricature that Ronald Searle did of him from photographs for the recent 'New Yorker' Profile gave him an Eiffel Tower neck and made him look a cheerful 100. In fact he looks a cheerful seventy, if that. The doctor is making him take pills to get his weight down, and he has recently shed a stone. He is down to 12st. 10lb. now, only a few pounds over his boxing weight at school. His trousers still feel insecure even now that he's on the tightest hole in his leather belt. His wife will find someone in Speonk to punch a new hole or two.

Wodehouse's favourite caricature of himself is the one Low did in the thirties, and a copy hangs near one of the numerous book-bulging alcoves in the house on Long Island. Low got him grinning, bald-headed, fiftyish, stoutish 'in creaseless grey bags': as it might be the jolly games-master, a Free Forester who had played for Sussex several seasons in the Hastings weeks, who had read for the Church, but had been floored by theology: that sort of chap.

Basket Neck Lane, Remsenburg, Long Island, New York. You might be in one of the boskier dells of Sunningdale or St George's Hill. The Speonk station taxi-driver had to ask her way twice. The house isn't named, but it has WODEHOUSE in big white letters on the black rubber mat outside the front door. The house is white, with scarlet shutters, standing in its own twelve acres of grounds. They bought land in every direction to ensure privacy, but forgot that corner by the road there. 'And now, dash it, they're building that house. A rich stockbroker . . . very nice people. But we ought to have made sure of that last corner.'

It is reminiscent, strongly, of Low Wood, the house they had at Le Touquet from 1935 to the day in 1940 when the Germans said 'Raus!' But Low Wood was on a golf course (see that report on Valerie Twistleton by private investigator Claude 'Mustard' Pott at the beginning of *Uncle Fred in the Springtime*). And, for variety, you should have seen the villa in the hills behind Cannes they rented in the summers mid-way between the wars: own big marble swimming pool, rows of statues and own vineyard. Very Capuan. Wodehouse could hardly hear his typewriter for the plashing of fountains.

Mrs Wodehouse bought the Basket Neck Lane house on an impulse one morning when they were staying with the Guy Boltons a mile away. She has pulled it apart and together and is still considering fresh improvements. It is cool and chintzy inside, with a small bar-room in the middle. It is very comfortable for Wodehouse: electric typewriter in the work-room – which is reminiscent, slightly, of that captain's cabin where Kipling wrote on blue foolscap at Bateman's, back to windows, eyes front, nose to grindstone: no slacker he, either – with many armchairs and sofas where, when not typing, he can flop with notebooks and pencils and pipes. Very comfortable house: for Ethel too, whose second care is the animals, four dogs, five cats, all, except the aristocratic old dachs, foundlings or strays who have looked in and, deciding the browsing and sluicing was regular and good, stayed for the duration.

Very comfortable too for Mrs Armine Wodehouse, widow of P.G.'s brother (cricketer, pianist, double first at Oxford and

Newdigate Poetry prizewinner, theosophist and teacher in India). She is a prop and pillar of the well-run house, official remembrancer, detail-tender, chore-minder, punctuality-at-meals-or-you'll-upset-the-staff-insistress. Her private Peke tends to attack the pacifist dachs and disrupt the quiet which she otherwise does so much to organise for all. A Polish maid, 9 am to 3 pm, with 'the best car in the district'. A college boy who comes twice a week to cut the grass, tend the garden, and sweep the leaves in season.

Bird-tables hang from the orchard trees, and blue jays, grey squirrels, orioles, red-wing blackbirds with vivid orange shoulders, and many others scramble for the everlasting food which Mrs Armine W. goes round topping up from buckets. A pair of bobtail quail ('I say, is that what they are? You do know a lot about birds!') walk in among the scatterings from the hanging tables, squirrels disperse blackbirds, jays dive-bomb squirrels, and all the time expensive groceries are flapped off on to the grass.

It was a hot day. Mentally I always put the endless hammocky weather of Blandings summers in the low seventies. Today on Long Island we were at least in the middle eighties before lunch, and on the patio I kept shifting the deeply upholstered armchair to keep myself in the shade. Wodehouse begged me to take my tie and coat off, and to keep them off.

'I say, what d'you make of *Punch* these days? Basil Boothroyd's book on Prince Philip . . . will that mean a knighthood for him? Guy Bolton's in London at the moment, and we may get news from him of the Jeeves musical that's been hanging fire so long. Musicals cost the earth to put on these days. They were hoping to get Derek Nimmo for Bertie in London, but *Charley Girl* proved a long-distance winner. What did you think of the Bertie/Jeeves BBC television series? I thought them awfully good. Someone wrote an article about me in a London paper saying I didn't like them. He got it all wrong. I did. No, they haven't sold in America yet. . . .

'I think that in the fifteen years we've been here, I've only slept three nights away. . . .' Ethel joined us. 'Plummie said, some years ago, that he was going to England with the Boltons. I went to Saks in New York and bought him seven pieces of new luggage, a whole set, and then he said he wasn't going. The luggage is all in the attic, never used.'

Plum continued, 'These chaps who came the other day and made me read a story into their cameras! That producer fellow. What a blighter! I hung up on him when he first telephoned. I hung up on him. I knew I didn't want to have anything to do with it. . . .'

Ethel took up the story. 'Well, then, the man phoned again within half a minute, and I had to answer it! He said "I was talking to your husband half a minute ago and got cut off. Can I speak to him again?" I said, "No, he's gone out for a walk," and he had. I said, "Can I do anything?" – and he said he wanted to come with his crew and get Plummie to read about 2,000 words of script into the cameras. So I innocently arranged a day, and Plummie wrote the 2,000 words. The crew came. The producer lay back in an armchair, with his feet on another chair, and he called me, what was it? "Baby doll". I rather liked that, being eighty-six next birthday. . . .'

'Blighter!'

'He told Plummie to start reading. First time a hammering started in that house they're building for the stockbroker there. The producer shouted "Cut!" and Plummie had to stop reading. The producer dug into his pocket and gave an assistant a handful of money. "Tell those guys to stop hammering for forty minutes!" he said, and the dollars did it. Start again, Plummie reading. Then one of our dogs started barking. "Cut!" yelled the producer. "Say, doll, can't you keep the dogs out?" So I took them off to the back quarters and shut them up. Plummie started reading again. "Cut!" This time it was me. I'd walked behind Plummie's chair and the producer didn't want me in the picture. Once again, and this time I had to cough! Poor Plummie! He was getting so tired and angry he could hardly see. "Just one more, and this time it'll be perfect!" said the producer, and this time Plummie did get through, to the end. I hurried him away from the producer and the crew and put him to bed.'

'What a blighter that fellow was!'

Russell Flint prints, a Canaletto copy, some ancestors in oils, four lovely Epstein flower paintings, originals ('the only valuable pictures we've got'). A colour photograph of an

5

English wedding group, their grand-daughter, a Cazalet, marrying a Hornby, in Kent. In the front row the Queen Mother, Princess Margaret, and others. No Plummie? 'No, he stayed home . . . felt he couldn't leave the dogs.' He has never been back to England, in fact, since the summer of 1939 when he came from Le Touquet to watch a Dulwich cricket match. He had been over just before to receive a DCL at Oxford.

'I say, what's happened to English cricket? I understand there aren't any amateurs any more. They pay people like Cowdrey? I wonder how that's arranged and how much they get. In my day the Fosters . . . I never understood how all of those brothers played first-class cricket all summer, every summer. Except Basil, of course. He was the actor. And the Gilligans and Crawleys and Ashtons. If I came back to England in the summer I wonder if I'd find cricket interesting. I love watching baseball here on the television.'

Had he seen his godson play cricket? No, silly question. In fact he hadn't even met him yet. Mike Griffith, son of Billy Griffith of Lord's and named from Wodehouse's fictional Mike Jackson: captain of Sussex cricket, international hockey cap and near-topmost rackets player.

'I say, what d'you make of the Queen asking for more money? I thought she was so rich, and with all those huge houses. . . . Have you read Alec Waugh's new book? What did you make of it? And his brother Evelyn's life at Oxford . . . in his autobiography . . . they do seem to have wasted their time there, that lot. . . . I remember coming away from a cricket match at Lord's one evening and seeing Somerset Maugham walking towards me. I thought, "O Lord, we shall stop and say 'Hullo', and have nothing more whatever to say to each other. And I bet he's thinking just the same." We both of us went down side-streets simultaneously . . . Milne, now there's a man whose books I can read. I love them.' (Milne, who wrote the beastliest letter of all in the papers about Wodehouse and those broadcasts he made from Berlin in 1941.) 'Dornford Yates' – extraordinary. Berry is a good, funny character, but I get the impression that his author was completely without a sense of humour. Fancy bringing himself in that way into *As Berry and I Were Saying*.

'Yes, I worked on *Vanity Fair* magazine in New York just after we were married. I sold them lots of things. You're right, Dorothy Parker followed me as dramatic critic on *Vanity Fair*. No, I never actually met her. I don't think I'd have liked her, would you? Those prepared *bons mots*. And she was a slacker too: any excuse not to work. Alexander Woollcott, yes, I remember him well, as a slim and very polite young man. Kaufman I knew well. He was very amusing to talk to. Robert Benchley, yes, a charming fellow. But I always thought he was slightly ashamed of being in the funny-writing business. I wonder why people feel that writing dull books about, say, Shakespeare's humour is respectable, but writing funny books themselves is *infra dig*. And those three-hour lunches at the Algonquin . . . when did those slackers ever get any work done?

'There's a new Jeeves book coming out this autumn [at last we shall learn Jeeves's Christian name], and now I'm working on a sequel to the Monty Bodkin book. Trouble is, I'm very slow these days, about 500 words a day. And I find I'm writing very *short*. A scenario section that fleshed out easily into a 5,000-word chapter of a novel before . . . now I get all the events down in 2,000 words. It's not enough. I have to go back and fill it out. . . . In the old *Globe* days in London, my first steady writing job, I had to get the whole "By the Way" column done between 10.15 and noon, six days a week. It was a discipline, you had to get it done. You learnt to skim the news and see things, well, wrong way up perhaps, for jokes. "By the Way" was a collection of jokes and bits and pieces. Some verse too.

'Jokes? What is a sense of humour? How does a joke get made in print? You ask me how . . . to express Jeeves's shock at seeing Boko Fittleworth's awful clothes, wasn't it? . . . You ask how "Jeeves clutched at a passing table" happened: had I read that misuse of words somewhere, forgotten it and reproduced it? No, I don't think so. I'm always re-reading and re-writing what I've written. You put it down straight the first time. Then you fiddle with it, change it, change it again, and it gets better.

'I much prefer writing books and short stories to writing dialogue for plays. There's no author's narrative in plays. I love writing song lyrics. I've had more than three hundred copyrighted, I think. Everybody asks me about "My Bill" which Helen Morgan eventually sang in *Show Boat*. You know, I can't remember now whether Jerry Kern wrote the music to my

7

words for that, or I wrote the words for his music. Generally with Jerry it was me writing words to his music ... Noël Coward is a great lyric writer. It seems a bit unfair for a man to write the words *and* the music. His rhymes are so good.'

I wanted to tell him about the enchanting verse, new to me, for the 'Mad About the Boy' song ... that Housman perhaps wrote 'A Shropshire Lad' about the boy. But Wodehouse seemed not to know that song, and it is easy to curb oneself from telling long jokes to the man who has put hundreds of the best into lasting print.

The Wodehouses have adopted, and been lavish angels to, a dogs' and cats' shelter and home in Speonk. Ethel drove me to see it on my way back to the station: kennels and cages for puppies and dogs, kittens and cats brought in by sad owners hoping to get them adopted; or collected as strays. A vet presides, with a girl assistant. Both in white coats. Ethel is the Lady Bountiful, bringing bones and bits and treats for them ... more than a hundred all told, and great is the barking and miaowing when she passes down the alleys. In Speonk and Remsenburg the name Wodehouse isn't widely recognised as belonging to one of the greatest humorists and busiest writers in our language. But it is known as being on the notice board: 'THE P.G. WODEHOUSE SHELTER FOR CATS AND DOGS'.

2
Honoured by Oxford

On 15th October 1981 a P.G. Wodehouse Centennial Exhibition was opened at The Pierpont Morgan Library in New York: a treasury of first editions, autograph letters, posters for Broadway shows and Hollywood films, pictures, sheet music and many other memorabilia, mostly from the great private collection amassed by the American James Heineman.[1] Ethel (Lady Wodehouse), deep in her nineties, had come in from Long Island, other members of the family from England and Italy, the British Ambassador, Sir Nicholas Henderson, and his wife from Washington, the British Ambassador to the United Nations, and 'a great many more of lesser degree, in sooth a goodly company'. In the evening, a black-tie occasion: a large dinner party, with speeches and toasts – photographers flashing – and a performance in the theatre by Edward Duke of his brilliant one-man show encompassing Bertie, Jeeves, Gussie, Florence and her ferret-faced brother, Edwin the Boy Scout.

We had hoped that Queen Elizabeth The Queen Mother, a known Wodehouse addict, would come and cut the ribbon at the Morgan. She couldn't, but she sent a goodwill message from London. It was brought over personally by Iain Sproat, then a junior minister in Mrs Thatcher's government, and it was read out at the dinner. When, in 1975, she had heard that Wodehouse, given a knighthood in the New Year's honours, was, aged ninety-three, not strong enough to come to Buckingham Palace to receive the accolade from her daughter, she had suggested going across herself to say 'Arise, Sir Pelham' or whatever it is that royalty says these days. Plum would certainly not have been able to kneel, nor Sir Pelham to rise – not with those old arthritic knees of his. But that visit too had been impossible to fit into the Queen Mother's long-prearranged schedules.

The exhibition was at the Morgan for three months, and then it came over to London's South Bank. The Queen Mother did come to the opening ceremony there, and was shown round by Jimmy Heineman himself. There was, at the South Bank, one exhibit that had not been at the Morgan – the seated wax figure of Plum from Madame Tussaud's. We put spectacles on his wax nose, and a pipe (mine) into his wax left hand. The pipe was looted, and a wax finger broken in the process, by some visitor who

9

probably now thinks he possesses a pipe that Plum had owned and smoked.

I gave the following address in the Morgan Library theatre one afternoon during the show there.

I have nothing new to say about Wodehouse, and I'm going to say it for the next half-hour, at least, of your valuable time. I had, in fact, for the purpose of this paper, picked out a single day in Wodehouse's ninety-three years: a day in which, with research, I would try to follow his movements closely. But now I find, in the splendid catalogue that Jimmy Heineman, Eileen McIlvaine and Don Bensen have put together for this splendid centenary exhibition in this splendid library, that two people have written about that exact day, in June 1939, on which Oxford University made Wodehouse into Dr Wodehouse. These two people, whose accounts you will have read in the catalogue, are Letty Grierson and the late John Hayward. They were both there, at the 1939 Encaenia at Oxford. I wasn't.

But I shall rise above such expert interference, and stick to my chosen subject, at least off and on.

Edward Gibbon, in his *Decline and Fall of the Roman Empire*, had occasionally to write frankly about sin: sins in the plural – the sins that some Roman emperors, some foreign satraps, some early Christians, and, indeed, some ladies of various courts indulged in. And when the going became too hot, Gibbon would write footnotes – these enormities were generally kept to the footnotes – in Latin. So he was able to claim at the end, 'My English text is chaste – and all licentious passages are kept in the decent obscurity of a learned language.'

At Oxford and Cambridge universities, and many other academic foundations in England, much ceremonial is still performed in 'the decent obscurity of a learned language'. The ceremonial language, written and spoken, is Latin. At Oxford certainly, the high office of Public Orator passes from one Classics professor to another, and his big moments come each summer when, in the Sheldonian Theatre, designed by Christopher Wren, the University, with considerable pomp and show, gives honorary fellowships to eminent men and, occasionally, women. The honorands, six or more of them, sit

10

in the aisle of the theatre, and the Public Orator brings them forward one at a time, raises his mortar-board and his voice, and introduces them to the Chancellor or Vice-Chancellor, who is sitting aloft – each with a panegyric of anything up to five minutes of uninterrupted Latin.

At the end of the Latin introduction from the Public Orator, each honorand mounts the steps to where the Chancellor, or Vice-Chancellor, is sitting enthroned, and he gets a few more sentences – Latin of course – from the great man, a handshake, and a parchment scroll commemorating the occasion, hand-lettered in a lot more Latin. All this to the accompaniment of much doffing of bonnets and mortar-boards, and bowing.

The Chancellor of Oxford has, for a record number of years now – twenty-one – been our one-time prime minister, Mr Harold Macmillan. He is an old, old man, but he says he enjoys the office and that nobody, by the rules, can sack him from it. He is very short-sighted, and, having been at school and Oxford a long, long time ago, he pronounces his Latin differently from what the moderns are taught. He is also very stiff in the physical joints. He was the guest of honour this year at the Gaudy at our mutual Oxford college, Balliol; a gathering for dinner of such Old Boys as could be found still alive who had come to the College before 1930. He made an extremely witty speech at the dinner on the Saturday night, slept at the Master's Lodge and, on Sunday morning, before breakfast, we found ourselves, he and I, next to each other at the altar rail in the chapel for Holy Communion. I may say I have myself, these days, difficulty enough in kneeling appropriately. But Mr Macmillan had to be helped down and up by friends, and his walking sticks – two of them – seemed to complicate rather than assist his determined genuflection.

At Encaenia in June this summer it was a task to get him up the eight steps to his throne in the Sheldonian, and then to get him turned round to face the ceremonials in the well of the theatre. One of the perquisites of the office of Chancellor is a page – he can choose a nephew, or grandson, or such to carry the train of his, and I quote, 'elaborate and distinctive robe made from heavy black brocaded silk with gold-lace trimming on the collar, facings, back and sleeves'. And a boy page – Mr Macmillan's page was dressed in a courtly outfit of black, with

11

white lace ruffles – could not be expected to hold that heavy robe up from trailing on the carpet *and* help its wearer up eight steep steps alone. It needed two strong men from among the beadles to lift Mr Macmillan to his rest aloft.

One of the honorands this year was Sir Peter Pears, the great singer for whom Benjamin Britten wrote his operas. And Sir Peter was also, in June, very wobbly on his legs. In fact he was held up on his feet by two strong sidesmen during the Orator's Latin introduction of him. But *non tali auxilio nec defensoribus istis*, one lifting him under each arm, was he able quite to get up all the steps to shake Mr Macmillan's hand. And Mr Macmillan, once aloft, couldn't descend. With a charming courtesy, and smiles on both sides, Mr Macmillan *waved* his greeting to Sir Peter, as it were forgiving him the last two steps. Sir Peter waved back, took his scroll from another's hand, and the two strong men sat him down, at last, clutching his scroll, comfortably for the rest of the ceremony.

Macmillan and Peter Pears waving to each other reminded me of the story of our General Montgomery, then in command of the Allied Eighth Army against the German general Rommel in the Western Desert. In command of Monty's New Zealand division – magnificent fighters – was General Bernard Freyberg, and Monty complained to Freyberg that his New Zealanders seemed not to have been taught to salute. Freyberg said, 'That's all right, Monty. If you wave to them, they'll wave back.' In passing – and still nothing to do with P.G. Wodehouse – New Zealander Bernard Freyberg won medals for gallantry in large numbers and in both world wars: as a young man in the 1914–18 show and as a general in the 1939–45 one. Stormed at with shot and shell, he survived, but was scarred by many wounds. There is a story that in 1917, during one of his many brief visits to hospitals as a patient, he was introduced to Queen Mary as a soldier who had been wounded in twenty places. The Queen said, 'I didn't know that a man *had* that many places.'

I read recently – it was in a letter to *Time* magazine – that when the thirteenth president of the United States, Millard Fillmore, was offered an honorary degree by Oxford, he said, 'I had not the advantage of a classical education, and no man should, in my judgement, accept a degree that he cannot read.'

Mr Albert C. Leighton, of Oswego, who wrote the letter,

ended it, a shade sententiously, I thought, 'How many honorary degrees the world would have been spared if others had followed his (the President's) example.'

Well, yes. I suppose President Fillmore had a point, though hardly strong enough, I'd have said, for its being offered to the world as a general principle. *'Don't touch any degree that you can't read. I'm saying No to Oxford. You should too if you don't understand Latin.'* Surely the document, the scroll, is not the degree. It's only a record of the occasion. Had Mr Fillmore accepted the degree, but lost the scroll afterwards, he would still have been able legitimately to sign himself 'DCL (Oxon)'. (Doctor of Civil Law: that's what they generally give to statesmen. It comes second in the list of academic precedence and standing – the first being Doctor of Divinity, and the last, or thirty-second, Bachelor of Education.) And Mr Fillmore could still have worn, if he was feeling flamboyant, and if he had bought them rather than what is usual, borrowed them off the peg, the (and I quote again) 'full scarlet robe with bell-shaped sleeves – the body made from scarlet cloth, with facings and sleeves of crimson or art silk – and a black velvet bonnet'.

Having brought President Millard Fillmore into the context of P.G. Wodehouse, I discovered that it was the autograph signature of President Fillmore, sent, at the boy's request, to fourteen-year-old J. Pierpont Morgan in 1851, that started Morgan collecting, started the whole Morgan collection: the seed from which this great library has grown. There is a lesson for us in this, I am sure.

I don't know what American income tax rules say now – let alone what they said then – but I know that the upper crust of the academic hierarchy at English universities, professors, doctors, masters and bachelors of arts and so on, must buy their first set of academic robes and cannot charge them against income tax. If such finery gets lost, stolen or worn out, they may buy replacements – and *can* charge these against tax. But I expect that, had President Fillmore accepted the honorary degree with which Oxford hoped to honour him and itself, he would have, like all transient honorands, borrowed his robes and bonnet from the store the colleges and University keep for such occasions. And he would have been expected to tip the hall porter, or beadle, or wardrobe master, or whomever, one or two guineas. The going-rate for borrowing the finery of a mere Master of Arts when I took my degree was £3. But my college gave me, and its other alumni up for their MAs, a splendid lunch, with ample sherry, claret and port – so I was well on the right side of the ledger. President Fillmore would, in his earlier day, have been wined, lunched and dined sumptuously, to say nothing of a garden-party tea, given by the Chancellor or Vice-Chancellor, usually in the grounds of his own college and, for this . . . I quote yet again, 'members of the University' (of which for the time President Fillmore would have counted as one) 'wear full academic dress, with the exception that, by custom, ordinary ties may be worn instead of white bow ties.' Relaxed, you see; ordinary ties instead of white bow ties with your scarlet robe and bell-shaped sleeves of crimson silk. What a permissive society Oxford is!

In the summer of 1939, as Letty Grierson and the late John Hayward have told you in the catalogue, Pelham Grenville Wodehouse, who had gone straight from school into a bank, was, at the age of fifty-eight, at Oxford up before the Vice-Chancellor's throne getting what was coming to him: an honorary Doctorate of Letters. The robes he had borrowed and was wearing were even flashier than those of the Doctor of Civil Law. Wodehouse's scarlet robe had facings and sleeves of grey silk, though his hat wasn't a bonnet, but a plain mortar-board with black tassel. He had to wait in the aisle of the Sheldonian while eight other honorands, one of them Letty Grierson's father, another the American Supreme Court Justice Felix Frankfurter, received the treatment from the Public Orator. All these got their panegyrics in Latin prose, though it was liberally larded with clever quotations from the Greek and Roman poets, especially Lucretius, Lucretius being the current Public Orator's special subject. Justice Felix Frankfurter got a hexameter straight out of Lucretius, a line which started with the word *felix* and which, by the Orator's crafty addition of a single letter, produced a Latin pun of inexplicable complexity, describing the honorand as a great philosopher and advocate in the Law. I have no doubt that Dr Cyril Bailey (he was the Public Orator) read the line out with the same smile – and the same extra emphasis – as signalled the jokes in his lectures on Lucretius to us undergraduates. In the manuscripts of these

14

lectures – I saw them in his rooms – the jokes were underlined in red. He was a very good lecturer and Balliol Hall, where he gave his Lucretius lectures, was always overcrowded for him.

Back to Encaenia 1939, and Cyril Bailey, the Public Orator, speaking (again I quote, but translating from the Latin this time). 'Last, but in the opinion of the University far from least, Pelham Grenville Wodehouse: Behold a magic writer, than whom none is more expert to delight men's spirits and get them laughing . . . ' And so on for nineteen lines of Latin hexameters in the manner of Horace – though the last three words of the last line had been stolen from some verses written by none other than Julius Caesar – *the* Julius Caesar. Did you know that Julius Caesar wrote verse in Latin, and that some of it has survived? I didn't. But he did, and it has, and Doctor Cyril Bailey slotted in half a line of it most aptly to refer to Wodehouse. The foregoing eighteen and a half hexameters spoke of Bertie, and Jeeves, and Mr Mulliner, and Lord Emsworth, and his pig, and Gussie Fink-Nottle, and his newts, and Psmith. And the Latin for Psmith – in case you want to use it – is *Psmintheus* . . . at least that's the way Mr Macmillan and I would pronounce it. I wonder how Dr Bailey said it. Neither Letty Grierson nor John Hayward tells us.

I have been more than usually troubled by the *-eus* ending for classical names. At the age of five and six I sat at my mother's knee while she read me *Tanglewood Tales* and Kingsley's *Heroes*. My father being in India at the time, there was nobody to correct her pronunciation of Zeus in two syllables. At preparatory school I gradually came to accept Zeus as a single syllable, to rhyme, roughly, with goose. Then, in the Sixth at my public school, we were ordered to adopt the new pronunciation of Latin, and the master allowed no shirking of the rules in proper names. Orpheus, for instance, became *Orrp-haus* (as near as I can write it) with a cockney twang to the second syllable. One day when the headmaster was taking the Sixth a boy had to read some Virgil in which the name Orpheus occurred, and he did it Mr Irvine's way. *Orrp-haus.* The headmaster went rigid and then said, 'What did you say, boy?' '*Orrp-haus*, sir.' 'What?' '*Orrp-haus*, sir. That's the way Mr Irvine says we have to pronounce it.' The headmaster shook his bald head and said: 'I have too much respect for the ancient

Romans to think they made noises like that. Get on with your translation, boy.' Heaven knows what would become of *Psmintheus* in Mr Irvine's pronunciation.

Wodehouse in 1939 had the advantage of President Fillmore. He had had a classical education, at Dulwich College. Wodehouse (P.G.) would probably have easily won a scholarship at Oxford (where his elder brother had had a distinguished career as a scholar and poet). But by the time young P.G. came to university age, his father's pension, payable in Indian rupees, had suffered from devaluation, so that young Pelham went straight from school into the City. But forty years later he could have followed the Public Orator's panegyric without too much difficulty. Indeed, as in those days the Latin that the Orator was going to speak was printed in advance in a leaflet, Wodehouse had probably had time to read it. These days the Orator's speeches are printed beforehand, in Latin and in English translation. Wodehouse in 1939 had, for the last twenty years, given his Latin to Jeeves, but as a boy he had been a good, if idle, Latin scholar and Latin verse (he said) was his favourite subject, at which he got his best marks. Yes, standing in the aisle of the Sheldonian Theatre, the last, but not the least, to be honoured while the first seven of his company sat with their scrolls, Wodehouse would have listened in embarrassment, but in fair comprehension of what was being said. And when he went up to get the blessing and handshake of the Vice-Chancellor (the Chancellor had not been able to attend) on his throne, he was meeting again the admirer who had put his name up for the honours and with whom he, Wodehouse, was anyway staying the night – at the President's Lodgings in Magdalen – the President being the Vice-Chancellor, Doctor George Gordon.

It was Gordon, an expert in the Wodehouse books, who had briefed Cyril Bailey, the Public Orator, in what he should say (in Latin) about Wodehouse in introducing him to *him*, the Vice-Chancellor, as an excellent man to be given a Doctorate of Letters. Cyril Bailey was, more permanently if less spectacularly, a Classics don at Balliol and he was my tutor for what was called Honour Moderations. He was a charming, quiet, gentle man, and many a Sunday lunch or tea I had at his house which overlooked the College playing fields. No invitation was needed for Sunday tea, but for lunch he sent you a printed card saying that Gemma and Cyril Bailey hoped you could come on such and such a Sunday at such and such a time. And, printed at the bottom of the card was an iambic of three very long words in ancient Greek 'Come in whatever clothes you like'. Dear Gemma, Cyril Bailey's wife, daughter of a bishop, had been his pupil once, I think. She was extremely deaf and she put a sounding box between herself and you when you were sitting next to her. Rather formidable. It seemed to say, not so much 'Speak into this' as 'You've got to talk to me, and it had better be worth listening to because all the table will hear you roaring into this hearing aid.'

In 1955, when I was beginning to work on *Wodehouse at Work*, I went to see Cyril Bailey, well into his eighties then, to get him to recall what he could of the 1939 Encaenia. He was retired, living in a cottage in a village near Oxford. Gemma, deafer than ever, must have been in her late seventies. Those were stringent post-war years in England – petrol was rationed and there were still some shortages of food in the shops. Certainly, for a retired don of whatever age, it was Do It Yourself – or Get Your Wife To. No servants, no car and no gardener. When I arrived, I found Gemma digging potatoes in the frost-bound garden. Cyril was wrapped in rugs in the sitting room in front of a tiny and inadequate fire. Doubtless Gemma had collected and sawn the logs that sputtered in the grate. I told Cyril, as I sat down, that I had encountered Gemma hard at work in the potato patch. He said, 'Yes, poor Gemma . . . she works so hard and I am so feeble. I found her digging in the garden once and I said to her, "Gemma, you oughtn't to be doing this heavy work," and she said, "I have to. And I do it much better because I read Latin and Greek when I was at Oxford."'

Gemma came in and made tea and toasted scones for us. I am sorry about this Christian name business. It probably sounds very casual, or presumptuous, to be calling my tutor by his Christian name, ditto his wife. But it was a habit in our college, and Cyril was very quick, the first fortnight almost, to tell you that his name – to his pupils and friends – was Cyril. And Gemma was Gemma. And it was so, for generations and generations of undergraduates at Balliol.

I asked Cyril about the 1939 Encaenia and, particularly,

about Wodehouse. As near as I can remember, Cyril said, 'Ah, yes, P.G. Wodehouse. An odd fish. I don't read him much myself, but George Gordon gave me details about him. They printed my verses about him in *The Times* next day in full – rather flattering – they didn't print any of my other introductions in full. But Wodehouse himself . . . you know, nobody could get a word out of him. I was paired with him in one of the processions, from All Souls to the Sheldonian. I suppose we were walking through the streets side by side all told for about ten minutes – and he didn't say a word. I remember asking him if he was any relation to the E.A. Wodehouse who had been a bit of a star scholar at Corpus when I was a young don. Wodehouse didn't say a word – didn't seem to hear. I later learnt, though not from Wodehouse, that this had been his elder brother. Then, at the grand dinner in Christ Church that evening (they do you very well there) we had speeches with the cigars and port, and, when the final formal speeches were over, people right the way down to the far end of the Hall began hammering with their coffee spoons and chanting, 'We want Wodehouse! We want Wodehouse!' So the Vice-Chancellor had the microphone carried down the High Table and put in front of Wodehouse. And not a word did he say. Well, yes, he shuffled to his feet, looked at the microphone as though it might have been a cobra ready to strike, murmured 'Thank you very much' into it, and sat down. An *odd fish*. Even Gordon, who rated him very high as a writer and whose guest he was at his Lodgings, told me he said practically nothing from the moment he had met him off the train at Oxford station to the moment when he put him on the train to go back to London.

In fact – or let's say 'As far as I know' – Wodehouse could never be persuaded to speak in public, make speeches, I mean. But here I must partly take back what I said about Wodehouse remaining totally silent on that visit to Oxford for his honorary degree. He himself records that he did say at least a few words, if not to his host, the President of Magdalen, then to the late Hugh Walpole, the popular English novelist. This is a passage from a letter Wodehouse wrote to his old schoolfriend Bill Townend. It is in the English book *Performing Flea*, and I expect it is also in the American version titled *Author! Author!* He, Wodehouse, is trying to comfort and advise Townend, a

18

persistent, but not very successful, writer of novels and short stories.

I'll tell you what's the whole trouble with you, Bill, and that's that you have never done anything except write the stuff, and are competing with all these birds who hang around authors' lunches and go about lecturing and presenting prizes at girls' schools. I don't think it matters in the long run, but there's no doubt that all these other fellows who shove themselves forward and suck up to the critics do get a lot of publicity, and it helps them for a while. I always think Hugh Walpole's reputation was two-thirds publicity. He was always endorsing books and speaking at lunches and so on.

I can't remember if I ever told you about meeting Hugh when I was at Oxford getting my D.Litt. I was staying with the Vice-Chancellor at Magdalen and Hugh blew in and spent the day. It was just after Hilaire Belloc had said that I was the best living English writer. It was a gag, of course, but it worried Hugh terribly. He said to me, 'Did you see what Belloc said about you?' I said I had. 'I wonder why he said that.' 'I wonder,' I said. Long silence. 'I can't imagine why he said that,' said Hugh. I said I couldn't, either. Another long silence. 'It seems such an extraordinary thing to say!' 'Most extraordinary,' I said. Long silence again. 'Ah, well,' said Hugh, having apparently found the solution, 'the old man's getting very old.'

We went for a long walk in the afternoon, and he told me that when somebody wrote a stinker about some book of his, he cried for hours. Can you imagine getting all worked up about a bad notice? I always feel about the critics that there are bound to be quite a number of them who don't like one's stuff and one just has to accept it. They don't get a sob out of me.

I never cared much for Walpole. There was a time when I seemed about to be registered as about number fourteen or something on his list of friends – did you know that he used to list all his friends in order? – but nothing came of it. He wanted me to come to Majorca with him, but I backed out and this probably shoved me down to number thirty or off the list altogether . . .

No, you remember the story – it's the only one told by Jeeves – of Bertie Wooster's visit to a girls' school and his being made to address the girls: his terror beforehand and his dismal, hilarious failure on the platform? I am sure that Wodehouse here was writing from his heart, and Bertie's terrors would have been his own. So would Gussie Fink-Nottle's terrors, when Bertie's Aunt Dahlia made him address the boys of Market Snodsbury Grammar School at their annual prizegiving. You will recall that teetotal Gussie's terrors were cured by alcohol, laced privily, and in large quantities, into his orange juice by Bertie and Jeeves.

I met Wodehouse only once, though we corresponded a good deal. I expect there are people in this gathering who knew him personally much better than I did. But I haven't heard anybody (and that includes Bill Townend and Guy Bolton themselves, his two greatest friends) claim that Wodehouse was a *merry* companion. Charming, sympathetic, generous, but never scintillating except in print via the typewriter. The history of Wodehouse the Clubman seems to bear this out. Friends in England used to put him up for their clubs, and other members, thinking, 'Wodehouse . . . yes . . . he'll keep us in stitches of laughter', supported his candidacy and he was elected; and in weeks, rather than months, he would resign politely. But I have learnt, from an exhibit in this centenary exhibition, that Wodehouse lasted at the Garrick Club at least long enough to have it printed as his address on his calling cards. But he was not a clubman in any accepted sense of the word. The London social club to which he belonged longest was one in Northumberland Avenue where he knew nobody and nobody knew him and he was able to work uninterruptedly in the library. He enjoyed the amenities of the club – warmth, service, food – but he enjoyed them all the more because he knew nobody would bother him.

But there was, and still is, one club in London – a dining club – to which Wodehouse was elected in 1930, and of which he kept his membership to the end of his life. The Other Club, so called. I was astonished to learn, only recently, that he had been a member of this very exclusive dining club. I have found no mention of it in any of his books or letters, published or unpublished. You'd have thought he would have swanked about it to *somebody*. Oh no. Not Wodehouse.

The Other Club was started, in 1910, by three friends – two future prime ministers, Winston Churchill and David Lloyd George, and a future lord chancellor, F.E. Smith, later Lord Birkenhead. There has been, since 1764 when it was founded by Sir Joshua Reynolds, the painter, and Dr Johnson, of dictionary and much other fame, a club called simply The Club. This became political rather than literary/artistic in the next century and a half, and in 1910, when Winston Churchill and F.E. Smith were proposed for membership, they were considered too rambunctious and controversial as politicians, and turned down. So they started their own club, and called it The Other Club, and they would dine once a fortnight, in a private room at the Savoy, when Parliament was in session. The membership, limited to fifty, included politicians of all persuasions, and eminent men from all walks of life and several countries. Churchill's criterion was simple – he would accept for membership anyone with whom he thought it would be his pleasure to dine. The rules of the club are read out at each dinner, and the first rule is: *The purpose of this Club is to dine.*

The last rule, which Churchill and Lord Birkenhead both claim to have composed, is: *Nothing in the rules or intercourse of the Club shall interfere with the rancour and asperity of party politics.*

When the last rule is read out, it is customary for the symposiasts to cheer.

In the sixty years since the club's foundation it has included as members six or seven prime ministers, some field marshals, admirals of the fleet, ambassadors (our ambassador in Washington, Sir Nicholas Henderson, is a member), artists, actors (Sir Laurence Olivier is a member), newspaper barons, several trade union leaders, and authors: H.G. Wells, for instance, Arnold Bennett, A.E.W. Mason, Anthony Hope and yes, P.G. Wodehouse. He was proposed by Lord Birkenhead and seconded by Anthony Hope (author of *The Prisoner of Zenda* and inventor of the country of Ruritania). Wodehouse attended his first dinner in November 1931, when Winston Churchill himself was in the chair.

Sir John Colville, who was Churchill's private secretary and became president of The Other Club, tells us something about it in his book *The Churchillians*. As you can imagine, with two such founders as Churchill and Lord Birkenhead (and here I quote Colville): 'there was heavy consumption of champagne and cigars. There was also a Betting Book, with wagers varying from the serious to the ridiculous. For instance Lord Beaverbrook laid £500 against £1,000 that he would beat Lord Birkenhead in the best of three sets at lawn tennis, Beaverbrook to receive fifteen a game.' Colville doesn't say whether this was serious or ridiculous: nor, alas, who won. It is a pleasant grace-note that ever since Churchill's death, in his memory the Savoy subsidises the dinner. The hotel gives of its best (and the Savoy's best is still the best in London) but the members pay only a fraction of what such a dinner would properly cost.

There are a few references to Churchill in Wodehouse's letters. Somewhere he said that he had met Churchill on several occasions, but Churchill never knew who he was and he couldn't think of anything to say to Churchill. I remember only one reference to Lord Birkenhead, in a Wodehouse letter, I think a letter to Townend. He said he had found himself next to Birkenhead at a dinner and asked him a few polite questions – about the Law and the House of Lords, but couldn't rouse him to conversation. Then Wodehouse said something about a rugby football match in which he had seen Birkenhead play (he would have been F.E. Smith still if he was playing football) or perhaps a long-ago school match in which they had both played, on opposite sides. This perked the great lawyer up no end – literally, no end. He never stopped talking – about rugby football and his own triumphs in it in his youth – till the end of dinner.

They do not have after-dinner speeches at The Other Club, except that, when a member dies, someone speaks a tribute to his memory. Lord Birkenhead, a fearless drinker (Otard's brandy was what he preferred, I believe), could be a brilliant after-dinner speaker. It is alleged that when the President, or Chancellor, or Mayor, or whoever the man at the Top Table in charge of a dinner was, noticed that the brandy had produced the whitening of a certain vein that pulsed near Lord Birkenhead's eye, then any other speaker of the moment should be asked to sit down. That was the moment when Lord Birkenhead should be called upon to speak: the moment when he would be at his best for what would be a memorable fifteen minutes.

As Bertie Wooster says somewhere – changing from the particular to the general – 'It just shows . . . what any Member of Parliament will tell you . . . that if you want real oratory, the preliminary noggin is essential . . . unless pie-eyed, you cannot hope to grip.'

I think Wodehouse never let his clergymen drink anything stronger than Buck-U-Uppo, did he?[2] Perhaps Otard's brandy would have improved the prospects of the congregation had it been given to that bishop at that Old School dinner which Wodehouse described, without undue reverence, in the novel *Big Money*. Do you remember it?

> At the top table, on either side of the President, were seated some twenty of the elect; and it now flashed upon him [*him* being the hero of the novel] that at least eight must be intending to make speeches. And right in the middle of them, with a nasty, vicious look in his eye, sat a bishop. Anybody who has ever attended Old Boys' dinners knows that bishops are tough stuff. They take their time, these prelates. They mouth their words and shape their periods. They roam with frightful deliberation from the grave to the gay, from the manly straightforward to the whimsically jocular. Not one of them but is good for at least twenty-five minutes.

I am still astonished that Wodehouse was elected to so political a sodality as The Other Club, and that he remained a member for the last thirty years of his life, when he lived in America and could never have gone to any of the club's revels at the Savoy. Perhaps that was *why* he let his name stay on the list?

In 1960 it was rumoured in London that Wodehouse was coming to England – I think primarily for a family wedding. A dinner of honour to its oldest living contributor was immediately arranged for him at the magazine *Punch*, and he was to carve his initials on its sacred table. Another such dinner of honour was to be given at the Garrick Club: Sir Alan Herbert (A.P. Herbert) was arranging it. And Sir John Colville told me that he had seized the opportunity and asked Wodehouse to take the chair at a dinner of The Other Club, at the Savoy. All of these occasions would have required Wodehouse to stand up and say something: perhaps a speech at the wedding too, as grand-stepfather or uncle of the bride or groom. I was not a bit surprised to hear that Wodehouse had changed his mind and had decided that he couldn't leave his dogs and cats at his home on Long Island. He never did come to England again after the war.

I have taken a long time to state a case for something that is more quickly arguable from the great body of Wodehouse's published books, the plays he collaborated in for the theatre, the films for which he wrote scripts in Hollywood. A man with that output would have to have sat more at his typewriter than in clubland's leather armchairs. He was a great worker, and, when his room was tidied up in the hospital in which he died, Lady Wodehouse found typescript and pencilled notes for a new Blandings novel and two pages of scribbles where he was composing new verses for an old song, 'Kissing Time', from one of his musical shows. He was ninety-three then: Sir Pelham Wodehouse, Knight of the British Empire, citizen of Britain and citizen of the United States of America.

I am very much honoured to have been asked to speak in this august institution. I'm afraid I haven't advanced the frontiers of anybody's knowledge of Wodehouse, the man or his books. I have not discovered the exact site in Shropshire of Blandings Castle. I have not discovered the source of Bertie Wooster's happily unearned income. In fact I have rambled self-indulgently round the subject, as, in a sense, and very attractively, the exhibition here at the Morgan Library does – the subject being Plum Wodehouse. His great friend, Guy Bolton, who became a good friend of mine in his late eighties, wrote me a long letter about something or other, in his own handwriting, near the end of his life. He apologised, at the end of the letter, for its being untidy in patches and explained, 'The fact is, I kept falling asleep whilst writing it.' There: I have been rambling again.

I will end up quoting something I have quoted before, and

may quote again. It comes at the end of one of the (now) many books entitled *P.G. Wodehouse* – this one by Owen Dudley Edwards.

When Wodehouse died, I asked a Carmelite friend of mine to remember him at mass. He replied, 'Well, I will, since you ask me. But in the case of someone who brought such joy to so many people in the course of his life, do you think it is necessary?'

Postscripts

1. James Heineman, at present a resident of New York, is the major collector of Wodehouse treasures in the United States. He also collects originals of New Yorker *cartoons – Charles Addams, James Thurber, Peter Arno, George Price and others – as well as those of Charles Schultz (*Peanuts *and* Snoopy*), Ronald Searle, Rowland Emett and David Low. By the time this is printed, he may be chasing other quarry. By then, too, the great Wodehouse bibliography that he and Eileen McIlvaine have been working on for years may be out – the last word until Vol 2 – monster, definitive, comprehensive. Every self-respecting public library should have one by now. Tri-lingual (English, French, German) from his play-pen onwards, Heineman is also producing a series of volumes of translations into an infinite number of languages, from ancient Greek to modern Icelandic, of a single Wodehouse short story, 'The Great Sermon Handicap'.*

2. I assume that Buck-U-Uppo was non-alcoholic. But the bishop and headmaster had been drinking port in the story 'Mulliner's Buck-U-Uppo' in Meet Mr Mulliner.

3
My Blandings Castle
Norfolk in film and fancy

The piece following, published in Blackwood's Magazine *in 1972, takes you back to the early 1930s and to me in my early twenties. It is much more about me than about Wodehouse, but the Wodehouse family has squirearchic roots in Norfolk.*

If you have seen Joseph Losey's film, *The Go-Between*, you will remember the great Norfolk country house which was the setting for the events of that summer month of 1900: the secret love affair between the rich man's daughter and the rustic tenant farmer on the estate; with the twelve-year-old guest, friend of the girl's young brother, acting as the lovers' messenger and, eventually and innocently, the cause of their tragedy.

In the film, and in the L.P. Hartley novel from which Harold Pinter had scripted it for Losey, the house was named Brandham Hall, and was located nearly fourteen miles from Norwich. The house they used in the film was, and is, Melton Constable Park, twenty miles from Norwich.

The film was particularly interesting to me, for two reasons: a harmony of fact and fiction. In the summer holidays of 1930 and '31 I lived in this house, employed as tutor to Simon Astley, the schoolboy younger son of Lord and Lady Hastings. And for forty years this house has, for me, had a somnambulistic, but vivid, existence as Wodehouse's Blandings Castle: a notion which happily remains with me to this day, undislodged by Wodehouse's sometimes divergent descriptions of Blandings or his location of it in Shropshire. Nor has the imprint of Melton Constable Park on the retina of my inward eye faded, even though Wodehouse himself told me in a letter that the Methuen house, Corsham, near Bath, had given him, when skating on a lake there as a boy, a profile for the later Lord Emsworth's home. I am equally unmoved by the scholarly grass-roots researcher, Colonel Norman Murphy, who, in his *In Search of Blandings*, says, 'It must be Sudeley Castle.'

My own tutor in the ways of English stately homes had, till 1930, *been* P.G. Wodehouse. I took my cues and views about the landed gentry from the Wooster/Jeeves stories and the four Blandings Castle novels that constituted the then canon. (I count *A Damsel in Distress* as a Blandings novel even though the nice old hen-pecked peer in it is named Lord Marshmoreton and the stately home is named Belpher Castle.)

I have recently, in *Burke* and *Debrett*, dug deep into the Wodehouse lineage. The name, thus spelt, first occurs in 1402, when a John Wodehouse was made Constable of Castle Rising, a Norfolk village twenty-five miles from Melton Constable. Wodehouses have married Astleys (Astley is the family name of the Barony of Hastings) for centuries. Indeed P.G. Wodehouse's elder brother shared an unusual family Christian name with a sister of the small Astley whom I tutored. The spelling of the name is slightly variable. Armine Wodehouse was P.G.'s brother. Armyne Astley was the elder of the two then unmarried daughters at Melton Constable in those two summer holidays of 1930 and '31.

Lord and Lady Hastings and their offspring were kind to me, and I involved nobody in any tragedy. But it was my first wage-earning employment, and it was the first time I had dwelt in marble halls. And, lacking the advantages of birth, wealth or previous experience, I took Wodehouse as mentor. He is the least snobbish of authors. He writes of stately home life, yes, but from the point of view of the underling and the downtrodden: the tutor, the secretary, the curate, the chorus girl – even, if you like, Lord Emsworth, downtrodden by almost all.

I admit I had problems at Melton Constable in 1930 to which no reading of Wodehouse gave unequivocal answers. Should I, a paid tutor, tip the butler when I left? (Beach had objected to Baxter leaving without crossing his palm with money. 'The great door of the castle closed with a soft but significant bang – as doors close when handled by an untipped butler' in *Leave it to Psmith*. But Baxter had been Lord Emsworth's secretary in that book. When he came back as a tutor many books later, he left in a hail of airgun pellets and he certainly did not tip Beach.) Then, which arm, left or right, does a gentleman offer to a lady to lead her in to dinner? (Beach offers his arm to Mrs Twemlow, the housekeeper, heading the procession to dinner in the Servants' Hall in *Something Fresh*. But the lazy author does not say which arm.) Does a tutor go in to dinner in front of, or after, the chaplain to the Archbishop of Canterbury? How does a tutor address a French governess? How can a tutor know, unless told, that his employer has a sensitive nose and does not like the smell of Virginian cigarettes anywhere on his premises? But even though Wodehouse evaded these issues in his books, he did give me a confidence that, with normal goodwill on both sides, my employer's and my own, I could play it by ear without disaster. Wodehouse did not let me down.

In *Something Fresh*, the first Blandings novel, Wodehouse had explored, in greater detail than elsewhere, life in the servants' quarters beyond the green baize door at Blandings. And resident staff then included a butler, a housekeeper, an under-butler, a groom of the chambers, two footmen, a head gardener, a chef, housemaids, chambermaids and kitchenmaids, a bootboy/buttons and, Lord Emsworth's bane and bugbear, Rupert Baxter. Though Melton Constable in 'my' day did not keep quite that abundance, Wodehouse gave me my bearings for my tutoring months there.

Actually it was from Wodehouse, in the Wooster/Jeeves short stories, that I had got the idea of being a holiday tutor at all. Ashe Marson, hero of *Something Fresh*, had dabbled in private tutoring and he referred to it as 'this dreadful trade'. But Bertie Wooster's friend Bingo Little was, on at least three occasions, holiday tutor to sons of the gentry: Oswald Glossop, Egbert Wickhammersley and Young Thos Gregson, Bertie's own first cousin. Bingo describes Young Thos as 'a kid who requires not education in Greek and Latin languages but a swift slosh on the base of the skull with a blackjack'. Young boys in Wodehouse are always fiends, and Aunt Agatha's son Thos was the toughest of them all. But Bingo found these tutorings restorative financially after he had suffered reverses in his investments on the turf. And, even if the boys were menaces, they generally had elder sisters with whom Bingo fell ridiculously in love.

In the summer term of 1930 at Oxford I decided that I would have to earn some money during the Long Vac. And, preferably at the same time, I would have to find peace and solitude for reading the stuff – the whole of Homer and Virgil for a start – that my college tutor expected me to have absorbed by the beginning of the pre-Christmas term. I would see if I could get a tutoring job.

My old preparatory school, Summer Fields, is just outside Oxford: a ten-minute bus ride from the Martyrs' Memorial up the Banbury Road. The new headmaster (not the old terror who used to cane me as a boy) was a friend of mine, and I told him that I was in the market for a tutoring job any vacation, especially that summer. If he had a boy for whom he was recommending to the parents holiday coaching, would he bear me in mind? He said he would.

Near the end of the university summer term, one Sunday morning in early June, I was sitting in my room in Balliol, listening to the organ of the chapel service across the front quad. I was drawing in a sketch-book. (My mother had always been keen that I should keep up my drawing.) My model that morning was a small plaster figure of a naked but decorous girl sitting on a rock: one of a pair of book-ends that as a freshman I had bought for my rooms, along with a china tobacco jar with the Balliol crest on it, and a reproduction of a Leonardo sketch. I heard some steps coming up my staircase, which was uncarpeted stone.

There was a knock on my door and, with no pause for my 'Come in', a well-dressed gentleman entered. He was of medium height. But his appearance was, for a second, forbidding. First, he had a fierce moustache. It was of a shape I associated with the glittering Guards officers who came to inspect the Charterhouse OTC when I was an awkward ranker swathed in scratchy khaki; a moustache from behind which would come an imperative bark of authority. Second, he was carrying a bowler hat. A bowler hat was almost never seen in Oxford except as part of the uniform, mandatory head-gear, of the proctors' bulldogs or 'bullers', a nightprowling pocket police-force of two, swift to capture the miscreant undergraduate and bring him back for identification and booking. Authority again.

29

For me, that Sunday morning at Oxford, the moustache and bowler hat produced, by association, a momentary smell of danger.

'Usborne? I'm Lord Hastings, y'know.'

I rose quickly and asked him to come and sit down. I wished I had not been drawing a naked girl figure at the main table. But I was thankful that I was dressed, even if she was not. And I was shaved. On some Sunday mornings at that hour I might have been still in bed. In any case it was unusual for outside visitors to walk straight up to a man's rooms in College without a previous post-card or a warning messenger sent from the Lodge.

'I've come from Summer Fields. My son Simon's there now,' continued Lord Hastings. 'The headmaster tells me you might be available to coach Simon next holidays.'

'Yes, sir. I did tell them there that I would like to be considered for tutoring jobs in my vacations.'

'Simon's a good boy, but they tell me he is a bit backward in one or two subjects, especially Latin. He must get through Common Entrance for Eton in two years' time. I want someone to take him in hand in the mornings for perhaps a month of his summer holidays. Would you consider it?'

'I certainly would, sir. What part of the holidays have you in mind?'

'I thought perhaps three weeks of August and the first one or two of September. But you've probably got plans.'

I had no plans except to play a bit of cricket in July. Lord Hastings continued, 'We live in Norfolk. I'll write to you and we'll see if we can come to a satisfactory arrangement, shall we?'

'I hope we can, sir.'

'Good. Simon's eleven now, and we don't want him to fail for Eton in 'thirty-two. His brother Edward has just finished there. I'm sure you will get on well with Simon.'

'Well, if it's Latin chiefly that he wants, I think I can do that, sir. I'm still reading Classics here.'

Lord Hastings shook me by the hand and said I was not to bother to see him down the stairs. I would be hearing from him.

Four days later I got his letter, written on very thick, white, deckle-edged cartridge writing paper, with coronet and address

30

die-stamped in red and envelope to match. The handwriting, in black ink, was characterful and clear: 'Dear Usborne, my wife and I hope that, etc, etc.' He gave me the dates, said the Summer Fields headmaster had recommended £5 a week as payment, and hoped I would agree to that. He gave me the best times of Saturday trains from King's Cross (change at Peterborough on to the Midland and Great Northern Joint Railway). I would be met at Melton Constable station. 'If you confirm that this suits you, I will write again, or get Simon to, to suggest things to bring in case you need them.' Signed 'Hastings'.

In those days I did not know how to use *Burke* and *Debrett*, and indeed wonder whether they kept them in the Balliol library. Today I learn from them that the Lord Hastings who employed me then was the twenty-first baron. The first was born in 1262, was in Parliament in 1290 and tried to become King of Scotland. One of his splendid subsidiary titles was Seneschal of Aquitaine. The Fourth Baron married the daughter of King Edward III of England. The Astleys had been Norfolk landed gentry since 1236, when Sir Thomas Astley came from Warwickshire to marry Editha, heiress daughter of Maelton the Constable, from whom the place was named. The barony lapsed in 1391 when a seventeen-year-old baron died from a wound received in tilting. The title went dormant for four hundred and fifty years. It was brought out of abeyance by a decision of the House of Lords in 1841, and thus awarded posthumously to the intervening successors. The Christian name Armine, however spelt, came into the Astley family in a marriage to a Wodehouse in 1746. A forty-year-old John Wodehouse became the first Earl of Kimberley in 1866. Kimberley is a Norfolk village, and the South African diamond town was given that name from the then Colonial Secretary, John Wodehouse, first Earl of Kimberley. The first earl's third son married the daughter of Matthew Arnold. And so on.

I managed to go up the road to my old prep school to meet young Simon before the end of the university term. And a very nice boy he seemed to be, with red hair, freckles and a great grin. He might turn out to be a fiend, but he would be a cheerful fiend. Although his father was writing to me as 'Dear Usborne', Simon instantly called me 'Dick'. He may have been prompted to do this by the headmaster, but I liked it. I said I hoped he would have all the school books his masters thought he would need in the holidays. He said he would remember to bring them home with him. Simon looked to me as though he would bear up under the yoke of holiday Latin, and French, Maths and (as they called it in Entrance Exams) Divinity, if those were required.

His father wrote to me again, giving me a run-down on clothes:

We change for dinner except on Sunday evenings. We go to church on Sundays in the morning. If you would like a game or two of cricket – and they tell me you do play a bit – bring your kit. We have estate matches on our ground most Saturdays. Bring your bathing things and a tennis racket. Lots of old clothes. You will find we live very quietly, and you will have plenty of opportunity for your own reading. We think three hours with Simon at his books in the mornings, and an hour's recreation of some sort with him in the afternoons, will be right. Saturday and Sunday will be holidays from his books, but perhaps we could ask you to keep an eye on him for periods during those days if we, his father and mother, are not here. . . .

I had visions of Wodehouse's Bingo Little, come as tutor to Honoria Glossop's kid brother Oswald in the summer holidays. In order to curry favour with Honoria, Bingo pushed the boy into the lake while he was fishing from a bridge during his 'recreation' hours. Bingo hoped that by rescuing the dear boy from a watery grave he would win the fawning thanks, love and hand in marriage of the adored object, viz. Honoria. These were the wilder shores of Wodehouse. I did not propose to behave so idiotically. On the other hand I did not at all mind the thought of this freckled, grinning boy having a few elder sisters: preferably with red hair and freckles, too. In fact he had three, one married, one soon-to-be-married and one a child with governess.

A chauffeur in a large black car met me at Melton Constable station. (In the correct Wodehouse image, the station had a single porter and about a dozen huge milk-churns on the otherwise empty platform.) We drove a mile and then up a long avenue of trees, and there was the large, three-storey house of *The Go-Between* film. It trailed off towards the stables in a long two-storey wing. The car stopped under a copper beech tree, at a small door in that wing, perhaps a hundred yards from the main block and twenty yards from the stables. The door was opened by a butler, and he had a footman with him to carry my luggage.

As I came through the front door the butler (Wodehouse was wrong; the Hastings butler was slim and dark and sinewy – Jeeves, not Beach) showed me a room just off the hall, saying, 'This is where you will work with Master Simon, sir: the Justice Room. His books are here already. I'll take you upstairs to your bedroom now, sir. Then Master Simon will come and fetch you down to tea. They are having tea on the lawn, sir.' (Wodehouse was right; the gentry did have the sort of weather for tea on the lawn. But, I thought, the butler is calling me 'Sir'; he *will* expect a tip. Keggs the butler at Belpher Castle, showed shilling-a-head visitors round the sights on one day a week. He longed to be tipped by everybody in his crocodile when he came to the end, but he found that his great stateliness tended to make visitors feel he would be insulted by a silver coin of thanks. It was one of Keggs's problems.)

Simon, in shorts and cricket shirt, came up and banged on my door. 'Can I come in, Dick?' When I had finished washing and brushing my hair, he led me down the corridor, down the stairs and out on to the lawn. There I met his father again, his beautiful, but awe-inspiring, mother for the first time, his kid sister Jean with freckles and pigtails, and Jean's Mademoiselle, whose name I never got. Thinking that 'Ma'm'selle' sounded rather forward, I used to call her 'Mademoiselle' with all four stately syllables. She spoke excellent English with a strong French accent. I learned that she had been a governess in a number of noble English families. 'When I was with Lord and Lady Brrradford . . .' was a frequent beginning for reminiscences, and the French roll to the first 'r' in her late employers' name is what remains with me now that all the anecdotes have gone. Mademoiselle was in her fifties, I guess now. She never called me anything. Simon, when he was not in my charge, seemed to be in hers.

33

The house we see, inside and out, in the film is the three-storey stately part. In the 1930s the whole of this part was kept under wraps unless there were house parties for weddings, shoots or cricket. Lord and Lady Hastings and their children and servants lived in the long two-storey 'family wing' that led off the main stately block and ended in the stables. Only once when I was at the house did they open up part of the big house. That was when an old friend of the family, the Archbishop of Canterbury, Cosmo Lang, and his chaplain came for the night. There was a large dinner party, mostly other Norfolk lords and their ladies, and, a little to my surprise, the tutor was included. We dined in white tie and tails and in the state dining room. (In the film, the room in which they ate was in fact the Hastings drawing room.) After dinner we danced to the gramophone, with the carpets rolled back, in the salon, so-called (where they had family prayers in the film). Noticing the skill and agility with which the Archbishop's chaplain performed on the dance-floor, I was reminded of one of Wodehouse's clerical stories in which a young curate, feeling yeasty because he had been offered a vicarage and his girl had said yes, gave the office in church 'with a good deal of stomp in it'.

White tie and tails. That I, a tutor, should have taken my evening tail coat, white ties and waistcoats to Melton Constable in 1930 sounds to me very odd now, and I am less inclined to curl the lip when Wodehouse, in a novel of the 1950s, has a moment when Bertie Wooster (temporarily without Jeeves, I think), dressing for dinner in a country house, considers putting on tails simply because he is feeling rather festive. In 1930 I possessed tails, and though Lord Hastings's 'We change for dinner' specifically meant black tie, tails would have been correct, if not obligatory, even for any informal country dance to which I might have been asked to go. In those days evening shirts and collars were starched anyway. So 'tails' meant the addition of a tail coat, white ties and white waistcoats to the luggage I packed. It occurs to me that I have not even possessed evening tails now for thirty years. That lot got a bomb in the London blitz, and I have never replaced them or needed to wear them.

But in spite of my correct clothes for the archiepiscopal dinner party, I was caught out in embarrassing ignorance of which arm to give a lady when taking her in to dinner. When Lady Hastings said to me, as she sorted us out to go from the salon to the dining room, 'Dick, will you take Lady I-forget-her-name in?' I ranged myself on whichever her wrong side was. Lady Hastings quickly re-ranged me and, I had no doubt at the time, my gaffe was widely noted and I was a hissing and a byword. I had never before, and have never since, taken a lady in to dinner on my arm in procession, and now I have forgotten which the correct side is.

I do not worry about my gaffe now. The agony has abated. I do not mind that, even with Wodehouse's help, I was so ignorant of so many aspects of stately home life. I do mind that I was not then more curious, that I did not keep a diary, that my memory is blank on the big things, vivid, if inaccurate, on the small.

I was ignorant about flowers and trees. Of the Melton Constable gardens I remember the landscaping and the shapes, but not the colours or contents. There must have been a covey of gardeners and gardeners' boys (there had been eleven gardeners when Lord Hastings inherited in 1904). There were, I have read, great vineries there. Where? Was that a dilapidated vinery in which, in the film, Marian Maudsley and Ted Burgess were caught in the act by Marian's mother?

The architecture of the house? I was not educated enough to be interested. The pictures and furnishings . . . they have all gone from my mind's eye. If there were Gobelin tapestries, Titians or Rembrandts, they were in the state rooms and I missed them. Were there splendid wines in the cellars? I knew nothing about wine. When Field, the butler, asked me what drink I would like brought to the Justice Room after dinner when I went there to read, I said, 'Whisky, please,' and I used to find, waiting for me, a small decanter of Scotch, the equivalent of about two doubles, with a soda-water siphon. There was no gathering before dinner for cocktails or sherry. I expect we had wine at dinner. The food? Always good and beautifully served, the footmen wearing white gloves. The butter pats were pressed with what I took to be the baronial coronet. I later learned that this was a splay of five white ostrich feathers granted to Ralph Astley when he was knighted by the Black Prince after fighting at Crécy. (He later gave up his knighthood and went into a monastery.)

Lady Hastings had a red cocker spaniel named Roy. There were hunters in the stables, but it was not the hunting season when I was there, and I knew nothing about horses or hunting. It was only the other day that I read that Lord Hastings's father had owned and bred Melton, winner of the Derby in 1885. In the 1930s Lord Hastings had, beside Melton Constable, the Vanbrugh mansion, Seaton Delaval in Northumberland, but I am sure there was no racing stable anywhere.

In my years of reading Blandings novels, old and new, with Melton Constable as its portrait in a mirror, I have idly wondered where this and that were located. Eternal summer gilds both Blandings of the books and, for me, Melton Constable of those Augusts and Septembers. But where was the pigsty? Where would Lord Ickenham have slung the hammock in which he liked to weave his plots between breakfast and lunch? Where would the Duke of Dunstable have put his deck-chair? Under which tree? In which parts of the terraces was Baxter when shot at with airguns? Was there a family spectre at Melton Constable?[1] There was at Blandings. Did Lord Hastings get his robes for coronations from the Brothers Moss,[2] as Lord Emsworth and Lord Ickenham did? Was there a public house equivalent to the Emsworth Arms at Melton Constable, with (apparently) freedom to serve its home-brewed beer, very potent, at all hours, and with a tea-garden in which people from the castle could come and hear impostors plotting? If there were fêtes, school treats and campings of the Church Lads Brigade in the park, where would the tents have risen? They lived very quietly at Melton Constable when I was there. But I was disgracefully uninquisitive, too.

A footman brought me a tray of tea and bread and butter (in the Jeeves manner) when he called me at seven a.m. Field and a second footman hovered over the sideboard at breakfast in the dining room. Breakfast was generally at eight for Simon, Jean, Mademoiselle and me. Sometimes Lord and Lady Hastings were there; sometimes Simon's two elder sisters; sometimes Edward, his elder brother. Lunch was punctually at one o'clock, and I believe it was called lunch, not luncheon. Two footmen helped Field with the serving. It was the same at dinner, even though there might be only Lord and Lady Hastings and myself dining. Sometimes, when Edward and the elder sisters were at home, they took me into the 'nursery', a pleasantly untidy room where, after dinner, Armyne played an upright piano, or we played the gramophone, or we played inexpert three-handed bridge till a reasonably late hour. But most evenings I went down to the Justice Room, to my Homer or Virgil and my small decanter of whisky. I was perfectly content either way, and managed to get a lot of Oxford reading done in the Justice Room in the late hours.

I was warned that if I heard footsteps on the gravel outside, or in the corridors inside, during the night, it would probably be Moore, the night-watchman. I did hear his footsteps, and they were a comforting sound. I never met the noctambulant Moore, who was also captain of the estate fire brigade. It seems that he wore a sort of fireman's uniform for his lonely night-watching. The horse earmarked for pulling the fire engine was the one which, with leather boots over its hoofs, pulled the lawnmower.

P.G. Wodehouse's novels had not alerted me to night-watchmen. But the novels and stories were, as I say, a good rough and ready guide to gracious living for me. And not only did I come to give Blandings a Melton Constable shape, but my wayward memory muddled things from t'other to which. At Melton Constable there was, in the main stately block, a library (it is the smoking-room in the film). During my tutoring job I once peered into the library. It was dark and leathery and cold and full of books and I do not know what I was doing in that part of the house then anyway. Until recently I believed that I had read in the papers just after the war that some great incunable, a Gutenberg Bible or a first-ever Chaucer, had been found in the library shelves here. Reading Wodehouse's *Something Fresh* again, I see that it was Lord Emsworth's fictional library at Blandings Castle that contained the Gutenberg Bible. I had unscrupulously transferred it to the factual Melton Constable library.

My memory also places in a, or the, stately dining room there two particular period pieces. A horse-shoe 'sociable' table had been designed to encompass the fireplace. The diners (and I pictured them to be all male and their dinner parties to have followed days of fox-hunting in pre-Victorian times) sat round the outer rim of the table, looking at the open log fire. All along

37

the inner rim of the table were hooks to which a net had been attached. Into this net the symposiasts had pushed their wine bottles when empty. And the huge sideboard in this dining room contained a side-cupboard in which, still, there resided a huge pewter chamber pot. And somewhere were wooden shafts which fitted under the gentlemen's chairs, so that footmen could carry the incapacitated up to bed, chairs and all.

How was Melton Constable heated in the thirties? I do not know. It was summer when I was there. Was there a museum? Was there a portrait gallery? I think neither. There were both at Blandings in *Something Fresh*, though Wodehouse seems to have forgotten them, along with the Gutenberg Bible in subsequent Blandings books. Was there a billiard room? There must have been, but where? What cars did they have? Several, but I remember none by name. Were there prize pumpkins in the kitchen garden? Was there a disused gamekeeper's cottage in the woods as (unknown, oddly, to Freddie Threepwood, son of the house) there was at Blandings? A summer house? An arbour? A bowling green? A yew alley? Probably there were all of these at Melton Constable. I have forgotten.

In the hall of the family wing, outside the Justice Room, was a table on which one was allowed to leave gloves, hats, hunting crops and letters for the post. Someone took the letters to the post twice a day, and the times of collection were marked on the box. The cloakroom under the stairs had ivory-backed masculine hairbrushes. There were Alken sporting prints on the wall as one went up the stairs to the main corridors (the family wing had attics above and servants' quarters below) leading to the main block. And along the inward side of the final corridor before the main block was a row of vast, Ali Baba-type blue-and-white Chinese porcelain urns. Lord Hastings came on Simon and me playing some mild indoor football in this corridor, with Roy the spaniel and a tennis ball, and there was a sharp explosion of disapproval; the Chinese urns were at risk.

On one side of this corridor were windows overlooking the gardens. On the other side were the family dining room, a bathroom and my bedroom. I did not have far to go for breakfast. Simon, Jean and Mademoiselle did not come to dinner. They presumably had supper earlier, in the nursery; and perhaps there the children were allowed to be grubby and to sit back in their chairs. In the dining room finger-nails had to be utterly clean, hair brushed; and never, never might an Astley back touch the back of a dining room chair. The whole family had excellently straight backs, and carried themselves like guardsmen, perhaps through this unbreakable rule about sitting up straight at meals. Compare the sad bonelessness of the owner of Blandings Castle: 'he seemed to work on a hinge somewhere in the small of his back, and people searching for something nice to say of him sometimes described him as having a scholarly stoop.'

I myself learned to be punctual, to be tidy, to sit up straight at meals and to keep my shaving things in my bedroom and not leave them in the bathroom. I regarded it as 'my' bathroom as nobody else in the family used it. But when people came to play tennis, it was the handiest for the men to wash in before tea, and men guests apparently did not like to see my toiletries there. Lord Hastings asked me to remember this, and I remembered it then and have remembered it to this day.

At the end of lunch and dinner Field or a footman brought round a silver tray on which were a silver box of Turkish cigarettes and a silver lighter with a paraffin wick alight. (I think there was a decanter of port after dinner, and that we smoked with our port.) I would never have brought out my own cigarette case at the dinner table, since the silver box of Turks was so clearly part of the ritual. But I did smoke my own in the Justice Room and elsewhere, and my own were Virginian 'gaspers'. Lord Hastings politely but firmly objected to those on about my third day in the house. He said he had a very sensitive nose, and did not like to smell anything but Turkish cigarettes, cigars or pipe tobacco in his house. He said I was welcome to smoke his cigarettes at any time – but please, no more gaspers. I sent for a box of two hundred cheap Turkish from Rothmans in London. When I left Melton Constable that summer, I had got used to smoking Turkish, but people at home objected to them as strongly as Lord Hastings had objected to gaspers, and I switched back. Next summer I took Turkish only when I went back to tutor Simon again.

To me, hardly able to remember my father and brought up by an indulgent mother, the Melton Constable parental discipline seemed strict. Whatever the children did, they had to take seriously and do well. There was no encouragement to ragging. Simon and I had a short break in our morning's work, and we ran outside to enjoy the open air. We played a mild sort of one-a-side cricket on the grass on the terrace, with an old tennis ball and a child-size bat. Simon's game was to try to hit my bowling into a certain clump of nettles so that I would sting myself in retrieving the ball. But to get it there he had to do some mighty slogging, which was not the way he would have played if he had been having lessons from professionals at Lord's. It seemed to me quite a pleasant way of getting the lungs expanded between periods in the Justice Room; but Lord Hastings decided that it was bad for Simon's cricket, and, even with a soft ball, we were required to make a lesson of it: straight bat, no cow-shots, watch the ball, no laughing.

I was asked to play cricket for the estate team one Saturday early in my stay. This I was delighted to do, and for this I had brought proper clothes and equipment as Lord Hastings had suggested. But that first Saturday, on the estate ground near the water-tower (not the cricket ground in the film – that was the ground of the nearby village, Thornage. The Melton Constable ground was ploughed up for food-growing in the war), the standard of skill of neither side was up to much, and the match had taken a cheerful knockabout turn (we were playing against a neighbouring estate, I think) when Lord and Lady Hastings came to watch. I happened to be batting then, and I was trying, and enjoyed trying, to play with the same abandon as the previous batsmen. They had sloshed about with happy cries and got out with friendly curses. I was out fairly quickly for a paltry score. I found that Lord Hastings had not liked the spirit of the game from what he had seen of it. And he made this clear to the tutor. I ought not to have swung my bat across that last shot, and anyway the estate would probably be beaten. It was.

I am able to say, truthfully, that in the next Saturday's match I played to my employer's rules and scored a great number of runs, more than I had ever in my life scored in a single innings before. Lord Hastings was pleased, and the estate side won. They would have, even if I had scored a duck.

Cricket, for me at Melton Constable, came at most once a week. I needed more activity than that to counteract the succession of good meals. I asked Lord Hastings whether he would let me go out with a gun in the afternoons to shoot pigeons. He seemed pleased at the idea, whether because the pigeons were going to be stirred up or because I would look less pasty-faced, I don't know. I wrote home asking to borrow my uncle's old hammer gun. It arrived by rail within a few days. I asked someone who was going into Norwich to buy me cartridges. After that I used to go out into the woods and fields of the estate with the gamekeeper, Vout, every afternoon. I shot pigeons and rabbits and walked miles. It must have been boring for Vout but, with the game-shooting season approaching, he may have had to inspect his boundaries, and I could have been some company in addition to his dog.

Vout showed me a poacher's trick for getting rabbits. He had a wheel of a toy train, a disc about an inch across with a hole in the middle. With this between his lips he produced a whistling noise that was very similar to the cry of a rabbit in pain or facing a stoat. Vout would take me to a rabbit warren in a wood; and there were lots of woods and lots of banks with rabbit holes in them. Then we would stand quietly and watch the holes while Vout whistled through the train-wheel. Very quickly the rabbits would appear at the mouths of their holes and look round to see where the danger was. I shot them as they moved, or even as they sat. Vout had no objection to my shooting sitting rabbits. It was his job to keep the vermin down. I much enjoyed my long tramps with Vout. I never slew much in the way of pigeons or rabbits, but it was an excellent way of getting tired and hungry to justify a good bath and a good dinner.

In September Edward, the elder son, and I were sometimes asked to go out and get a specified number of partridges for Mrs Coatsworth, the cook, to prepare for a meal. The sunset shot in the film, with the wedge of geese flying low over a hedge, was authentic. I am glad Losey liked it and got his cameramen to catch it. A flock of Canada geese had for many years regarded themselves as guests of the estate. They liked the ponds and lakes, they liked the barley fields. They were fruitful and multiplied. Farmers are not too fond of wild geese grubbing up their fields, and in 1930 word had got to Lord Hastings that the Canada geese were a nuisance. So Edward and I were instructed to shoot them if they came over while we were out for

41

partridges. We killed a few of the geese. They flew so low and so slowly that they seemed to be unsporting shots. Yet, astonishingly, we could both miss them with both barrels, and often did. There was a story that, during one of the big shooting days a year or two earlier, a skein of these Canada geese had winged low along a whole line of guns waiting for a partridge drive, and the bag of geese made by these expert shots had been prodigious. Lord Lascelles, husband of Princess Mary, had had a formation of them exactly in line as they crossed in front of him, and he had brought down eight or ten of them with two shots. Or so I remember being told, perhaps by Vout. It was for me very nostalgic seeing the geese again in the sunset in the Losey film.

The deer in the park, they were authentic too. There were Japanese sika deer, red deer, fallow deer and some small Sardinian *mouflon* sheep in the three-hundred-acre walled home park round the house. Any day of the week except Thursdays you could see them from the house, grazing, lying down, sometimes the bucks fighting. On Thursdays you could not see a deer from one end of the park to another, for on that day Lord Hastings or Edward, or both, went out to cull. It was kept to Thursdays because, with the squire using rifle and ball cartridge, the neighbours, estate hands and others had to be alerted. Everybody knew that Thursdays were deer-culling days. The deer knew it too.

On what principle the deer were culled, I do not know. The gamekeeper who looked after the deer was 'old' Colman, with a red face and mutton-chop whiskers. Doubtless he reported to Lord Hastings on the numbers of the deer and their weaklings, and on his reports the cullings were planned. On Thursday mornings, if Simon and I looked out over the park from our books, we could see Colman's pony and trap, with one or two 'rifles' (Lord Hastings and/or Edward), driving to where Colman thought the proscribed beasts were hiding. Very, very occasionally during the morning we heard a distant shot. But always on Thursdays Lord Hastings, and Edward if he was at home, came to lunch flushed and, I thought, in bad temper. I suppose they did sometimes get the deer they were after. Their morning had been a duty, not a pleasure. I never saw a dead beast; corpses were probably taken immediately to the larder.

The venison, I know, was distributed to estate servants. But I cannot remember any Thursday lunchtime when the riflemen, singly or together, appeared happy about their morning's cull. The deer are still in the park at Melton Constable. I wonder whether Losey's cameramen got their shots of them on Thursdays.

To have chimed properly with Wodehouse's novels, the lake at Melton Constable should have had an island in the middle, and the island should have had nesting and angry swans. (How often in a Wodehouse novel or short story is a man marooned on one such island because some fiendish boy has cast his boat adrift!) We bathed in the Melton Constable lake, as Ted Burgess and, later, Marian and her friends did in the film. But there was no island, no boat visible. And no swans.

We played tennis. There were three courts, two grass and one hard, at the bottom of the garden below the terrace. In one Wooster/Jeeves story Bingo Little, the tutor, is so excited about putting it across the local curate on the Woollam Chersey tennis court that he forgets his charge, Young Thos Gregson, the boy he is tutoring. And Young Thos is out marooning a pompous member of Parliament on the swan-infested island in the lake. There was no tennis-playing curate when I was tutoring Simon.

At the end of my weeks there in 1930, I left, with pleasant memories, with about £30 of pay in my pocket and with friendly farewells. I had worried about my tip to Field, the butler, and to Vout, the gamekeeper who had walked me round after rabbits and pigeons. I gave Field a pound and Vout twenty-five shillings. I had some absurd idea that they might compare tips in the Club after I had left and that, if I had given them the same amounts, Vout would think that he was hard done by, having borne the burden and heat of the afternoons – about twenty of them in all – walking me miles after things to shoot.

In the summer term of 1931 at Oxford I received a letter in an envelope I recognised, with coronet in red on the flap. But I did not know the writing. It was Lady Hastings writing to ask if I would like to repeat the visit and give Simon more coaching. So I spent another pleasant and rewarding month or more at Melton Constable. Nothing seemed to have changed. The food was as good as ever. The butter pats still had ostrich feathers on

43

them. The sun shone all the time. Simon and Jean were taller. I had brought my uncle's gun, and Vout and the pigeons and rabbits were at risk again. In 1930 I had been reading Homer and Virgil for my next Oxford examination. That past, in 1931 I was reading Plato and Kant. I was trying to be a philosopher for my finals. If I ever open any of the few books by or about Kant that remain with me from that period, and of which I never understood a word, they are memorially redolent of the Justice Room and whisky and Turkish cigarettes.

Melton Constable has passed into the same sort of haze for me as you see in the film over the deer in the park in the long shot of shimmering summer heat: Wodehouse weather. I never saw Simon again. He passed safely into Eton in 1932, and thence to Sandhurst and a career as a soldier. He married Joan, youngest daughter of Lord Wavell, Commander-in-Chief of our Middle East armies and later Viceroy of India. They had a daughter, Diana. Simon fought in the Western Desert (Mentioned in Dispatches) and in Burma, and then became ADC to his father-in-law in Delhi. In 1946 he was killed in a motor accident in Quetta. There are photographs of Simon, and of Joan Wavell, in the second volume of John Connell's *Life of Lord Wavell*.

The Lord Hastings, Simon's father, who employed me, died in 1956. In 1936 there had been celebrations at Melton Constable to mark the seven hundred years of father-to-son succession in ownership of the estate. But by 1948 the succession had to be broken. Lord Hastings found the post-World War Two costs of keeping up a house of that size in the country excessive, and staff impossible to replace. Edward, his son and heir, had bought a farm in Rhodesia, and he would keep Seaton Delaval. Melton Constable had been going to go to Simon and his family; and Simon was dead. Lord Hastings sold the Norfolk house and about four thousand acres of land to the Duke of Westminster's Grosvenor Estates company. For a period the house was occupied by a tenant. But then the Duke's company resold house and land to a farmer. The farmer has never occupied the house. He lives in one of the flats which have been made out of what was the family wing and the stables. He put an advertisement in *The Times*, offering his herd of deer for sale, because he wanted to farm the home-park acres. But he got no takers and the deer are still there.

Edward, the present Lord Hastings, has a house (much smaller and more manageable) with three thousand good farming acres of the old estate. But the home of his ancestors is empty and cold, and awaits the occasional Losey or purchase as a girls' school or institutional retirement home. Who can privately keep up a place that size, or find staff to run it, these days?

Moore, the Melton Constable night-watchman of the 1930s, is dead. He had a heart-attack while on his rounds of the corridors in the early hours of one morning during a cricket week when a number of Edward's friends from Eton days were at the house. As Moore collapsed, he fell against a grandfather clock and brought it down with him. The crash and the subsequent non-stop chiming of the clock, albeit in the small hours, woke the house, but not Moore. Tibbles, the chauffeur, died after forty-six years with the family. Mrs Coatsworth, the cook, retired after thirty years. Field, the butler, died in 1947. He had been Lord Hastings's valet before the First World War, and his batman in the trenches, where he was wounded. How can you replace that sort of loyalty?

I gathered some extra details of family, house and staff since those early days of the 1930s from Armyne, middle of the three Astley sisters. But she will not let me keep the horseshoe 'sociable' table in the dining room, or the chamberpot in the sideboard. She says there was no such table, nor chairs with slots for shafts to be pushed in so that footmen could lift drunken diners. She is sure I have been reading too many of Georgette Heyer's Regency romances.[3] The big sideboard had a cupboard for a chamberpot, as most gentlemen's sideboards had from Sheraton's period onwards; but there had been no chamberpot in the Melton Constable sideboard within accurate living memory. I wonder where I got that table from into my *inaccurate* memory. There is one like it, though smaller and without the hooks for a bottle-net, in the Jawleyford house in *Mr Sponge's Sporting Tours*. Armyne tells me, too, that the story of Lord Lascelles shooting all those geese is new to her, and thus almost certainly apocryphal.

Armyne and her elder sister shared, as girls, that bedroom at

45

the top of seventy-four stairs that Marcus Maudsley and Leo Colston shared in the film. Up those stairs all nursery meals were brought on trays by a youth known as the hall-boy. There had been no central heating in the house, and the children were allowed a fire in the grate of their bedroom only if one of them was ill. The family upbringing had indeed been strict, but Armyne has nothing but pleasant memories of the house and home life ... much more pleasant, she says, than the Maudsleys made of it in the book and film. She was married in St Peter's Church, which was the one we went to across the park on Sundays. (It is not the one the house party walked to in the film. That was the Heydon village church, six miles from Melton Constable.) St Peter's stands by itself in the park. It is nearly nine hundred years old. When it was built, it had a village round it. But after the Black Death of 1348 and the other outbreaks of plague in the fourteenth and fifteenth centuries, villages were often burnt down to destroy infection; but churches were left standing. St Peter's is one of a number of solitary churches in Norfolk.

Wodehouse, in some earlier stories and later novels, makes the great English country house, which has become impossible to heat, to staff, to sell or to rent, a hinge in the plot. Shall the impoverished owners contrive for some careless guest to burn it down and thus enable them to collect on insurance? Or shall they take paying guests, preferably Americans, paying handsomely? Or shall they, if bachelors, look for American million-airesses to marry and thus save the old home? Melton Constable, for cricket weeks and such occasions, could 'sleep fifty' as the advertisements might say. It is still windowed and watertight, and would be, at great cost, habitable. But by whom? Armyne, in a recent letter to me, says:

It had stood empty for several years before it came to life again briefly for the filming of *The Go-Between*. Now the old house has relapsed once more into silence, and dry rot is beginning to gnaw at its heart.[4]

Postscripts

1.   *Why did I say there was a family spectre at Blandings? I can't remember any such in the books now.*

2.   *His daughter Armyne later told me that her father Lord Hastings had had his own robes and had had to replace them in the 1920s when a forgetful valet had left them un-moth-proofed and unvisited in the wardrobe for more than a year. The outburst of several generations of gorged moths when Lord Hastings himself opened the wardrobe, and the trembling repentance of the valet had been one of her father's best stories.*

3.   *I still (1990) have not read a single Georgette Heyer. But Armyne's mother confirmed that I had remembered right. There had been a chamberpot in the sideboard, as stated.*

4.   *1990. Good news. The old house, with its grounds (except for the deer-park and the deer) has been bought, re-designed, largely re-built and renovated by a Norwich businessman, at an estimated cost of £1 million. Parts of it have already been rented for apartments, conferences and the occasional Elizabethan-style dinner, with wenches, syllabubs and mead. The acres of dilapidated greenhouses and hot-houses, in one of which, yes, Alan Bates and Julie Christie were caught* in flagrante *by her mother in the film, are being restored.*

4
Laughter in Church

Thelma Cazalet-Keir, sister of Peter Cazalet who married Plum's much loved stepdaughter, Leonora, edited a book, Homage to Wodehouse, *published in 1973: a collection of essays (and a poem from John Betjeman) by friends and admirers. Plum was ninety-two when he received this book, and shortly to be ninety-three and a knight. The piece that follows (I have cut a bit of it) was my offering. Other contributors were Lord David Cecil, Claud Cockburn, Henry Longhurst, Basil Boothroyd, Richard Ingrams, Malcolm Muggeridge, Guy Bolton, William Douglas Home, Compton Mackenzie and Auberon Waugh.*

Dear Mr Wodehouse,

It is a question fans and interviewers often ask authors: how do you get started? Do you wait for inspiration or write by the clock and the calendar as Trollope did? His advice was sealing-wax applied to the trousers, to keep them attached to the chair. You have given one or two evasive answers in your time – that you sharpen pencils and clean pipes; that you sit down at your typewriter and curse a bit. But then?

There is a Bentley/Chesterton clerihew:

Brahms
liked to be tickled under the arms;
but what caused Schubert to compose
was to be stroked on the nose.

Kipling said he encouraged the approach of his daemon by getting out his blue unlined foolscap paper and blackest ink.

I was reading the other day, in a book called *The Creative Process* by Brewster Ghiselin, about the ways in which certain other masters summoned their muses or turned themselves on. Tunes came to Mozart when he was travelling in a carriage, or

48

walking after a good meal, or when he couldn't sleep. He hummed them to himself, and when it came to writing them down at his desk, that was easy, because by then everything was finished. Coleridge dreamed up two to three hundred lines of 'Kubla Khan' when, having taken an anodyne for 'a slight indisposition', he fell asleep after reading two specific sentences about the Khan Kubla in a travel book. He got fifty-four of the lines down when he woke up three hours later, but the rest disintegrated when the man from Porlock called. Well, that was Coleridge's story, though I understand it has recently been proved a fabrication.

Housman said he had seldom written poetry unless he was rather out of health, or extraneously stimulated. He might have had a pint of beer at luncheon, a walk of two or three hours to follow, and then the stuff started coming ready made: a physical process rather than an intellectual. Afternoons, he said, were the least intellectual portions of his life. Schiller liked to have rotten apples in his desk: the smell got him going. De la Mare had to smoke. Auden has endless cups of tea. Spender needs coffee and cigarettes: sometimes he finds he has three cigarettes alight at the same time.

What are your rotten apples, Mr Wodehouse? I have known a number of the *Punch* writers and artists of the last thirty years. Their vague answer to this question, 'How do you find your jokes?', is 'Controlled wool-gathering'. Well, yes. But what starts the wool-gathering? James Thurber, I believe, sometimes went silent and distant during dinner parties, and his wife would shout down the table to him, 'Stop writing, Thurber!' But what had started him writing?

But, before I forget, an instant change of subject. One of the clichés of adventure-story writers that obviously amused you was 'was the work of an instant'. You bring it into gentle disrepute from time to time. I found rather a fine specimen of it recently, in an English translation of the *Memoirs* of Eugène Vidocq, that French crook-turned-cop (1775–1857).

... in the earnestness of my grasp we both rolled on the passage floor, onto which I had pulled him: to rise, snatch from his hands the shoemaker's cutting knife with which he had armed himself, to bind him, and lead him out of the house, was the work of an instant . . .

C'était l'affaire d'un instant would, I am assured, be the French original.

But to more serious things. What about that girl Angelica Briscoe, the parson's daughter in your story 'Tried in the Furnace'? I don't know when you wrote the story: *Young Men in Spats*, in which it is collected, was published in 1936. But I put it to you that a real parson's daughter was the model for Angelica Briscoe, and that you, in your tempestuous teens or torrid early twenties, had been in love with her, as Pongo and Barmy were in the story. I also guess you would have sent her the story when it was published, as a fond retrospective tease, if you had only known what had become of the girl. Speak up, please. Am I right?[1]

You don't bring Angelica on stage much. She is a short vision in the grocer's shop ordering five pounds of streaky bacon at the beginning, and a voice-off in the car outside the pub later. But she and her cousin (to whom she was engaged all the time, as the barmaid could have told Barmy and Pongo) pulled some very raw work on those two rusticated Dronesmen: the Mothers' Outing on one, the School Treat on the other.

Their love for Angelica died. Pongo listed her failings, and ended with '. . . in a word, a parson's daughter. If you want to know the secret of a happy and successful life, Barmy, old man, it is this: keep away from parsons' daughters.'

Am I right about Angelica Briscoe? Was there such a girl in your heart once? Did you meet a parson's daughter buying streaky bacon for the vicarage, and did it occur to you (and go into your notebook immediately) that one of the advantages that a Dronesman might have in marrying into the Church was expressible in this bit of eventual dialogue:

> Pongo ate a piece of cheese in a meditative manner. He seemed to be pursuing some train of thought.
> 'I should think,' he said, 'that a fellow who married a clergyman's daughter would get the ceremony performed at cut rates, wouldn't he?'
> 'Probably.'

50

'If not absolutely on the nod?'

'I shouldn't wonder.'

'Not,' said Pongo 'that I am influenced by any consideration like that, of course. My love is pure and flamelike, with no taint of dross. Still, in times like these, every little helps.'

'Quite,' said Barmy. 'Quite.'

In a short story a Drones character says of a girl with whom Freddie Widgeon has been disastrously in love:

You needn't let it get about, of course, but that girl, to my certain knowledge, plays the organ in the local church and may often be seen taking soup to the deserving villagers with many a gracious word.

The Rev. Anselm Mulliner at one moment says to his fiancée, Myrtle Jellaby, 'I have a Mothers' Meeting at six,' and Myrtle says, 'And I have to take a few pints of soup to the deserving poor. Amazing the way these bimbos absorb soup. Like sponges.'

And Stiffy Byng, in *Stiff Upper Lip, Jeeves*, gets excited at the pre-vision of herself as the perfect vicar's perfect wife, 'doling out soup to the deserving poor and asking in a gentle voice after their rheumatism'.

I think that to you this soup-for-the-poor picture was one you took with affection and mild mockery from Trollope, Dickens and the sort of novelette serials that appeared in those bound copies of parish and Sundayish magazines that you found in your clerical uncles' libraries in the holidays.

But Ursula Bloom, whose father was a country parson, wrote in a book about him that she remembered taking soup out herself to the poor at their gates. Which, for me, chimes with the idea suggested by that hymn

> . . . the rich man in his castle,
> the poor man at his gate . . .

i.e. that the poor didn't come to the house, like tradesmen, but stayed at the gate waiting for little Miss or Mrs Bountiful to bring the soup to them through the snow. I wish you would tell us one day the exact circumstances of soup distribution for the poor in country parishes: what sort of soup, how hot, how carried through the snow. Ursula Bloom doesn't tell us much. You tell us nothing.

Have you read Cecil Woodham Smith's *The Great Hunger* about the potato famine in Ireland which peaked in 1846–8? Alexis Soyer, the famous French chef of the Reform Club, produced a recipe for a soup costing, to make, three farthings a quart, a soup which, he said, 'has been tasted by numerous noblemen, members of Parliament and several ladies . . . who have considered it very good and nourishing':

¼ lb. of leg of beef
2 oz. of dripping
2 onions and other vegetables
½ lb. flour (seconds)
½ lb. pearl barley
3 oz. salt and ½ oz. brown sugar
2 gall. water.

M. Soyer tested this concoction daily on two or three hundred of London's poor who, presumably, received it gratefully. Perhaps this recipe was in Ursula Bloom's father's vicarage and all the vicarages in your books.

I would like to ask you many questions about the background to, and breeding ground of, your literary churchmanship. You had many years of English schools and, in the holidays, I understand, stayed a lot with aunts married to country clergymen. I think I can claim close kinship with you, a generation later, in receipt of the Anglican Church message and in exposure to its devoted evangelists, in school chapel and country church. I had ten years of boarding school, with community prayers twice a day, chapel once a day and twice on Sundays, Bible-readings, Divinity classes and Latin graces before and after meals. Like Bertie Wooster, I won a Scripture prize. I sat for a scholarship to my public school primed with the 'contexts' of seven 'I have sinned' statements in the Bible.

My family – four brothers for a start – lived a stone's throw from a country church. The backstop of our tennis court was a high wall with the graveyard and vicarage garden on the other side. (To get tennis balls that had gone over, I dragged the spaniel on to the chicken-house roof and thence, surmounting the wall, dropped on to holy ground to search the long grass. The spaniel was indispensable.) My mother was devout and it was Sunday morning church for all of us . . . no shirking . . . and a pew with our name on it.

The curate, a cheerful young red-head bachelor who had been a padre in Gallipoli, came to supper with us every Saturday. This was his bath-night, too, because his digs in the village had few amenities, and those were in the garden. The curate liked his whisky . . . or rather our whisky . . . or rather whisky. We got a bottle in, for him alone. He had a glass before supper after his bath, a glass with supper and a glass after supper. He taught us that you could always get twenty-seven more drops out of a bottle you thought empty. He taught us that Lenten fasts and self-denials didn't apply between dusk on Saturday and dawn on Monday. He taught us auction bridge, showed us how to blow smoke-rings, played, on our schoolroom upright, and sang from the *Oxford Song Book*. He smoked Turkish cigarettes: the first of the day before breakfast, while shaving. He had been a member of the Archery Club at John's, his college at Oxford. He said the advantage of that was that you could have girl guests and, to teach them how to shoot a bow and arrow, you had to stand behind them and put your arms round their shoulders. He was very fond of pretty girls.

My mother, reporting in regular letters to *his* mother in Tunbridge Wells, tried to find the right girl for the curate to marry. He wasn't a great intellectual. He said he had passed his Divinity and Theology exams at Oxford only with the help of a benzedrine equivalent. He had, at least equal to his curate's stipend, a private income from an inheritance invested in distilleries and crematoria. He had a hoarded sermon, ready for emergencies, on Dives and Lazarus. We all liked him very much, and he prepared me for Confirmation.

I always think of that curate and his Oxford benzedrine-sniffing when I read your Buck-U-Uppo stories. I take it you know (I've only just learnt, from the *New Yorker* of all sources) that in East Africa there is a small plant, *ol-umigumi*, that is taken as a stimulant with meat before a lion hunt by Masai warriors to give them courage behind their spears and shields.

You have your Buck-U-Uppo, something formulated by the analytical chemist Wilfred Mulliner for putting into the bran mash of elephants in India, to give them courage to stand their ground when out hunting and charged by tigers. And the pale young curate, Augustine Mulliner, gets some bottles of this stuff mistakenly sent to him as a tonic by his aunt, Wilfred Mulliner's wife. Under the influence of Buck-U-Uppo Augustine knocks sense and humility into the head of his landlady. Under the influence of Buck-U-Uppo the clerical headmaster and the Bishop of Stortford paint the statue of 'old Fatty' pink in the school close at midnight, and leave the bishop's shovel hat on top. Under the influence of Buck-U-Uppo the same bishop goes to a fancy-dress dance at a night club and, when this is duly raided by the local police, socks a policeman in the eye . . .

'. . . So I biffed this bird. And did he take a toss?
Ask me!' said the Bishop, chuckling contentedly.

The bishop remembers proudly that he had won the Curates' Open Heavyweight Championship two years in succession.

Good stuff, all of this. But the eye of the critic is not blacked or closed. You, the storyteller, want to divide your plot this way and that at planned intervals. One of any storyteller's ways of ravelling a plot is to have a character, or all the characters, get tight. Your good taste told you that you could not have the clergy alcoholically inebriated. They can do almost anything else human – preaching about Naboth's vineyard to shame Sir Watkyn Bassett for dirty work to a rival collector of *objets d'art*, lying, pinching policemen's helmets, visiting Blandings under false names, knocking out Roderick Spode, the amateur ex-dictator. But they must not get tight. So you invent Buck-U-Uppo, specially for the use of the clergy. It makes them elated and irresponsible, brave, young and foolish, able to bring about a story's high spots without causing shocked tut-tuts from the aisles.

'That's what today's Church needs,' says the sententious Gussie Fink-Nottle. 'More curates capable of hauling off and letting fellows like Spode have it where it does most good.' Spode had known that the hefty Rev. 'Stinker' Pinker had played rugger for England, but not that he had boxed heavyweight for Oxford. But Spode, when he came round, forgave him, and was full of praise for the blow that had floored him:

> ... He was more or less a revelation to me ... because I didn't know curates had left hooks like that. He's got a knack of feinting you off balance and then coming in with a sort of corkscrew punch which it's impossible not to admire. I must get him to teach it to me some time.

Most of your clean young curates are pin-heads, but full of zeal. In one of your stories you describe a country hamlet pithily as 'mostly honeysuckle and apple-cheeked villagers'. I forget whether that was Walsingford-below-Chiveney-on-Thames, where Augustine had the cure of souls. It might well have been:

> It was a lovely night, and Augustine opened the French windows, the better to enjoy the soothing scents of the flowers beyond. Then, seating himself at his desk, he began to work.
> The task of composing a sermon which should practically make sense and yet not be above the heads of his rustic flock was one which always caused Augustine Mulliner to concentrate tensely. Soon he was lost in his labours and oblivious to everything but the problem of how to find a word of one syllable that meant Supralapsarianism.

Mulliners apart, your country curates have probably rowed, boxed or played rugger for their universities. They love, and are loved by, the vicar's daughter or the girl up at the big house. They get down to their old boxing or rowing weight in Lent. At other times they fatten up on country butter and tithes. Vicars have a low opinion of curates, especially as prospective sons-in-law. What curates most want is to get vicarages of their own. Then they can marry and have families, nurses, governesses, and butlers.

They are not double Firsts, your men of God, but they are 'gentlemen'. And if they have to live on their stipends as curates, they have rich uncles in the background and ambitious fiancées keen to drag them by the surplice up the financial ladder.

Here's the adorable young Stiffy Byng pleading the cause of her beloved, the curate Harold 'Stinker' Pinker, to her guardian, Sir Watkyn Bassett. Sir Watkyn, once a London magistrate and now retired and a country gentleman, can, according to Stiffy, 'spout vicarages like a geyser'.

'You know that vicarage you have in your gift, Uncle Watkyn! What Harold and I were thinking was that you might give him that and then we could get married at once. You see, apart from the increased dough, it would start him off on the road to higher things. Up to now, Harold has been working under wraps. As a curate, he has had no scope. But slip him a vicarage, and watch him let himself out. There is literally no eminence to which that boy will not rise, once he spits on his hands and starts in.'

Stiffy wiggled from base to apex with girlish enthusiasm. But there was no girlish enthusiasm in old Bassett's demeanour.

In your books owners of advowsons dish out or withhold benefices as the whim takes them. Sir Watkyn won't spout a vicarage for Harold, but someone else will – a squire is determined to build up his village rugby football team. When he hears that the saintly Harold was once prop-forward for England, Harold gets the vicarage. Beefy Bingham gets his vicarage, at Much Matchingham, because Lord Emsworth, in whose gift the vicarage is, wants to plant a thorn in the flesh of Sir Gregory Parsloe-Parsloe, squire of Much Matchingham. Lord Emsworth, quite unjustly and for several books, suspects Sir Gregory of all sorts of skulduggery as a rival grower of champion pigs and pumpkins. One man who can't give vicarages where he thinks vicarages are due (ie to the Rev. Augustine Mulliner, who has rescued him in many dire straits) is the Bishop of Stortford. The bishop's wife insists that the vacant living of Steeple Mummery go to her cousin, '. . . a fellow,' said the bishop bitterly, 'who bleats like a sheep and doesn't know an alb from a reredos'.

Freddie Threepwood, I recall, says that at one stage his family had tried to get him to go into the Church. And I know, from your story 'The Metropolitan Touch', that an earl's younger son who becomes a parson is properly addressed on an envelope as 'The Hon. and Reverend'. I like to think of Freddie as The Hon. and Reverend Frederick Threepwood. He might have been a go-getter at that, too.

Your country churches are ivy-mantled. At summer evensong Mr Mulliner arrives in a topper, and Miss Postlethwaite, the lady behind the bar at the Anglers' Rest, returns moony with sanctity:

> The quiet splendour of her costume and the devout manner in which she pulled the beer handle told their own story. 'You've been to Church,' said a penetrating Sherry and Angostura.
> 'Beautiful in every sense of the word,' said Miss Postlethwaite . . . 'I do adore evening service in the summer. All that stilly hush and whatnot . . .'

That's the beginning of 'Anselm Gets His Chance', a story which, you told me, you put among your best three. Mr Mulliner here takes the Sunday evensong subject a little further:

> . . . in the rural districts of England vicars always preach the evening sermon during the summer months, and this causes a great deal of discontent to seethe among curates. It exasperates the young fellows, and one can understand their feelings . . . There is something about the atmosphere of evensong in a village church that induces a receptive frame of mind in a congregation, and a preacher, preaching under such conditions, can scarcely fail to grip and stir. The curates, withheld from so preaching, naturally feel that they are being ground beneath the heel of an iron monopoly and chiselled out of their big chance.

And

> At supper that night Anselm was distrait and preoccupied.

57

Busy with his own reflection, he scarcely listened to the conversation of the Rev. Sidney Gooch, his vicar. And this was perhaps fortunate, for it was a Saturday and the vicar, as was his custom at Saturday suppers, harped a good deal on the subject of the sermon which he was proposing to deliver at evensong on the morrow. He said, not once but many times, that he confidently expected, if the fine weather held up, to knock his little flock cockeyed. The Rev. Sidney was a fine, upstanding specimen of the muscular Christian, but somewhat deficient in tact.

However, thanks to Myrtle's sensible generalship, Joe the burglar comes to the vicarage that Saturday night to steal Anselm's heavily insured collection of stamps. The vicar tangles with him in the dark and gets a black eye. With one hand on that eye, he addresses Anselm in the small hours:

> . . . the sermon that I had planned to deliver at evensong tomorrow, Mulliner . . . a pippin, in the deepest and truest sense a pippin. I am not exaggerating when I say I would have had them tearing up the pews. And now that dream is ended . . . I cannot possibly appear in the pulpit with a shiner like this . . .

So Anselm gets his chance. Every curate, says Mr Mulliner, keeps by him a sermon for emergencies like this. (All your clergymen seem to *read* their sermons, or other people's sermons: 'the old stockpile', Stiffy Byng calls it. Once or twice you use it as a plot-hinge, that if the script is stolen there can be no sermon delivered.) Anselm preached that evening his Brotherly Love sermon . . . the same subject as Old Heppenstall's in 'The Great Sermon Handicap' . . . and it went over so big that (a) Joe the burglar, who sang in the choir ('looking perfectly foul in a surplice'), brought the stamp collection back with sobs of repentance, and (b) Myrtle's uncle, the millionaire philatelist, also with sobs of repentance, confessed that he had offered £10 for the collection as a normal business precaution. He now admitted that its true value was £5,000 and he would, in remorse, make that double. He wrote the £10,000 cheque, and Myrtle decided to motor up to London to be there when the

uncle's bank opened at 9.30 next morning, to cash the cheque.
She had had experience before of her uncle cancelling cheques.
Myrtle explained to Anselm:

'You know how Uncle Leopold feels about business pre-
cautions. This way [the 9.30 am presentation of the cheque
for cash] we shall avoid all rannygazoo.'
  Anselm kissed her fondly.
  'You think of everything, dearest,' he said. 'How right you
are. One does so wish, does one not, to avoid rannygazoo.'

Summer Sunday evensong in the country . . . you have
written two or three superb evocations of the stilly hush, soon
probably to be broken up dramatically. Steggles, making a
book for the School Sports, is singing in the second row of the
choir, and he puts a beetle down the collar of the choirboy in
front of him – Harold, the page-boy at the Hall. Harold has
been heavily backed by Bertie Wooster and his syndicate for
the Choir-Boys' Handicap 100-yards sprint for (and how often
I have seen this quoted!) 'a pewter mug presented by the vicar –
open to all whose voices have not broken before the second
Sunday in Epiphany'.
  Here's Bertie Wooster's description of the scene:

There's something about evening service in a country
church that makes a fellow feel drowsy and peaceful. Sort of
end-of-a-perfect-day feeling. Old Heppenstall was up in the
pulpit, and he has a kind of regular, bleating delivery that
assists thought. They had left the door open, and the air was
full of mixed scents of trees and honeysuckle and mildew and
villagers' Sunday clothes. As far as the eye could reach, you
could see farmers propped up in restful attitudes, breathing
heavily; and the children in the congregation who had
fidgeted during the earlier part of the proceedings were now
lying back in a surfeited sort of coma. The last rays of the
setting sun shone through the stained glass windows, birds
were twittering in the trees, the women's dresses crackled
gently in the stillness. Peaceful, that's what I'm driving at. I
felt peaceful. Everybody felt peaceful. And that is why the
explosion, when it came, sounded like the end of all things.

59

(Harold in the choir starts yelling and squealing.)

Well, I mean, you can't do that sort of thing in the middle of the sermon during evening service without exciting remark. The congregation came out of its trance with a jerk, and climbed on the pews to get a better view. Old Heppenstall stopped in the middle of a sentence and spun round. And a couple of vergers with great presence of mind bounded up the aisles like leopards, collected Harold, still squealing, and marched him out. They disappeared into the vestry, and I grabbed my hat and legged it round to the stage door, full of apprehension and whatnot.

So Harold is dismissed from the choir, and is thus not able to compete in the race. It is left to Jeeves to recoup the group fortunes by a colossal counter-nobbling operation in the Girls' Egg and Spoon Race.

And ... back to Barmy Fotheringay-Phipps at Maiden Eggesford. Under the influence of evensong he decides that he must make the great sacrifice and give up Angelica to his dear old friend Pongo Twistleton-Twistleton, who loves her too.

There is something about evening church in a village in summer time that affects the most hard-boiled. They had left the door open, and through it came the scent of lime trees and wallflowers and the distant hum of bees fooling about. And gradually there poured over Barmy a wave of sentiment. As he sat and listened to the First Lesson he became a changed man.

The Lesson was one of those chapters of the Old Testament all about how Abimelech begat Jazzbo and Jazzbo begat Zachariah. And, what with the beauty of the words and the peace of his surroundings, Barmy suddenly began to become conscious of a great remorse ...

... It was a different, stronger Barmy, a changed, chastened Cyril Fotheringay-Phipps who left the sacred edifice at the conclusion of the vicar's fifty-minute sermon ...

You play country evensong for excellent laughs, and as a

plot-hinge: a way of giving the story-line a jerk, changing someone's mind and attitude (in the last case, Barmy's). Welsh preachers, too. Ukridge's boneheaded boxer, Battling Billson, all trained up to hammer the stuffing out of his opponent that night, wanders into a Welsh revivalist meeting, and a powerful preacher converts him on the spot to be gentle in all his ways: with the result that he can't hit his opponent in the ring as intended, and Ukridge, his sponsor, once again fails to win a colossal fortune. In your recent *Do Butlers Burgle Banks?* you have Basher Evans, a four-square Welsh pug, suddenly preached into repentance and going straight, much to the embarrassment of the gang of crooks who have him signed up to help in a big burglary.

Your men of God are nearly all absurd, but none despicable. Perhaps the Rev. Aubrey Upjohn, your prep-school head-master, is a stinker. But I notice that in your last book about him, *Jeeves in the Offing*, he has lost his 'the Rev.' appellation (except in the leader-page synopsis) and is trying to get nominated as Conservative candidate for the by-election at Market Snodsbury. Probably you defrocked the old horror to make this possible, it being against the rules for a C. of E. clergyman to stand for Parliament. But whatever he may be called officially, when he is last heard, in *Jeeves in the Offing*, he is getting from Bobbie Wickham over the telephone a splendid commination starting, 'Listen, Buster . . .' Bertie Wooster says, reverently, to Jeeves, 'If anyone had told me that I should live to hear Aubrey Upjohn addressed as "Buster" . . .'

Your Bishop of Bongo-Bongo is rather sanctimonious at first, as is his cat Webster. But Webster restores things by getting tight. A bishop mustn't. A bishop's cat can. And it's the best thing that has ever happened to Webster, lapping that spilled whisky. A man at the Anglers' Rest public house, having heard the first story, of Webster's fall from grace, asks Mr Mulliner how it turned out:

'As I see it, there is a great psychological drama in this cat. I visualise his higher and lower selves warring. He has taken the first false step, and what will be the issue? Is this new, demoralising atmosphere into which he has been plunged to neutralise the pious teachings of early kittenhood at the

61

Deanery? Or will sound churchmanship prevail and help him to be the cat he used to be?'

'If', said Mr Mulliner, 'I am right in supposing that you want to know what happened to Webster at the conclusion of the story I related the other evening, I can tell you. There was nothing that you could really call a war between his higher and lower selves. The lower self won hands down. From the moment when he went on that first majestic toot this once saintly cat became a Bohemian of Bohemians. His days started early and finished late, and were a mere welter of brawling and loose gallantry . . .'

So when Percy, the loathsome cat owned by the widow who's trying to get the bishop to marry her, arrives on the scene, Webster engages him in a great fight, and the bishop backs his own cat and the widow sails out of his life forever. And Lancelot, the bishop's nephew, who had spilled the whisky that changed Webster's life . . . he gets a nice cheque from his grateful uncle and is able to marry, therewith, his ink-spotted Chelsea artist girlfriend.

I would vote you a literary gold medal of some sort for being so very funny about Church and churchmen, so very often, without ever being unkind to the Church or mocking the faith of its ministers. You show us clergymen in all manner and states of dress, undress and fancy dress (Sinbad the Sailor). You show us them in anger and jealousy, in fury and joviality, in sorrow and triumph, in night clubs, in love, in danger of arrest ('nothing retards a curate's advancement in his chosen profession more than a spell in the jug') . . . and in drink: Buck-U-Uppo, that tonic 'with a slightly pungent flavour, rather like old boot soles beaten up in sherry'.

You give us clergy treed by snarling dogs, bullied at Theological College, forced by their wives to keep their thick woolly underwear on in sweltering summer, getting their eyes blacked by burglars, giving policemen black eyes, stealing policemen's helmets, and in many other human, ordinary-mortal occupations and predicaments. When the headmaster, next morning, discovers that he may be unveiled as having painted that statue pink the night before, he says, 'I will be asked to hand in my resignation. And, if that happens, bim goes my chance of ever being a bishop.' With his crony, the (already) bishop, he is saved by the bought 'confession' of a young Mulliner at the school, and the bishop, who had been writing a rather sceptical article for a religious journal on miracles, corrects its attitude, removing the scepticism, before sending it in.

That was the early Bishop of Stortford, in *Meet Mr Mulliner* (1927). It is sad to find, many books later in *Cocktail Time* (1958), that this same bishop, now 'venerable' and having presumably conquered his addiction to the Buck-U-Uppo bottle, can't stomach a modern novel. He had grabbed it away from his daughter and,

> At 12.15 on the following Sunday he was in the pulpit of the church of St. Jude the Resilient, Eaton Square, delivering a sermon on the text 'He that touches pitch shall be defiled.' (Ecclesiasticus 13–1) . . . The burden of his address was a denunciation of the novel *Cocktail Time* in the course of which he described it as obscene, immoral, shocking, impure, corrupt, shameless, graceless and depraved, and all over the sacred edifice you could see eager men jotting the name down on their shirt cuffs, scarcely able to wait to add it to their library list.

When a bishop denounces a novel as obscene, it stays denounced. *Cocktail Time* became a long-distance bestseller in a book of the same name, one of your very best.

You take us into the church with your men of God, and at the lectern, in the pulpit or the choir-stalls anything may happen, from choirboys getting beetles down their backs to curates tripping over hassocks. But you never try to take us beyond the altar rails. No clergyman of yours, I think, is ever shown on his knees – at least, not in worship. And none is shown being unctuous. If he does act like a stage parson, we can be sure he turns out to be an impostor: the clergyman Hemmingway that Bertie Wooster met in the South of France and that Jeeves unmasked as a confidence trickster, and the stuttering clergyman who interrupted Ukridge's Buttercup Day in his (absent) aunt's Wimbledon garden. He was a crook, too . . . an even greater one than Ukridge.

You have given us a benign Barchester, with a little Bab Ballads in ragtime. And you do a lordly job of verbal mimicry: of Old Testament and New (authorised version), of the Prayer Book, of the parlance of pulpits and of the table talk of curates, vicars, bishops and their loved ones, their wives and their landladies. I said earlier that I suspected that you had absorbed some of your churchmanship as a boy in the vicarage libraries when you were spending school holidays with clerical uncles. As well as bound parish magazines and other improving Sundayish periodicals, I am sure there were many of those devotional journals that all Victorian clergy were apparently encouraged to keep and that far too many published: also bound volumes of sermons. I get some confirmation of this hunch of mine from your recent novel *The Girl in Blue* (1970), in which the impoverished owner of the big house is made uncomfortable by the 'seven or eight hundred bound volumes of early Victorian sermons eyeing him with silent rebuke' in the stuffy library. They have nothing to do with the plot. As room furniture I think they must come from your visual memory right back into the 1890s. But as furniture for a type of mimicry of clerical jargon they have been serving you excellently since your earliest school stories.

God is not mocked, nor is the Church. But you are affectionately irreverent about the Church's ministers all right. Thank you, especially, for the many human failings of your many men of God.

Yours sincerely,

Postscript

1.   I never did discover whether there had been a vicar's daughter in Plum's love-life.

64

5
Fives-bats and the Young Wodehouse Villains Who Deserved Six of the Best with Them

The following appeared in Blackwood's Magazine *in July 1974.*

It started with fives and fives-bats.

I was re-reading Bernard Darwin's 1941 book, *Pack Clouds Away*. In the chapter headed 'Mr Bultitude Looks Back' he returns to the end of the 1880s, when he was a boy at his preparatory school, Summer Fields, Oxford, where I was also, thirty years later. Darwin wrote:

> I remember it [the school] with extraordinary clearness. The dullest and most absurd little details have stuck in my head. If I were now set down in the lobby with its floor of coloured tiles and its row of squash rackets (we called that game 'Fives') in a rack. . . .

What did Darwin mean by 'we called that game "Fives" '? What game? The school archives do not reveal. Conceivably they had then a (Rugby) fives court in which the boys played with a soft (squash) black rubber ball and with (squash) rackets, and conceivably they still called the game 'fives'. In which case, did the boys also play the statutory fives game, with gloved hands and a harder, white, leather-bound ball? And in any case, what was a fives-bat? There was no knowledge of fives-bats at the school when I was there.

Among the William Hazlitt (1778–1830) entries in the *Oxford Book of English Prose,* edited (1925) by Sir Arthur Quiller-Couch, is one, from his *Table Talk,* about John

65

Cavanagh 'the famous hand fives player'. I am not a Hazlitt scholar, and I do not know why 'Q' attributed this piece to Hazlitt. Hazlitt quotes it, at length, from an obituary of Cavanagh that had appeared anonymously in the *The Examiner*, a Sunday paper, in 1819. Perhaps Hazlitt, who was himself a fives player, had written the *Examiner* piece. At all events the fact that Cavanagh is described as a famous *hand* fives player does suggest that there was a fives game played with something else, presumably a bat. And it might be the same implement as described in the Badminton Library 1890 edition of *Tennis, Lawn Tennis, Rackets and Fives*. In the 'Rackets' section of that one, E.O. Pleydell-Bouverie follows his excursus into the origins (at Harrow School) of squash rackets with:

> A game somewhat similar with regard to local conditions was, and is still, much in vogue at Winchester. Lord Penzance, who was in the Winchester eleven in the fourth decade of this century, well remembers such a game being played with a bat shaped somewhat like a racket but entirely wooden, thin in the middle and thick at the end, and with a hard ball. Rugby can also boast a like institution. . . .

And this is where my wool-gathering mind switches to P.G. Wodehouse. He mentions fives-bats in at least two contexts. And both times they are weapons of chastisement inflicted, in fact or in dream, by authority on the young. In *Uncle Dynamite* the sixty-year-old Lord Ickenham remembers that, when they were at school together, he, then 'Barmy' Twistleton, had administered the fives-bat as corporal punishment on young 'Mugsy' (later Sir Aylmer) Bostock for bullying a smaller boy.

Where had Lord Ickenham been at school? Almost certainly Eton. His nephew Pongo had been at Eton. It says so. And Lord Ickenham (see *Cocktail Time*) goes to Lord's for the Eton and Harrow match and is saddened to see so many of his contemporaries looking like centenarians. But here is the snag. The Eton-fives game is played in a court copied from the enclosure made by a buttress of the Henry VI Chapel and the end of a balustrade at the bottom of the steps. The court is full of nooks, crannies, ledges and other excitements (or impediments). It is difficult enough to winkle the ball out of these

66

hazards with the gloved hands. With bats it would be impossible. Why, then, would they have had fives-bats at Eton in Lord Ickenham's day? Only for chastisement?

The fives-bat is certainly a disciplinary weapon in Wodehouse's short story 'The Passing of Ambrose', though Wodehouse, or his surrogate Mr Mulliner, does not tell us what school Ambrose Wiffen had been at that made him mentally reach for a fives-bat when faced with a pestilential small boy. Ambrose, silly ass, had fallen for the beautiful and unscrupulous Bobbie Wickham. She, for nefarious reasons of her own, got Ambrose to take her little cousin Wilfred and his friend 'Old Stinker' to a cinema in London. Ambrose's first view of Old Stinker was unfavourable. He was 'goggle-eyed and freckled . . . an officious little devil who needed six of the best with a fives-bat'. But very soon Ambrose had changed his mind: 'not six with a fives-bat, he felt. Ten. And of the juiciest'.

And that is how it started. With fives and fives-bats. I read 'The Passing of Ambrose' again, and was hooked into a week's pleasant research into Wodehouse's treatment of children in the ninety or so books he has so far given us.

There were no fives-bats about that afternoon. And it was little Wilfred, not Old Stinker, who was at the receiving end of Ambrose's later wrath. 'The next moment, above the roar of London's traffic, there sounded the crisp note of a well-smacked head.'

Ambrose's crisp smack to little Wilfred's head is, I would now say, typical of Wodehouse's fearless attitude towards small boys in his major works. Just recently I saw on television that W.C. Fields film, *The Great McGonigle*, and witnessed again the heroic moment when Fields catches his old enemy, Baby LeRoy, bending, and boots him to the ground. I was glad to note the fellow-feeling between the two great artists, Wodehouse and Fields.

Ambrose Wiffen was accustomed to regard small boys with a slightly jaundiced eye. It was his simple creed that they wanted their heads smacked. When not having their heads smacked, they should be out of the picture altogether.

Wodehouse, in his *floruit* period from 1920 onwards, uses

children as mercilessly and hilariously as he uses the clergy. But, with the exception of the Rev. Sidney Gooch's black eye inflicted by the burglar ('Anselm Gets His Chance'), Wodehouse's men of God never, I think, get struck in anger. Wodehouse's children are being struck, or in danger of being struck, all the time. The head smacked with the hand (Ambrose *v.* little Wilfred), the behind whacked with the fives-bat (Ambrose's dream *v.* Old Stinker). And there are plenty of other methods of assault, executed, planned or threatened by right-thinking grown-ups on fiendish boys. I can recall the swift slosh on the base of the skull with a blackjack (contemplated by Bingo Little *v.* Young Thos, whom he was tutoring), ditto with a stocking filled with sand (ascribed to a mother *v.* her infant in an imaginative simile in *The Old Reliable*), the boot on the behind, as prescribed by W.C. Fields (Bertie Wooster *v.* Edwin Craye), the nose pushed sideways (threatened by Jane Bates *v.* her son Braid), the walking-stick or hunting crop across the behind (Mr Anstruther *v.* Young Thos, and Lord Worplesdon *v.* the younger Bertie Wooster), the mashie-niblick across the behind (Rodney Spelvin *v.* his son Timothy).

Bertie Wooster describes his cousin Young Thos variously as 'Aunt Agatha's loathly son' and 'England's premier fiend in human shape'. Young Thos lives on, from story to story, a careless maker of mayhem, a gangster in embryo. Apart from a few whackings from his mother, he suffers nothing worse than that whacking from old Mr Anstruther. More of that later.

The recipient of Bertie Wooster's boot is much older than W.C. Field's opponent. Edwin Craye (surely he must, as only son of the Earl of Worplesdon, be Lord Something; his sister is Lady Florence Craye; the Earl of Emsworth's elder son is Lord Bosham) is about fourteen, but he is wearing shorts because he is a devout boy scout. And he gets Bertie's boot behind him in the garden of his father's country residence at Steeple Bumpleigh in Wodehouse's alpha-plus novel, *Joy in the Morning*.

'Young ruddy Edwin' is, as a recent convert, obsessed by the boy scout's code of doing at least one good deed a day. He is constantly falling behind the calendar, and he makes life hell for those on whom he tries to inflict his good deeds. He burns Bertie's cottage to the ground, trying selflessly to clean its chimney. He selflessly blacks Bertie's best brown shoes. And he selflessly pastes the cuttings of the reviews of his sister Florence's new book into the wrong album with the wrong paste and the wrong way up. Bertie, to his anguish engaged to be married to Florence, does not know about Edwin's review-pasting 'good' deed. What Bertie wants is for Florence to see him booting her kid brother in the behind and, infuriated by this, to hand him, Bertie, back the engagement ring. So Bertie, choosing the time and place exactly, with Florence watching, tells Edwin there is a sixpence under that bush on the edge of the drive.

My subtle appeal to the young blister's cupidity had not failed to achieve its end. Already he was down on all fours, and if I had posed him with my own hands, I could not have obtained better results. . . . I drew back the leg, and let him have it just where the pants were tightest.

It was a superb effort. Considering that I hadn't kicked anyone since the distant days of school, you might have thought that the machinery would have gone rusty. But no. All the old skill still lingered. My timing was perfect, and so was my follow through. He disappeared into the bush, travelling as out of a gun, and as he did so, Florence's voice spoke.

'Ah!' she said. . . .

It all goes wrong. Instead of Florence flying into a rage and handing Bertie's ring back to him, she is delighted to see her brother precipitated into a bush. She looks at her fiancé with extra adoration. The plot of *Joy in the Morning* is extremely complicated. It is not only Florence who gives it a twist by approving of her brother being kicked. Edwin's father, Lord Worplesdon, twice gives it more twists by changing his moods, from grave to gay, when he learns that someone has kicked his son in the shorts. Poor Edwin. Bertie kicks him. Florence dislikes him. His father dislikes him. We rather like him. So, obviously, does Wodehouse.

Wodehouse likes almost all his fiendish boy characters. They are admirable hinges in his plots. They are splendid trouble-makers for the fat-headed, pure-in-heart grown-ups, the

Ambrose Wiffens and Bertie Woosters of Wodehouse's enchanted world.

Was there any child, important in any Wodehouse story, whom Wodehouse did not present as a rogue or a thug, due for someone's smack, whack or boot? And is there a child, rogue or thug, important in any Wodehouse story, whom Wodehouse himself actively disliked? First question, answer Yes – two, but both in very early works. So they cannot be held in evidence against the mature Wodehouse. Marjory Merevale comes in a public-school story, 'Welch's Mile Record'. I do not think the story was ever collected into a book. In my mind's eye, I see it illustrated, which means I probably read it in a bound collection of *The Captain Magazine*, date about 1904. It probably netted the young Wodehouse two guineas – enough, in those days, to keep him in food and lodging for a fortnight, with a quarter of a pound of tobacco for his pipe thrown in.

This is the story. Welch is the best athlete in Merevale's House, and one night, in his study, he is asleep after rubbing himself with embrocation in preparation for the morrow's great Sports Day. Somebody shakes him awake, and there, at his bedside, is his housemaster, Mr Merevale, 'with a look on his face so ghastly that it woke Welch far more efficiently than the shaking had done'. Mr Merevale is in pyjamas and a Balliol blazer.

Mr Merevale has a daughter, Marjory, much loved by all. She is about eight, and Merevale's House 'worships her to a man'. And she is devoted to the House; she had worn out vast supplies of gloves applauding the doings of Merevale's House teams on the football and cricket fields. Beloved little Marjory . . . and here, now, near midnight, is her father, haggard and horror-struck. He blurts out his story to Welch, the athlete. *Will Welch go and get a doctor?* Marjory has got diphtheria and is slowly choking to death. It is before the days of telephones, of course, but the bicycle is in vogue. Welch says: 'Can I borrow your bicycle, sir?' And Mr Merevale, more haggard than ever, says: 'Punctured yesterday! Not another in the house.'

Well, you see what is going to happen, remembering the title of the story. Welch gets on his running things and darts out of the house, up the road to the doctor's. It is exactly a mile. He routs the doctor out of bed, Marjory's life is saved and,

70

checking times – Welch's departure from the house to his arrival at the doctor's – Welch and Mr Merevale find that the former has set up a new school record for the mile.

Marjory Merevale stands almost alone as an important Wodehouse child who is not a maker of mayhem. Perhaps another one is Bill Winfield, the Bill of *The Coming of Bill*, an early, and an almost totally serious, novel. But the boy Bill breaks through the shackles of touch-me-not cleanliness, hygiene and mollycoddling imposed by his mother's imperious aunt, by having a rough-and-tumble fist fight with a neighbouring boy-thug and winning it. I find the chronology of *The Coming of Bill* a bit difficult. It seems as though young Bill has this, his first scrap, and gets this, his first black eye, at the age of about two.

Second question: is there a child in the books whom Wodehouse himself seems actively to have disliked? Yes. You can probably count the boy Blumenfield ('a pest, a wart, a pot of poison, and should be strangled'), to whom Bobbie Wickham gives the Scottie dog that Bertie is housing for his Aunt Agatha. But you must certainly name Ogden Ford, in *The Little Nugget* and *Piccadilly Jim*. Ogden is a good plot-maker (he is the little nugget that all the kidnappers are after), but Wodehouse presents him as a stinker. American Ogden, thirteen-year-old chain-smoker, son of a silly mother and a millionaire father, deserved all the cold baths, starvation, five-mile runs, compulsory games, chilblains and chapels that an English boarding prep-school could inflict in those pre-1914 days. In an introduction to a new edition of *The Little Nugget*, Wodehouse writes about the multiple editor of American magazines, Bob Davis, who gave him the plot for the novel. Bob Davis had ended: 'and be sure to make the kid sympathetic and touching, you know the sort of thing – blue eyes, golden hair and all that. . . .'

I think [says Wodehouse] he must have been a little disappointed in Ogden, who may, for all I know, have had golden hair, but whose best friends could not have called him sympathetic and touching. I used him again in a book called *Piccadilly Jim*, and he was just as repulsive there as he had been in *The Little Nugget*. I should imagine that, when he

71

grows up, if he is ever allowed to, he will be the sort of man who kicks dogs, grinds the face of the poor and takes three hours for lunch at expensive restaurants. He was not drawn from any boy of my acquaintance. . . .

Otherwise, with the possible exception of little Timothy Spelvin (see below), Wodehouse's children are composed of admirable young fiends and felons. Harold, page-boy at Twing Hall, on whom Bertie and his friends had plonked their bets for the Choir Boys' hundred-yard handicap sprint, streaks through the story 'The Metropolitan Touch'. He is a fast runner, but a headache to his trainers and backers. Bertie thinks he should be watched and guarded against nobblers twenty-four hours a day. He has read stories about cobras being sneaked into the loose-boxes of Derby favourites, and he suggests to Jeeves that he (Jeeves) should sleep in Harold's room. Jeeves says No, and tells Bertie that if anybody introduced a cobra into Harold's sleeping quarters, his (Jeeves's) anxiety would be entirely for the snake. Then there was that movie-soaked bootboy at Ukridge's aunt's house in Wimbledon: he wanted them to capture the aunt and keep her in a dungeon, putting lighted matches under her fingernails to persuade her to write cheques for them. There was Lord Emsworth's grandson George, who owned the airgun that caused the 'Crime Wave at Blandings'. There were that fine brother and sister, slum children from London, in the story 'Lord Emsworth and the Girlfriend'. Young Ern bit Lord Emsworth's sister Lady Constance Keble in the leg, and young Gladys copped McAllister, Lord Emsworth's crusty old gardener, on the leg with a stone. Another young tough was Braid Bates:

Braid Bates at that time was a young plug-ugly of some nine summers, in soul and temperament a combination of Dead End kid and army mule; a freckled, hard-boiled character with a sardonic eye and a mouth which, when not occupied in eating, had a cynical twist to it. He spoke little as a general thing, but when he did speak seldom failed to find a chink in the armour.

It is a poignant story, 'Rodney Has a Relapse'. Rodney is a bad but enthusiastic golfer and an enthusiastic and very successful writer of thrillers. But he has relapses into writing poetry, as when younger. He gives up his profitable thriller-writing and starts in again on poetry. And he uses his son Timothy as *jeune premier* in his poetry – Timothy Bobbin, he calls him. Timothy, the little beast, acts up to the Timothy Bobbin character. When he says his prayers at night he squints through his fingers to 'count the house', and he thinks that beetles are fairies' horses. It is all very sad. Worse. Timothy's first cousin, Braid Bates, son of two golfing champions and himself being trained to championships, decides that his father ought to be writing poems about *him*, and he demands it as his right, otherwise he will give up training for the Kiddies' Cup, soon due. The story must be read in all its pitiless detail. But Timothy Bobbin makes his father fluff an anxious, match-winning putt, and he gets what is coming to him, with a father's well swung mashie:

Rodney Spelvin's eyes were alight with a hidden menace. Quickly and silently, like an African leopard stalking its prey, he advanced on his son. An instant later the stillness was disturbed by a series of reports like pistol shots.

I looked at Anastatia. There was distress on her face, but mingled with the distress was a sort of ecstasy. She mourned as a mother, but rejoiced as a wife.

Rodney Spelvin was himself again.

That night little Braid Bates, addressing his father, said: 'How's that poem coming along?'

His father cast a hunted look at his helpmeet, and Jane took things in hand in her firm, capable way.

'That,' she said, 'will be all of that. Daddy isn't going to write any poem, and we shall want you out on the practice tee at seven sharp tomorrow, my lad.'

'But Uncle Rodney writes poems to Timothy.'

'No, he doesn't. Not now.'

'But. . . .'

Jane regarded her son with quiet intentness.

'Does Mother's little chickabiddy want his nose pushed sideways?' she said. 'Very well, then.'

I reckon that Young Thos was twelve, Bonzo Travers eleven and Sebastian Moon eight or nine at the time of the story 'The Love That Purifies'. Bertie Wooster is the narrator, and, though Jeeves pulls the strings, Bertie, at the end of the story, has seen three boys sorely tried, tested in the furnace and emerging with credit. He says to Jeeves: 'Jeeves, this Younger Generation is hot stuff.' Young Thos, Bonzo and Sebastian prove each to be in love with a *princesse lointaine*: respectively, Greta Garbo, Lilian Gish and Marlene Dietrich.

A crotchety old guest ('a rather moth-eaten septuagenarian' is Bertie's description of him), Mr Anstruther, is staying at Aunt Dahlia's house, Brinkley Court. Among the other guests are Lord and Lady Snettisham, Bertie (without Jeeves who, the slacker, has gone off for his summer holidays to the seaside) and the boys, Bonzo (Aunt Dahlia's son) and Young Thos (Aunt Agatha's). Mr Anstruther, anticipating trouble with two such boys about the place, proposes to give them good- and bad-conduct marks for a final prize of £5. He hopes thus to keep them on their best behaviour, and to provide a quiet life for himself.

The Snettishams and Aunt Dahlia bet on the result. Aunt Dahlia wagers her peerless chef, Anatole, against the Snettishams' peerless kitchen-maid. Aunt Dahlia bets that her son Bonzo will win Mr Anstruther's good-conduct prize. Villain that Bonzo is, she thinks, he is not in the same class of villainy as his cousin Thos. The Snettishams bet that Young Thos will prove better behaved than Bonzo. And on both sides they are prepared to pull all sorts of dirty work to make sure of winning. The Snettishams, for instance, offer money in an attempt to persuade Bonzo to climb on the roof and boo down Mr Anstruther's chimney; and, that failing, they offer him more money to burst a paper bag behind Mr Anstruther's deck chair when he is taking his rest. Neither inducement works, because Bonzo is in love with Lilian Gish and is determined to lead a pure life to make himself worthy of her.

So far, so good for Aunt Dahlia. But she is determined, in her turn, to make Young Thos misbehave, and since Bertie's methods of goading him towards misbehaviour fail (Young Thos, in love with Greta Garbo, is as full of saintly endeavour as Bonzo), Aunt Dahlia insists on Bertie bringing Jeeves back from his holiday to find a way. Jeeves comes back and suggests that if young Sebastian Moon, of the long, golden, curly hair, is invited to make a third small boy, Young Thos is sure to see red and beat him up, thus making Aunt Dahlia the winner of the bets – keeping Anatole and gaining the kitchen-maid from the Snettishams.

Does Jeeves ever fail on the last page? By his string-pulling, Sebastian Moon and Young Thos are in the stable yard and Sebastian makes a slighting remark about Greta Garbo and praises his own adored object, Marlene Dietrich. A fight breaks out. Young Thos seizes a bucket of water and chases Sebastian out of the yard, on to the lawns and right up to where Mr Anstruther is sitting. Then, near enough for the throw, Young Thos projects the contents of the bucket at Sebastian and scores a bullseye on Mr Anstruther. 'In one second, without any previous training or upbringing, he [Mr Anstruther] had become the wettest man in Worcestershire.'

So Aunt Dahlia keeps her precious Anatole and wins the kitchen-maid, and Young Thos, the popular loser of the good conduct prize, gets only Mr Anstruther's stick across his backside. Bertie's estimation of the younger generation goes up sharply.

It remains to add that by the time of the novel *The Mating Season*, Young Thos falls in love with yet another Hollywood star, though this time not so *lointaine*; they are fellow guests in her sainted uncle's vicarage at King's Deverill. Young Thos has been kidnapped by Bertie and Jeeves from his prep-school and brought to King's Deverill as a ruse to keep Thos's mother, Bertie's Aunt Agatha, busy looking for her son in Sussex, and well away from King's Deverill, where all the action is. Bertie is staying with some of Aunt Agatha's friends at King's Deverill, but not as himself. He is pretending to be Gussie Fink-Nottle, the real Gussie being in prison in London for having gone newt-hunting in a Trafalgar Square fountain at dawn. In his guise as Gussie, Bertie finds he is down to perform at the forthcoming village concert. He is to recite Gussie's fiancée's favourite 'Christopher Robin' verses.

Gussie's fiancée, Madeline Basset, was a threat to Bertie in several books. Like Florence Craye and Honoria Glossop, when any of her fiancés proved unworthy, she was far too ready to imagine that Bertie had been waiting for her all the time; and

Bertie, in such circumstances, could never say no, poor fellow. His views on Madeline, whose favourite reading was 'Christopher Robin' and *Winnie the Pooh*, were unequivocal:

> She is the sloppiest, mushiest, sentimentalest young Gawd-help-us who ever thought the stars were God's daisy chain and that every time a fairy hiccoughs a wee baby is born. She is squashy and soupy. . . .

Young Thos is only too happy to be away from school, away from his mother and in the same house as the adorable film star, Corky Pirbright, who gives him lots of her autographs. These he will sell at high prices when he gets back to school. But Bertie is shattered by the thought of reciting 'Christopher Robin' verses to a rustic mob at a concert. Gussie, his jail days over, comes to King's Deverill too (but of course he has to pretend to be Bertie Wooster). And Gussie is considerably relieved to know that he can pass on to the real Bertie Wooster the task of reciting those verses.

> 'I don't mind telling you Bertie, that I feel extremely relieved. There's one about the little blighter going hoppity, hoppity, hop which . . . well, as I say, I feel extremely relieved.'
> The slim volume fell from my nerveless fingers, and I goggled at him.
> 'But, dash it!'
> 'It's no good saying "But dash it!", Bertie. Do you think I didn't say "But dash it!" when Madeline forced these nauseous productions on me? You've got to do them. She insists. The first thing she will want to know is how they went.'
> 'But Gussie, the tough eggs at the back of the back row will rush the stage and lynch me.'
> 'I shouldn't wonder, Bertie. . . .'

Bertie was wisely afraid of those 'rustic standees, stern, implacable men, utterly incapable of taking the broad, charitable view and realising that a fellow who comes on a platform and starts reciting about Christopher Robin going hoppity,

hoppity, hop (or, alternatively, saying his prayers) does not do so from sheer wantonness but because he is a helpless victim of circumstances beyond his control. . . .'

On the printed page Wodehouse's view of children differs materially from A.A. Milne's. But perhaps the uses of 'Christopher Robin' in the short story 'Rodney Has a Relapse' and the novel *The Mating Season*, both published post-World War Two, were intended as something more than good comic business. Milne had, in 1941, written a very hostile letter to the Press about Wodehouse's broadcasts to America from Berlin after he had been released from internment. And, in that letter, Milne had made the mistake of suggesting that Wodehouse's own attitude to children was much the same as that of his fictional adults.

The Wodehouses were in their house at Le Touquet when the German armies swept across France in May 1940. Wodehouse spent nearly a year in internment camps and then, in June 1941, his voice was heard, at 4 am our time, speaking to America, on the Nazi radio from Berlin. He gave five talks, all funny and innocent in content, about his experiences in captivity. But one was enough to infuriate people in Britain. America was not in the war then. It seemed important to Duff Cooper, our Minister of Information at the time, that English Wodehouse should be publicly, officially and resoundingly disowned by Britain, lest America should think that we, alone against the Nazis, were not hurling total defiance across the Channel. Wodehouse got a terrible pasting on the BBC (against the unanimous wishes of the BBC authorities) from William Connor, the columnist 'Cassandra' of the *Daily Mirror*. The name Wodehouse was mud for the rest of the war and beyond, especially among those, MPs and others, who had never troubled to read the texts of the broadcasts he had given.

Wodehouse got a good deal of instant obloquy in the Press, too, not least in the letter to the *Daily Telegraph* from A.A. Milne. He said that Wodehouse had always been an escaper from responsibility, and he instanced a conversation he said he had had with Wodehouse between the wars:

He told me he wished to have a son, and added

characteristically (and quite sincerely), 'But he would have to be born at the age of 15 when he was just getting into his House eleven.' You see the advantage of that. Bringing up a son throws a considerable responsibility on a man: but by the time the boy is 15 one has shifted the responsibility onto the house-master, without forfeiting any of the reflected glory that may be about.

It was a pretty thin and unconvincing argument, and none the better coming from the father of the ever-profitable 'Christopher Robin', about a man who had never had any children of his own. But it was also quite unfair and untrue. It was putting words into Wodehouse's mouth that he had never spoken, but which Milne had misremembered out of a novel Wodehouse had written in 1910, *Psmith in the City*.

A dozen years after the war I was looking up the newspaper correspondence in England about the Wodehouse Berlin broadcasts in 1941. And I happened at the same time to be re-reading *Psmith in the City*. This is a paragraph about Mike Jackson, Psmith's friend:

> Mike got on with small girls reasonably well. He preferred them at a distance, but, if cornered by them, could put up a fairly good show. Small boys, however, filled him with frozen horror. It was his view that a boy should not be exhibited publicly until he had reached an age when he might be in the running for some sort of colours at a public school.

I wrote, then, to Wodehouse and asked him if my identification could be right, that Milne had been quoting from a novel of his, but had put the words into Wodehouse's own mouth. Wodehouse replied:

> You have cleared up a mystery that has been puzzling me for years. The thing he quoted me as saying . . . seemed familiar, but I was certain I had never said it to him. Evidently he must have read it in *Psmith in the City*. . . . Odd chap, Milne. . . .

I do not suggest that *The Mating Season* is a *roman à clef*. But you can find in it a few, tiny retrospective teases relating to some of the people, Milne among them, who had slated Wodehouse publicly in 1941. What name does Gussie Fink-Nottle give when hauled up in the Bosher Street Police court for wading about in the Trafalgar Square fountain? Alfred Duff Cooper, no less. Who is the girl at the King's Deverill village concert who plays the dreary violin solo? Eustacia Pulbrook. Sir Eustace Pulbrook was an important Old Alleynian, and he had sounded off pompously about Old Alleynian Wodehouse (P.G.) when the latter had done those broadcasts. And who wrote the dreadful verses that Bertie Wooster nearly had to recite at the village concert?

If you go back to *Psmith in the City*, you find that that summing up of twenty-year-old Mike Jackson's attitude to small boys prefaced his encounter with the ten-year-old son of a Mr Waller with whom Mike and Psmith were taking Sunday supper. Mike finds himself sitting next to the young, snub-nosed Edward Waller at the supper table, and virtually cornered by him conversationally. The boy 'had the peculiarly loathsome expression which a snub nose sometimes gives to the young', and Edward's first remark to Mike was: 'Do you know the principal exports of Marseilles?' Mike Jackson did not like young Edward. But Edward's father and Edward's author both did.

When the dust and small stones have settled and the smoke has cleared, what do we find as the sinews of P.G. Wodehouse's portrayal of childhood? When he is on top of his form, what is predictable about the children he brings into his books? I would categorise it like this:

1) *All babies are tremendously ugly.* Bingo Little thought his own first-born looked, in his pram, like 'a mass murderer suffering from an ingrowing toenail'. He cheerfully bet £10 of his infant's money that his infant would be held, by any impartial judge, to be uglier than the infant of another proud father in the park. And Bingo lost the bet. There is a description of another pramling as a 'mixture of Winston Churchill and Edward G. Robinson'. Yet another baby looks 'like a homicidal fried egg'. No hard feelings, but that is the way it is in Wodehouse.

2) *Small boys are fiends*, and those with long golden curls and innocent expressions should be beaten up by other boys or, failing other boys, grown-ups like Ambrose Wiffen.

3) *Bigger boys are monsters*. Of his step-cousin, young ruddy Edwin Craye, Bertie says: 'There's a boy who makes you feel that what this country wants is somebody like King Herod.'

4) *Girls need watching, too*. The schoolgirl Clementine puts sherbet in the ink. As a schoolgirl her godmother Bobbie had punctured her enemies' hot-water bottles by prodding them, at dead of night, through the bedclothes with a darning needle on the end of a stick. Wodehouse does not give us much in the way of young girls. But his favourites, and ours, are the delinquents who will obviously grow up into fizzy young heroines like Bobbie Wickham, Stiffy Byng, Pauline Stoker, Corky Pirbright and Nobby Hopwood.

I still do not know what a fives-bat is.

6
Three Good Books and a Query

During the run of the exhibition of Wodehouse material at the South Bank in London in 1982, we were allowed to put on cosy shows in the Lyttelton Theatre featuring, for example, Wodehouse songs from the musicals, in London and on Broadway, that he wrote with Guy Bolton and Jerome Kern, and lectures by, among others, Malcolm Muggeridge, Benny Green and William Douglas Home. The following was one of those lectures.

'Cats are not dogs!'

There is only one place where you can hear good things like that thrown off quite casually in the general run of conversation, and that is the bar parlour of the Anglers' Rest. Although the talk up to this point had been dealing with Einstein's Theory of Relativity, we readily adjusted our minds to cope with the new topic. In our little circle I have known an argument on the Final Destination of the Soul to change inside forty seconds into one concerning the best method of preserving the juiciness of bacon fat.

That's the opening of one of the Mulliner stories, as you may have recognised. In the next half-hour or so you will find me, too, changing my subjects, unpardonably often.

I have it in mind mainly to talk about three recent books. One is *Thank You, Wodehouse* by two Oxford dons, Doctors J.H.C. Morris and A.D. Macintyre, both Fellows of Magdalen. My second, *In Search of Blandings*, is by a serving army officer, Colonel Norman Murphy. I believe he is, to my embarrassment, in the audience out there. I have been afraid of colonels from the days when I was an awkward squaddie in the ranks of my school Officers' Training Corps, but I shall be frank and fearless about this excellent book. My third book is *Wodehouse at War*, by Iain Sproat, Member of Parliament.

These three books represent three main avenues of what I am pompously calling Wodehouse Scholarship.

1. The first avenue: with seeming innocence you take Wodehouse's fiction as fact, his characters as real people, and you assume that he never made any mistakes. This gets you into a lot of lovely problems, most often about dates, and you spend a lot of lovely time solving them, and teasing other critics who have either not tackled these problems or have not found the right answers to them. This makes a number of pleasant essays, and this is the method of those Oxford dons in their pleasant book *Thank You, Wodehouse*.

2. The second avenue: you accept Wodehouse's fiction as fiction, but you suspect that there is a lot of fact behind it, and you go after pairings – fiction based on fact. That's Colonel Murphy's method in *In Search of Blandings*.

3. The third avenue is purely biographical/factual, as in Iain Sproat's book, *Wodehouse at War*. Now that the Home Office has at last taken the wartime documents out from under wraps, Sproat spreads them on the desk and examines them, to learn just what did happen to poor Wodehouse in the 1940–44 wartime period, why did he make those five talks to America from Berlin (even the benign *New Yorker*, and only recently, referred to them as 'infamous'), what did the world say and – most important – why the hell did the Home Office keep it all under wraps for thirty-seven years? The result, of course, is a belated vindication of Wodehouse. He had been an ass but not a villain. And he suffered for it much more than he deserved, or ever let on.

In *Thank You, Wodehouse* the don authors ask themselves such questions as: What was Bertie's age? How many uncles had he? At which Oxford college was he an undergraduate? (He says, himself, that he was at Magdalen, and surely he should know. But how come he rode a bicycle round the fountain in the nude after a bump supper? Magdalen doesn't have a fountain.) How many girls had Bertie kissed when last heard of? To how many was he engaged on and off? (Remember, he was engaged for several days to Pauline Stoker in New York and he states specifically that he didn't kiss her, for various reasons – a cold in the head and the arrival of the waiter with the beef sandwiches.) What was the chronology of the Blandings stories? Which follows which and at how long a distance of real time? *Was* Ronnie the illegitimate son of General Sir Miles Fish and Lord Emsworth's sister Julia? With how many sisters was Lord Emsworth cursed? How many secretaries? How many pig-minders? How many calories per day did Lord Emsworth's prize pig, Empress of Blandings, consume in her diet? Where was Market Blandings? And what about the train service to and from Paddington? All these questions and many more . . .

Colonel Murphy's *In Search of Blandings* is not by any means all about Blandings. Its subtitle, 'The Facts Behind the Wodehouse Fiction', gives a truer description of its contents. Murphy goes deeply into Shropshire and the Threepwood clan. But he also noses round Norfolk, Sussex, Mayfair, Wimbledon and Emsworth (which is in Hampshire), playing a game of snap when a fictional place or person in the books echoes a real place or person in Wodehouse's own life. Murphy combs through the Wodehouse entries in *Burke* and *Debrett*, through Post Office guides, through parish registers of births and deaths. At Somerset House he dug out the names, addresses and wills of more than fifty of Plum Wodehouse's cousins and other relatives.

In his search for Blandings Castle, Murphy finds a useful starting-point in Stableford, a town in Shropshire where, we know, Wodehouse's parents took a house, and where Plum came from Dulwich for school holidays. But Murphy also keeps a wary eye on Cheltenham, where brother Armine and his wife Nella had a house for a period, and where young Pelham also spent some school holidays. What stately homes round these parts might have given him a shape for Blandings later, and a railway system similar to the one he postulates between Market Blandings and Paddington? I am revealing no secrets when I say that he makes a strong case for Sudeley Castle in Gloucestershire being the fictional Blandings Castle for its architecture and railway system, and Weston Park being Blandings Castle for its estate and gardens, with the village of Weston-under-Lizard as the probable Blandings Parva.

In the context of Blandings Castle, where is it? What was it? I want to slip in here a small contribution of my own. It is a vexed subject – what was the layout of rooms, the inner structure of the castle? Where were the dining rooms, the billiard room, the portrait gallery, Lord Emsworth's study? Wodehouse gives a number of conflicting pointers, but I have made this discovery – now known to Wodehouse scholars as the UCCWC, the Usborne Caveat of Confusion Worse Confounded. Briefly, it is that Wodehouse flitted carelessly between the English and American ways of describing floor-levels of a house. An American might say that the great front door of the castle opened on to the ground floor *or* the first floor – but the floor above is to him always the second floor. We in England say the first floor up is the first floor. Wodehouse writes it both ways, to the confusion of architects and anybody else who's trying to map out the geography of the castle. You've got to watch it carefully.

In many directions of research, other than in looking for Blandings, Murphy is able to claim 'Obviously Wodehouse was thinking of factual X when he wrote fictional Y.' A small example: in his first grown-up novel, *Love Among the Chickens* (1906), there is a handyman named Beale, ex-army. Murphy discovers that the Sergeant-Major in charge of the Officers' Training Corps at Dulwich in Wodehouse's time as a boy was named Beale. And I'll be telling you later, thanks to Colonel Murphy, about Wodehouse's cousin, Helen Marion Wodehouse, Mistress of Girton College, Cambridge from 1931 to 1942.

Fiction combed for fact, fact for illuminations on fiction. Murphy is specially good on the 'Pink 'Un' and Pelican Club background for Galahad's raffish youth and friends.

Iain Sproat's book, as I say, is all fact, no fiction. I nominate it as scholarship for the way Sproat went after his facts, picking locks and breaking down doors to get them. As you know, the Wodehouses at the beginning of the war, 1939, were living in their house – their only home – in Le Touquet in northern France. They were there when the German armies swept west in 1940, and Wodehouse, as a male enemy alien under the age of sixty – he was nearly fifty-nine – soon had to go off to civilian internment. He found himself released a few months before his sixtieth birthday and was brought to Berlin, where he accepted the invitation of a man in the German Foreign Office, whom he had known in Hollywood, to record five Talks to America for the radio . . . America was not yet in the war.

Many of us, including Frances Donaldson in the official *Life*, have written about this gaffe and the tons of bricks that were thrown at Wodehouse for it. I have given my own account, in fourteen pages, plus twenty-seven pages of the verbatim texts of the broadcasts themselves, in my *Penguin Wodehouse Companion* (1988). Wodehouse never came back to England after the war, but he was knighted – surely an official 'forgive and forget' as well as a tribute to his genius – at the age of ninety-three, and forty days before he died. But the Home Office, for reasons intelligible only to itself, had kept the papers of the interrogation of the Wodehouses in Paris after the liberation in the autumn of 1944 under wraps for several more years. And during all those years, before the full and innocent facts were known, one thought there *must* have been something despicable, not to say traitorous, that the Wodehouses had done, in Germany or France, and which we were not allowed to know.

The talks were cheerful, funny, completely Wodehousian . . . about his experiences, in various uncomfortable railway-trucks, and prisons, and barracks, and camps, on his way to the last camp, a converted lunatic asylum. Innocent though the talks were, it goes without saying that, as a British citizen in wartime, he should *not* have accepted the invitation to speak on the German radio. There was an immediate outcry against him in England and a good deal of disapproval in America. He never came back to England after the war and the cloud under which his name lay took a long time to disperse, largely because the official papers on the matter were not released to the public.

Iain Sproat, among others, had been trying to get the Home Office to unbelt the papers, or give the reason why not. And eventually, only last year, the Home Office did unbelt them, and Iain Sproat was the first to see them. Sproat gives the whole story: a diary of the events themselves, the documents, the five talks *verbatim*, the interrogation, the questions in Parliament and so on. You must read it, and not least the Home Office's strange reasons for not having let us have chapter and verse till years after Wodehouse's death.

The Sproat book, the Sproat scholarship, has done a fine job, for us, and for poor Wodehouse. And a curse on the faceless bureaucracy which kept a good man's reputation under a cloud for thirty-four unnecessary years!

Goodness, how sad the whole of that story of the Berlin broadcasts was! Wodehouse, in his post-war novels, did make pinprick teases of some of the people who spoke out against him in 1941. Gussie Fink-Nottle, you remember, up before the beak for newt-hunting after midnight in a Trafalgar Square fountain, gave his name as Alfred Duff Cooper. It was Duff Cooper who, as Minister of Information, had got the 'Cassandra' of the *Daily Mirror* – William (later Sir William) Connor – to spit that vile philippic against Wodehouse on the BBC radio. Let it be said that the BBC was all against it, but the Minister overrode them. And A.A. Milne again . . .

In the context of A.A. Milne and the damning letter he wrote about Plum's broadcasting from wartime Berlin, I commend to you a half-page of typescript in an upright glass-case in this exhibition – the case on the right as you stand with your back to the windows on the second floor. It was a stray page found in Wodehouse's study at home after his death. It is something he had typed, and then crossed out in pencil – and he had used the paper to type something on the other side. But the half-page he had typed and crossed out is an expert sleeve across the Milne windpipe. I don't know what it was for: something to be published in his memoirs? For a book to be called *Over Ninety*? Anyway, Wodehouse must have decided that he couldn't use it, perhaps that it was out of character for him to show that he had minded Milne hitting him below the belt during the war, out of character to be giving Milne the chop in reply. But I am delighted that this stray half-page of Wodehouse typescript should have been rescued, and its words made available to posterity:

Milne is the author of *Winnie-the-Pooh* and other works, and I have known him off and on for nearly forty years. He has never been a very popular man for one reason and another, and it was in the hope of giving him a rather wider circle of admirers that I once founded the Try To Like Milne Club. It never really caught on. After a great deal of canvassing I could find only one man who was willing to join, and he wrote me a week later saying, 'I'm sorry. I shall have to resign from the Try To Like Milne Club. I've just met him.'

The book, by the Oxford dons, *Thank You, Wodehouse*, puts Wodehouse among those much loved authors with whose works saints and scholars relax when they know they ought to be reading their bibles, or studying the works of Sophocles or Spinoza – the Sherlock Holmes stories, *Alice in Wonderland*, Stevenson's *The Wrong Box*, some Shakespeare and Trollope's Barsetshire. These saints and scholars produce specialist spoof scholarship as a 'displacement activity': what they hope will be taken as a justification for their laughing in an armchair when they should be at their desks surrounded by dictionaries, commentaries, concordances and things, like – to use a Wodehouse image – sea-beasts among rocks. Whatever their consciences may say, they are paying tribute to their beloved authors by giving their stuff the donnish treatment as though it were the Bible, Sophocles or Spinoza.

I don't say I know of any dons or divines whose displacement activities have been quite so time-consuming as those of a certain Bishop of Wells of the not too distant past. He is reported to have said, 'I like to get my golf over in the mornings so that I can have the afternoons for bridge.' I wonder how he relaxed in the evenings. He was of too early a date to have been tempted by the works of Wodehouse.

I suppose the grave of Conan Doyle, with the Sherlock Holmes stories, has come in for the most frequent and continuous laying on of such wreaths and bouquets by amateur and professional scholars. I possess those two monster and expensive volumes entitled *The Annotated Sherlock Holmes*, containing all the stories, all the *Strand Magazine* illustrations and acres and acres of solemn notes and essaylets such as Sherlock Holmes addicts exchange in their magazines, and at their dinners and club meetings. I read the other day, didn't I, that the Abbey National people in Baker Street, whose building might be said to stand where Number 221A stood, get – wasn't it? – some two thousand letters a year – or was it a week? Or a day? – addressed either direct to Mr Sherlock Holmes or to Abbey National for passing on, and they are all courteously answered, presumably by some Sherlock Holmes scholar. I remember that on the one occasion when I visited the Wodehouses, in their home on Long Island, I was shown into Plum's study, first by his wife Ethel – perhaps Plum was getting the drinks out. On his desk in the study was a big, neatly stacked basket of letters, mostly in air-mail envelopes. Ethel Wodehouse said, with an expression of wifely disapproval, 'Plummie insists on answering every letter. I wish he wouldn't.' Later I was in the study with Plum himself and he pointed to the letter tray and said, a little sadly, 'Ethel insists on my answering all the letters I get.'

I think the style of such spoof examinations of favourite books of entertainment is based on the plodding German scholarship of the early nineteenth century, when German pundits got into the Bible, the Greek and Latin classics and Shakespeare. I'm sure it is great fun, for the addict, to write in this style of spoof solemnity. The master of it – or, say, the man whose publications of such literary displacement activities I know best and have enjoyed most – is Monsignor Ronald Knox. He was a man of deep and reverent Catholic faith, of great industry and of restless brilliance, ingenuity and humour who, for relaxation, set himself awful problems of rhyme and reason for the pleasure of working them out, in English, Latin, Greek or (latterly) Hebrew – the more difficult the better.

Knox was one of the numerous dons and divines – he was both in his time – who read Wodehouse regularly and with great admiration. I wish he had included Wodehouse among his subjects for extramural publication. He was one of the first, perhaps *the* first, to apply this kind of scholarship to Sherlock Holmes and he clearly knew the stories backwards. There is a long essay in his book, *Essays in Satire*, entitled 'Studies in the literature of Sherlock Holmes'. He later goes on to study similarly Trollope's Barsetshire novels, Bunyan's *Pilgrim's Progress*, Boswell's *Life of Johnson* and, in the manner of Freudian psychoanalysis, the Struwwelpeter verses. For good measure he also – in imitation and mockery of the methods of those who prove, by cyphers, that Bacon, or a number of other people, wrote Shakespeare – proves, by cyphers, that Queen Victoria wrote Tennyson's 'In Memoriam'. I say Tennyson's, but that's wrong. The cyphers show that Queen Victoria wrote it and used Tennyson as a front man, just as Bacon had used Shakespeare.

Well, I'd like to read you a bit of Knox's introduction to his

Sherlock Holmes essay, because it exactly defines the approach of these Oxford dons to Wodehouse's works:

> If there is anything pleasant in life, it is doing what we are not meant to do. If there is anything pleasant in criticism, it is finding out what we are not meant to find out. It is the method by which we treat as significant what the author did not mean to be significant, by which we single out as essential what the author regarded as incidental. Thus, if one brings out a book on turnips, the modern scholar tries to discover from it whether the author was on good terms with his wife; if a poet writes on buttercups, every word he says may be used as evidence against him at an inquest of his views on a future existence. On this fascinating principle, we delight to extort economic evidence from Aristophanes, because Aristophanes knew nothing of economics: we try to extract cryptograms from Shakespeare, because we are inwardly certain that Shakespeare never put them there: we sift and winnow the Gospel of St Luke, in order to produce a Synoptic problem, because St Luke, poor man, never knew the Synoptic problem to exist.
>
> There is, however, a special fascination in applying this method to Sherlock Holmes, because it is, in a sense, Holmes's own method. 'It has long been an axiom of mine,' he says, 'that the little things are infinitely the most important . . .'

Then Knox goes on for thirty scholarly pages about why Dr John Watson's wife calls him James; about whether Holmes had been at Oxford or Cambridge and for how long; about the probable *two* Sherlock Holmeses, and the alleged death of one of them grappling with Moriarty on the Reichenbach Falls; about how a pencil marked with the maker's name, Johann Faber – two 'n's at the end of Johann – could be worn down to a stump with only the two 'n's left on it; about the dating of the stories; a comparison of a moment in 'The Speckled Band' with a moment in Aeschylus's *Agamemnon* play – and so on. Lovely, loving donnish stuff: the don at ease and at play.

I think that these essays of Knox were mostly, if not all, papers that he had prepared for the literary and convivial paper-reading societies which proliferate in public schools and universities (he had been a scholar at Eton and at Balliol, a classics teacher at Shrewsbury and a don at Trinity, Oxford). Indeed, he was an Oxford figure for half his life, and much invited to such societies. I would guess that it was he who made 'displacement activities' of this kind respectable, scholar yodelling to scholar across the groves of Academe as, in Wodehouse, aunt bellowed to aunt like mastodons across the primeval swamp. Still, if you look at the last item in the book Wodehouse had published in 1903, *Tales of St Austin's*, you will find Wodehouse himself, as early as that, applying to *Tom Brown's Schooldays* mock-German-Homeric scholarship, and showing that the second, soppy, half of *Tom Brown* was written not by Hughes but by a group calling themselves The Secret Society for Putting Wholesome Literature within the Reach of Every Boy and Seeing That He Gets it.

Other notable contributions to Wodehouse scholarship? Well, I hope you've seen, in the cases outside dealing with the Empress of Blandings, the picture found in a pig-breeding manual of the 1920s by a Wodehouse addict with the happy name of James Hogg; a picture of the Black Berkshire sow, painted by an artist named Wippell. It is very hard to argue for such a rare name, so appropriately connected, *not* having influenced Wodehouse. I personally believe, with James Hogg, that somehow Wodehouse had seen this book, this name and this picture of the black pig, and that the Empress was therefore specified as a Black Berkshire and Lord Emsworth's favourite author was given the crafty name Whiffle, his book being the immortal *On the Care of the Pig*. Go up top, James Hogg. And thank you, from all Wodehouse addicts.

By the way, another man, who shall be nameless because, alas, I have lost his letter, has discovered the author of *Types of Ethical Theory*. You will remember that this ghastly book was given to Bertie Wooster by the ghastly Florence Craye when they were first, and for the first time, engaged. And this is a passage that Bertie finds in it:

The postulate or common understanding involved in speech is certainly coextensive, in the obligation it carries, with the social organism of which language is the instrument, and the ends of which it is an effort to subserve.

Bertie's comment, as narrator, is:

All perfectly true, no doubt; but not the sort of thing to spring on a lad with a morning head.

Bertie does not tell us the name of the author of this ghastly book. Frances Donaldson tells me that she showed the sentence quoted to Sir Isaiah Berlin, that polymath philosopher, at Oxford, and he couldn't identify the book or the author. But he did say that in philosophic jargon – the way philosophers talked and wrote when they were on the job – the sentence made some sense: it wasn't a parody. I am happy to report that the author is, or was, a Dr James Martineau, 1805–1900, referred to in the *Dictionary of National Biography* as a 'unitarian divine', and author of many philosophic books and treatises including one long essay on Spinoza, which I expect Jeeves has read. I tried it and got stuck in the second page. Dr Martineau achieved the distinction of having a book written about his work, entitled *Dr Martineau's Philosophy*, by one C.B. Upton. Just for fun I'd like to read you one thrilling passage in Upton's book:

After distinguishing between a *spontaneity* and a *volition*, and explaining that for a voluntary act it is necessary that not less than two impulses should be present, Dr Martineau proceeds to express and establish a vital principle in his ethical theory, which is thus enunciated:
This plurality of simultaneous tendencies, however, would still present no cause for moral judgement were it not also felt to be a plurality of *simultaneous tendencies*. I must lay a separate stress upon each of those two words: a) the impulses must be simultaneous *inter se*: and b) they must be possibilities *to us*.

I could not bring myself to wade through *Types of Ethical Theory* to find the exact sentence that Bertie Wooster quoted. It is a very long book, and Dr Martineau is one of those philosophers who, for my money, disappear up their own hypotheses very quickly.

But I am delighted to learn, from Murphy again, that Plum Wodehouse's cousin, Helen Marion Wodehouse, Mistress of Girton College, Cambridge (where Florence Craye had been a student, of course) wrote books on philosophy too, and Murphy suggests, as a parallel to that passage from *Types of Ethical Theory* that Florence forced on to Bertie, this from Helen Marion Wodehouse's book, *The Logic of Will*:

> Of the two antithetic terms in the Greek philosophy only one was real and self-subsisting; and that one was Ideal Thought as opposed to that which it has to penetrate and mould. The other, corresponding to our Nature, was in itself pheno-menal, unreal without any permanent footing, having no predicates that held true for two moments together; in short redeemed from negation only by including indwelling realities appearing through.

To compare – or perhaps correlate is the *mot juste* – Cousin Helen Marion Wodehouse with Lady Florence Craye is, with Murphy, the work of a moment, and I think he's got a real find there.

And now, as I come to the end of all this, there is one item of, well, call it scholarship – linguistic scholarship – in which the problem remains to be solved, and I give it to you in the wild hope that someone may spot the echo and give me the answer. May I ask you to listen very carefully: it's a slighter thing than that quotation from *Types of Ethical Theory*. It's a phrase, an idiom, an image – yes, an echo. I don't really know what a grammarian would call it, but Wodehouse uses it at least half a dozen times over the vintage years between the wars. He's echoing something. I *know* he's echoing something, parodying something, gently mocking something for his own amusement. I'll give you three examples. First Bertie, who is his own narrator as usual: he writes ' "Oh," I replied, with a suavity that became me well.' There's the little phrase that I am trying to locate – 'that became me well'. It's fatuous, and funny, and Wodehouse repeats it often enough in other contexts to make it significant. Here's another example, from a Mulliner story dealing with the Church, the story 'Mulliner's Buck-U-Uppo'.

His vicar glared at Augustine.

'What do you mean by jumping through my window?' he thundered. 'Are you a curate or a harlequin?'

Augustine met his gaze with an unfaltering eye.

'I am a curate,' he replied with a dignity that well became him.

'With a suavity that became me well.' 'With a dignity that well became him.' I'll give you one more, from one of the golf stories:

'We want to settle a bet,' said James . . . 'will you please tell who . . . I should say whom . . . you are knitting that sweater for?'

'It's not a sweater,' replied Miss Forester with a womanly candour that well became her. 'It's a sock.'

I am sure this item of Wodehouse mimicry is not an echo of Malcolm's 'Nothing in his life became him like the leaving it' in *Macbeth*. I think, and it's a guess, that the turn of words has a pulpit provenance. There's a churchy ring about it: the school chapel, the short manly sermon by an Old Boy bishop? In my dreams I see young Wodehouse (P.G.) hearing it at Dulwich and making it part of a parody language for the study tea-party.

If you recognize and can identify this phrase, or turn of words, and tell me what it is echoing, I promise to see that your answer and your name is acknowledged, and distributed with gratitude to other Wodehouse scholars.[1]

Well, I've overshot my time, and my subject, if any. But let me read to you – even if you read it yourself last Sunday in the *Sunday Times* Colour Magazine – what Arthur 'Call My Bluff' Marshall said at the end of that 'A Day In The Life Of' piece about him:

I retire to bed very early, about half past nine. And every night before composing myself for sleep, I read a paragraph or two of P.G. Wodehouse. Because the writing is so perfect, the choice of words, the jokes, I always feel that I can go to sleep and, if I die in the night, there'll be this pleased expression on my face – a smile of quiet acceptance.[2]

Postscripts

1. *Nobody has yet convincingly identified for me this turn of phrase. I live in hope.*

2. *Arthur Marshall died, in his sleep, in 1989.*

7
Old Boy at Dulwich

Fifteenth October 1977 would have been Plum's ninety-sixth birthday had he lived another two and a half years. After his death, Ethel, his widow, had sent from Long Island to his old school, Dulwich, a number of items from his study: his desk, his chair, his typewriter, a painted portrait, a filing cabinet, many books, his own and others', old pipes and tobacco pouches, and smaller mementoes. A recess in the library at Dulwich had been built into The Wodehouse Corner. (The whole library is now The Wodehouse Library.) On 15 October 1977 The Wodehouse Corner was opened, in a short ceremony, by Edward (now Sir Edward) Cazalet, son of Plum's stepdaughter, Leonora. The Master had asked me to speak in the hall that evening.

In the afternoon, on the Dulwich ground in golden sunshine, there had been a fiercely contested school rugger match, Dulwich versus Haileybury. Dulwich was behind until three minutes before the end. Then they scored an unconverted try (10:15 to Haileybury) and, in the final minute, a converted try, to win 16:15. As the Master said that evening, this would have been a very happy occasion for Plum, who had played for the school as a boy and had followed Dulwich's fortunes at cricket and rugger ever since. In 1933 he had come down to Dulwich to watch the XV play against Sherborne. Dulwich was 0:3 down till near the end of the first half when they scored a converted try and held their lead throughout the second half. But Plum hadn't been able to stand the strain at close quarters. He had left and walked round the roads outside the school grounds until the huge cheering, and his watch, told him that it was all over successfully. He had then walked the seven miles back to his hotel, the Dorchester, in a haze of happiness.

Wodehouse had been a boy at Dulwich for six years and one term, and had loved it. He had come at the beginning of the summer term of 1894 and left at the end of the summer term of 1900. For his first term he was a day-boy, lodged at the house of an assistant master in East Dulwich. Then he became a boarder for two terms, until his parents returned from Hong Kong and took a house in Dulwich. The family moved up to Shropshire in the summer of 1896 and Plum became a boarder at Dulwich again. He

95

was in the College rugger team for a year and in the cricket for two. He was joint editor of the magazine the Alleynian, *a member of the Classical Sixth Form for two years, and a prefect.*

This is the text of my address in the Hall. The passages from Wodehouse books were read, excellently, by two Dulwich masters, Robert MacDowell and Peter Southern.

If you have read the book titled *Performing Flea* you will remember that it is composed mainly of letters that Wodehouse wrote, in the thirty and more years between 1920 and 1953, to his Dulwich schoolfriend, Bill Townend. They had shared a study in 1898 in one of the four boarding houses – Elm Lawn, which I understand is now the Master's house.

It is in a note by Townend in *Performing Flea* that we get a picture of Wodehouse on his last visit here to his old school – indeed his last visit to England for that matter. Townend writes:

> In the latter end of July 1939, Plum was over briefly from Le Touquet, where he lived, and on the Saturday he and I went to Dulwich together to see the school play St. Paul's, and it was the dullest cricket match, the slowest and most un-eventful that either of us had ever seen . . . . I said goodbye to Plum at about four o'clock, and left him seated in the pavilion, looking rather bored and rather disconsolate. That was the last time I saw him. Six weeks later war was declared.

So the two old friends never met again. Wodehouse went to America after the war and Townend died in, I think, 1962, in England. It's a sad last snapshot of Wodehouse out there in the pavilion, and I blame the schoolboy cricketers of the year. If it had been an exciting match, with hard hitting and Dulwich winning, the picture might have been of a smiling rather than doleful countenance.

In the late 1950s, when I was working on a book about Wodehouse's books, I asked Townend about his friend Plum Wodehouse at school. Was he a funny fellow? A wit? A cause of wit in others? A natural choice for Falstaff in the end-of-term school play? Or King Lear's Fool? Or King Lear himself?

Wodehouse was a very successful writer for the musical comedy stage in the years between the wars: but he was never an actor. At Dulwich he had written, for private circulation, a squib about the masters, in the manner and form of a Greek play. Well, I asked Townend, was the young Wodehouse an amusing boy? What had amused him? There was one story that Townend told me and that I put in my book: and I'll tell it again quickly now. Wodehouse (P.G.) had a habit of decorating, or, as schoolmasters would say, defacing, his school text books with little matchstick drawings of men and animals. You know the things. If you do them at the side of every page and then flip the pages, you get a primitive animated cartoon effect. (The boy in my classes at my preparatory school who did these best later became a bishop, deservedly. His 'Fight Between Hector and Achilles', with the chariot and corpse-dragging at the end, went half-way through the small Liddell and Scott Greek lexicon.) Plum Wodehouse had been a constant practitioner of this form of schoolboy art. And one day, in the Classical Sixth, they were doing Euripides with the Master, Gilkes. And Gilkes, striding round the room, wanted to check something in a text and he asked the boy nearest to him, which was Wodehouse (P.G.), to lend him his copy of the Plays. Wodehouse handed his book up, Gilkes flipped through its pages and handed it back, saying, 'No, *thanks*. This book has got a man in it.' At which, Townend told me, Wodehouse had laughed for about a year.

Another brief, and incomplete, memory that Townend had, and that I've remembered now – in answer to my question 'Was Plum Wodehouse a funny chap at school?'– was at some school group photograph. All the boys were trying to get into their rows and ranks, in chairs, on seats, on benches, on the ground: all that palaver, nerve-fraying for the prefects and masters, fraught with giggles for the rank-and-file, especially in the days when such photography was a matter of tripods, black cloths over the head of the cameraman, removal of a black cap from the spout of the instrument, and agonising time-exposures when everybody had to keep utterly still.

Well, the occasion that Townend could remember at Dulwich . . . just when the group had achieved the final

steadiness, silence and strained smiles, the low voice of Plum
Wodehouse, one of the rank-and-file, was heard. What he said,
Townend couldn't remember, alas, but whatever it was, it
caused the whole pack of cards to collapse in laughter and
disarray.

No, the boy Wodehouse hadn't been the school wit, nor a
comic, nor a buffoon. It can be shown, I think, that many
latterday professional humorists had, at school, or in a large
family, found that being funny was the best way of gaining
acceptance, respect and a rise in the pecking order in an age
group or among brothers and sisters, and had adopted humour
as a self-defensive, self-advancing technique. At school, if you
weren't good at games, if your parents didn't come down to
visit you in a Rolls-Royce (I am speaking of my own public
schooldays – and my parents didn't), if you were small, or
plagued with spots – you might still achieve popularity by
being funny. This idea – raise a laugh and raise your status – is
discussed interestingly by Old Alleynian Punch-writer,
Richard Price, in his *History of Punch* itself.

Clearly Wodehouse's humour was not of that sort, nor had it
self-defensive origins. He had status enough at school as a good
games-player, big, a good boxer, and with an elder brother a
considerable success-figure in the school already. I am sure
that Wodehouse Junior, though he was a light-hearted schoolboy, with a talent to amuse, already had deep reserves of
privacy. Certainly it was fairly late in his literary life that he
went flat out for farce and developed his talent to amuse into a
genius for sustained, word-woven absurdity.

But only at his desk, at his typewriter, in private. He was
never, as far as I know, a convivial, gregarious, clubland figure,
eager to set the table on a roar.

And speaking of privacy – and I'm sorry for going back to my
book for a moment – Old Alleynian cricketer Trevor Bailey told
me that, in his first year in the school team, aged fourteen, the
school won all its matches, and Old Boy Wodehouse enter-
tained them, the whole team, to a dinner in London and the
Palladium afterwards. That was a nice thought, and a nice act,
and a nice story, and I put it in my book fifteen years ago. It was
only in the last few weeks that one of the Dulwich masters here,
David Knight, who had also been in the team as a boy then,

happened to mention to me that Wodehouse himself had not been at his party. He had paid the restaurant bill and paid for the Palladium seats, but hadn't been with them. This hasn't much to do with Wodehouse the writer, but it squares very well with the image that I have now of Wodehouse the man: generous, self-effacing, private. I admit that it is somewhat impertinent of me to hold forth at all on Wodehouse the man – whom I met just once – in the presence here of people of his family, who really did know him.

There was something to which Townend, in his letters to me and at our infrequent meetings in London, kept coming back: Plum Wodehouse's constant generosity to him, a lesser writer, whose cheques from publishers and editors came in irregularly and in small figures. Plum Wodehouse was always available and willing to help Townend's writing, with advice and first-class criticism (see *Performing Flea* throughout). Wodehouse also went out of his way to encourage editors, publishers and critics to take notice of Bill Townend's work. And, in Townend's frequent lean periods – periods of anaemia of the bank balance – Wodehouse, without being asked, sensed it and provided money. It had to be done carefully: they both realised that.

I read somewhere that Arnold Bennett, when he was young and struggling, set himself two targets, of status and prosperity. First, always to be able to keep a pineapple on his sideboard: second, to get his bank manager to come and see *him*, not always the other way round. Bennett achieved both targets. But Wodehouse didn't need to go and see his bank manager, nor to ask his bank manager to come and see him. His bank manager lived in his house. It was his dear wife, Ethel.

Wodehouse as a boy had heard his parents quarrelling about money, and he had then and there determined that, when he got married, his wife would be the chancellor of their joint exchequer. And so it was. Wodehouse earned a great deal of money, loved doing so and was very content to let his wife look after it, spend it, invest it, sometimes pay the income tax people with it. But of course Wodehouse had a number of less prosperous friends – writers and artists and people in the theatre – and plenty of requests for loans. No wife, no bank manager, encourages a husband, or a client, to give the stuff away on all occasions. But Wodehouse broke the rules, discreetly and abundantly, with his less successful writer-schoolfriend, Bill. And Bill was never, repeat never, to refer to it in letters to Plum. The cheques came via publishers, editors, literary agents – never directly from the Wodehouse joint bank account.

It was a situation from which Wodehouse made one or two good plot situations in stories and novels: the joint husband-and-wife bank account, with the wife in control. Lady Ickenham kept a tight screw on her ebullient husband, Pongo Twistleton's Uncle Fred. And, in one of the last novels – I forget which – an American millionaire, a Hollywood tycoon, I think, had to ask his secretary for a small loan since he didn't dare tell his wife he needed cash from their millions. Quite funny, but Wodehouse knew what he was writing about – and was well content about it, except perhaps in the matter of helping Bill Townend. And Bill Townend, knowing I was writing about Wodehouse, but knowing, too, that I wouldn't write too blatantly, then, about this, insisted that, off the then record, I should know of this generosity of Plum Wodehouse's.

In fact, Bill Townend told me, when the Germans swept into France and over-ran the Wodehouses, Plum and Ethel, in their house in Le Touquet in 1940, Townend received an urgent call from Leonora Cazalet (Ethel Wodehouse's daughter by a previous marriage, adopted, loved and devoted daughter of her mother's new husband and later married to Peter Cazalet). Leonora, when France fell, hurriedly got in touch with Bill Townend and said, 'Don't worry. I shall be here to help you until Plummie comes back to us.'

Perhaps, after all, Ethel had known, but turned a blind eye to Plum's constant financial support of his great friend. Leonora died, tragically, before the end of the war. It was her son, Edward, Ethel's grandson, who opened the P.G. Wodehouse Memorial in the library this afternoon. It was her daughter Sheran who had unveiled the memorial plaque over the front door of the house in Guildford where Plum had been born.

Now, if I may revert to the young Wodehouse whose casual remark at a moment of high tension – the school group photograph – produced an explosion of laughter, it seems to me that laughter exploding out of suppression is very much a bonus of youth. At boarding school, someone has said, everything that is not forbidden is compulsory. It is, roughly, only in youth that one is regularly forbidden laughter, under pain of punishment. Those are the days when one has to be silent to order, serious to order: to suppress laughter, in chapel, in house prayers, in class, in the ranks of the OTC. But suppressed laughter, though painful, is an exquisite pain, its release a wild and abundant joy – that breathless, purple-faced, bottled laughter that constricts the stomach muscles, brings tears to the eyes and, sometimes, raucous agony through the nostrils. It is perhaps the best and most precious laughter of one's life, and it is granted to us most abundantly in our servile youth, when authority can say to us, sternly, 'Behave yourself or leave the room!'

I want to tell you of one occasion – a very sad, indeed macabre, occasion – when I, no longer in my youth by any means, had to suppress my laughter, laughter generated to explosion point by a book of Wodehouse.

It was in 1956 that I was lined up to write a book about Wodehouse's books. And it had to be ready for his eightieth birthday, 15 October 1961. I was glad of the five-year deadline, because I am a very slow and timid worker, and I had to read, or re-read, all of Wodehouse's books, more than eighty of them. One that I found I had never read before, at all, was *Something Fresh*, his first Blandings novel and his first farce, as opposed to light novel.

You probably don't remember it, but, even as late as 1956, eleven years after the end of the war in Europe, several commodities – some foods, drink, coal, petrol – were still in short supply in England. I decided to live for pleasure alone and take a fortnight's working holiday, with a bagful of Wodehouse books, in the south of France. I also took my bathing pants, and a sharp thirst and appetite. I needn't tell you that nothing was rationed in France, bless its Gallic heart. I fetched up in one of those Mediterranean villages which had been built perched on a hillside overlooking the sea: a small, off-the-main-beat place with a few not too expensive hotels, *pensions*, restaurants and *cafés*, an artists' colony, an enormous number of cats and, in the hot, velvet nights, absolute silence and stillness. Owing to the precipitous architecture of the village, its acoustics in the still night were astonishingly good and far-reaching, like that of a Greek theatre carved out of a hillside. You could hear pins drop five houses away. In my hotel at Bormes-les-Mimosas (that's what the village was called) at night, when the traffic had stopped, and the crickets, the swallows, and the accordion in the *café* near the Post Office – when these had finished, from the window of my bedroom I could hear couples whispering far up the hillside. I thought I could hear the *curé* saying his prayers before bed in his little house the other side of the church, and the mayor cleaning his teeth further away still. And I expect they could, if they listened, hear me turning the pages of *Something Fresh* in my hotel bedroom.

Now, this is the grim part. There was, in a house several streets away from my hotel, and within earshot of the whole village, an old lady who was bedridden, very ill and in great and constant pain. And, as I discovered from the man who ran my hotel, this old lady was looked after by a devoted daughter. The doctor had prescribed, and instructed the daughter in the administration of, pain-killing injections every four hours, night and day. Poor old lady, four hours were one hour too many for her comfort and oblivion, for a sleep and a forgetting. And her mounting pain was audible, between the third and fourth hour, in the night. For myself, I found it essential to go to sleep in the silence soon after the lady had had an injection, otherwise the crescendo, from sighs to cries, in the last hour before the next relief, plus my imagination of what she must be suffering, made sleep impossible.

I have a still all too vivid memory of reading, during one of those bad periods in the small hours, that chapter near the end of *Something Fresh* where, in the total darkness of the great hall at Blandings Castle, the efficient Baxter, suspecting that there is some devilry afoot, descends the staircase and meets, and grapples with, George Emerson, who is going up. Emerson is carrying a tray of supper, including a small cold tongue complete, to leave it, the tray, on the mat outside the door of the bedroom where his beloved Aline, the American millionaire's daughter, is, must be, George thinks, starving. Aline has, to encourage her father, who is on a diet for an ulcer *and* is a greedy pig, to refuse food at meals herself. So, in George's view, Aline needs secret midnight feeding. Hence the tray, and the cold tongue – and the sudden encounter with Baxter in the dark, and the fall of the tray, and the cold tongue, and the fall of both strugglers, interlocked, down the stairs into the great hall, sending chairs and tables flying and crashing. Hence Lord Emsworth's arrival, still in the dark, at the top of the stairs, in a dressing gown, with a revolver, to exercise a feudal right to shoot burglars – well, not on sight, because he couldn't see anything, but to shoot anyway and hope to wing, or even just frighten, the intruder or intruders. Hence, again, Baxter, cowering on the floor, lays his face up against something cold and corpse-like – he thinks it's a dead man. It's really the cold tongue.

That is a scene that I can re-read today with pleasure, but not explosive laughter. But that night in Bormes-les-Mimosas I was racked with laughter and – a thing I had not done since my school-days – I stuffed a handkerchief into my mouth to prevent my hilarity being heard through the village in accompaniment to the poor lady's cries for her tardy injection.

I was tempted – though only briefly – to write to Wodehouse and tell him of this ghoulish occasion and how very funny – mercifully funny – I had found that chapter of his early book. I'm glad I didn't. I learnt later that he was very sensitive to pain, in other people and in animals. You may recall that, in several novels and stories, *Something Fresh* amongst them, Wodehouse used dyspepsia for good comedy. Aline Peters's father in *Something Fresh*, Lord Tilbury in I forget which novel and, of course, Bertie Wooster's own Uncle Tom Travers. Old Tom Travers suffered from agonising stomach pains after meals until (a) his wife Dahlia, with Jeeves's help, lured the great chef, Anatole, from the Bingo Littles' employment and (b) Uncle Tom gave up having cold lobster at gentlemen's clubs for lunch.

Wodehouse's secretary, with whom I corresponded after his death, told me that she used to drive him on his routine visits to hospitals and dentists in Long Island, in his late eighties and early nineties. And once, while they were waiting for his doctor at the hospital, Wodehouse saw a man, doubled up and in great pain, being led down a corridor. Wodehouse asked someone on the staff what the man's trouble had been, and was told 'stomach ulcers', and it saddened him greatly – not only in sympathy for the man's pain, but because he had used ulcers as comedy in his books. Never again.

Which reminds me of yet another thing that Bill Townend told me: that Plum Wodehouse was a great reader, and admirer, of Dickens. But he simply could not face the novels, or the parts, where people were unkind to children: *Dombey, David Copperfield, Little Dorrit, Oliver Twist, Great Expectations*. I find it difficult to think of a Dickens novel (I don't include *Pickwick*) in which some child *isn't* beaten, starved, crippled, killed, frightened or humiliated. Wodehouse couldn't read all Dickens by any means. He thought Dickens was cruel. He himself, of course, put a number of children into his books – all, I think without exception, cheerful thugs, crooks, blackmailers and villains. But nobody was *cruel* to them, ever, as far as I remember. Chastisement, yes. As when Lord Worplesdon had caught the fourteen-year-old Bertie Wooster smoking one of his special cigars in the stables – and had chased him across difficult country with a hunting crop. As when the grown Bertie had booted the same Lord Worplesdon's boy-scout son Edwin Craye in the khaki shorts on the garden path, sending him flying. As when Mr Anstruther, the neurotic septuagenarian, set about young Thos, 'Aunt Agatha's loathly son', with a walking stick. But, as a rule, it was the grown-ups who suffered most in collision with Wodehouse's children.

I finally met Wodehouse on the eve of his ninetieth birthday, in Long Island, with television teams and reporters (and people like me) coming at him day after day and from all directions. In the long talk I had with him, and in the many television interviews with him that I have seen – Malcolm Muggeridge's, Robert Robinson's and others – it has always been hard work for the interviewer. Wodehouse, very courteous, always modest, always kind about and to other people, was always evasive about himself. He didn't much like being interviewed, and sometimes (well, those broadcasts from Berlin in 1941, for instance) got himself into trouble *viva voce*. He preferred to sieve his stuff through the typewriter for the printed page.

Wodehouse had been happy at Dulwich. He said that the six

104

years of his schooldays went like a breeze. And West Dulwich itself is fondly commemorated as Valley Fields in a number of his books. Even before he left school Wodehouse knew he was going to be a writer, and when he started writing, what did he know to write about except school life?

The first half-guinea he ever made by his pen (or perhaps already a typewriter) was for a contribution to *The Public School Magazine*, on 'Some Aspects of Game-Captaincy'. Next half-guinea, a short article on 'Cricket at Malvern': next, 'Cricket at Dulwich' – all of these for half-guineas for *The Public School Magazine*. His first break-through into the after-life and big money was when he sold to *Tit-Bits*, for fifteen shillings, an article entitled 'Men Who Have Missed Their Own Weddings'. I got all these fascinating trivia out of the first account book he kept, for six years, entitled *Money Received for Literary Work*. Wodehouse lent me this years ago and, though I gratefully sent it back when I had had its contents typed out and had absorbed what I wanted for my book, it has now, it seems, disappeared off the face of this earth. If ever there was a treasure that ought to be in the Wodehouse Corner of the Dulwich College Library, it is that.[1]

I see from this account book that the first two chapters of what became Wodehouse's first school novel, *The Pothunters*, appeared in *The Public School Magazine* in January 1902, when its author was still a bank-clerk. He didn't chuck the bank for another nine months. Then he went full time to be a free-lance writer. He became, as you know, a very successful, and great, one.

Wodehouse never regarded his school stories as anything but apprentice work, and he thought George Orwell – and I, for that matter – paid them too much attention. Orwell rated Wodehouse's *Mike* as possibly the best light school novel ever written. Orwell may have been right there, but I do not propose to check. I would *not* like the job of wading, for the purpose of establishing a chart of merit, through the hundreds of public-school novels that were written, generally with a high moral and evangelical intent, from the 1840s to the start of the First World War. I never want to read *Tom Brown's Schooldays* again. Nor *Stalky* for that matter.

It is good to know that Alec Waugh is with us this evening, a

105

friend of Wodehouse's and himself the author, at the age of nineteen, of a famous public-school novel, *The Loom of Youth*, which, published in 1917, did quite a lot to turn the serious public-school novel away from the paths of righteousness, evangelism, soppiness and cant, into something in which boys could recognise, with whatever fondness or embarrassment, their own schooldays rather than what school headmasters – all hoping to become bishops then – wanted parents to think a public school was like – just the place for little Johnny when the time came.

I certainly do *not* agree with Orwell that Wodehouse was 'fixated' in his schooldays all his life. 'Fixated' is the sort of horrid word that Sir Roderick Glossop, the great Harley Street loony-doctor in the later Wodehouse novels, might have used. Wodehouse himself thought his school stories weren't bad. But, as I said, they were apprentice work, adding to his income while he was learning the trade of writing.

Mind you, he got a lot of good, affectionate fun out of the public-school hangover, and public-school code, in dozens of his books, long after he had stopped writing public-school books. Incidentally, a very practical reason for Wodehouse stopping writing about public schools was that he was expanding his market into America, and in America a public school is a private school, and Americans don't understand cricket or rugger. Or they didn't then.

The public-school hangover. Do you remember, in *Money in the Bank*, young Jeff Miller (he has to be the hero in any book of Wodehouse's with that sort of name)? Young Jeff Miller has just qualified as a barrister, and has been given his first brief by the stern solicitor, who is also the father of the stern girl that Jeff is engaged to. Jeff tells his motherly housekeeper (poor bachelors in Mayfair flats had housekeepers then, if they couldn't afford valets). Jeff tells Ma Balsam about the case he has got to go and fight in court.

Yes, it's all settled, Ma. I appear for Ernest Pennefather, a licensed taxi-cab driver, who has invoked the awful majesty of the Law to help him pound the stuffing out of Orlo Tarvin, an interior decorator, claiming that in the course of a dispute about his fare Tarvin gave him a blow or buffet – whereby

106

the said Pennefather goes in fear of his life. Interesting, of course, as showing what highly-strung, nervous men taxi-drivers are, but a bit on the minor side, one would have thought, for a man of my gifts. Still, the disembowelling of Green may give me some scope.

It appears that a second interior decorator, of the name of Lionel Green, was present during the proceedings and maintains that the alleged blow or buffet was not a blow or buffet at all, but in reality more in the nature of a playful prod or tap. And the attitude of the defence, I gather, is 'Laugh that off, J.G. Miller.' Well, we shall see. I have been instructed to shake Green, and I propose to do it till he feels like a cocktail. I shall be very courteous, of course, very polished and suave, but by the time I've finished with him Green will know he's been in a fight.

You see, Jeff Miller and Lionel Green had been at school together, and now – here's Jeff, the budding barrister, with his schoolmate in the witness box.

COUNSEL: Is it not a fact, Green—
JUDGE: Mr Green, if you please, Mr Miller.
COUNSEL: Oh, sorry.
JUDGE: Not at all, Mr Miller. Pray continue.
COUNSEL: Right ho. Thanks. Is it not a fact, Mr Green ... Look at me, if you please, and not at the jury—
JUDGE: Witness is looking at you, Mr Miller.
COUNSEL: Oh, is he? Right ho. Is it not a fact, Mr Green, that at school you were known as Stinker, and that we were given a half-holiday the day the news came out that you had had a bath?
WITNESS: Your worship!
JUDGE: It is more customary to address me as 'My Lord', Mr Green, or, alternatively, as 'Me lud'. However, I find your emotion intelligible. Have these references to witness's apparently misspent youth any bearing on the case now before us, Mr Miller?
COUNSEL: I'm shaking him, me lud – showing what a louse he is.

107

JUDGE: Do not use the word 'louse', Mr Miller.

COUNSEL: As your ludship pleases. Well, anyway, Stinker, putting aside for the moment the question of your niffiness, wasn't it notorious that you couldn't tell the truth without straining a ligament? What I'm driving at is that this story of yours about the blow or buffet being really a prod or tap is a tissue of lies from soup to nuts. Come on now, come clean, you unspeakable wart.

JUDGE: The expression 'wart', Mr Miller—

There had been quite a lot of this sort of thing, culminating in Counsel requesting the Learned Judge for heaven's sake not to keep interrupting all the time, and His Lordship, ceasing to be urbane, speaking of contempt of court and advising Counsel to lose no time in adopting some other walk in life, for he, His Lordship, could see no future for him at the Bar.

The main proponent, and victim, of the public-school code is, of course, Bertie Wooster himself. How often does he get lugged into frightful perils, alarms and excursions because some old school friend or – more dangerous still, old school friend's fiancée – appeals to Bertie's old school loyalty! But don't start accusing Wodehouse of reverence, even to public-school loyalty. I must remind you of that lovely short story, 'Tried in the Furnace'. Barmy Fotheringay-Phipps, a pillar of the Drones Club, is in a grocer's shop in a country village when he falls in love, bang, at first sight with a beautiful girl, who is ordering five pounds of streaky bacon to be delivered to her – and Barmy hears the name she gives the man behind the counter, 'Miss Angelica Briscoe, at the Vicarage.' Later, Barmy is brooding in the bar of the local pub. And:

It was while Barmy was at the counter listening in a distrait kind of way to the barmaid telling him what cucumber did to her digestive organs that a fellow in plus-fours entered the bar and Barmy saw that he was wearing the tie of his old school.

Well, you know how it is when you're in some public spot and a stranger comes in wearing the old school tie. You shove a hasty hand over your own and start to sidle out before the chap can spot it and grab you and start gassing. And Barmy was just doing this when the barmaid uttered these sensational words:

'Good evening, Mr. Briscoe.'

Barmy stood spellbound. He turned to the barmaid and spoke in a hushed whisper.

'Did you say "Briscoe"?'

'Yes, sir.'

'From the Vicarage?'

'Yes, sir.'

Barmy quivered like a jelly. The thought that he had had the amazing luck to find in the brother of the girl he loved an old schoolmate made him feel boneless. After all, he felt, as he took his hand away from his tie, there is no bond like that of the old school. If you meet one of the dear old school in a public spot, he meant to say, why, you go straight up to him and start fraternizing.

He made a bee-line for the chap's table.

'I say,' he said, 'I see you're wearing a . . .'

The chap's hand had shot up to his tie with a sort of nervous gesture, but he evidently realized that the time had gone by for protective measures. He smiled a bit wryly.

'Have a drink,' he said.

'I've got one, thanks,' said Barmy, 'I'll bring it along to your table, shall I? Such a treat meeting someone from the dear old place, what?'

'Oh, rather.'

'I think I'd have been a bit after your time, wouldn't I?' said Barmy, for the fellow was well stricken in years – twenty-eight, if a day. 'Fotheringay-Phipps is more or less my name. Yours is Briscoe, what?'

'Yes.'

Barmy swallowed a couple of times.

'Er . . . Ah . . . Um . . . I think I saw your sister yesterday in Bridmouth,' he said, blushing prettily.

So scarlet, indeed, did his countenance become that the other regarded him narrowly, and Barmy knew that he had guessed his secret.

'You saw her in Bridmouth yesterday, eh?'

109

'Yes.'

'And now you're here.'

'Er – yes.'

'Well, well,' said the chap, drawing his breath in rather thoughtfully.

There was a pause, during which Barmy's vascular motors continued to do their bit.

'You must meet her,' said the chap.

'I should like to,' said Barmy. 'I only saw her for a moment buying streaky bacon, but she seemed a charming girl.'

'Oh, she is.'

'I scarcely noticed her, of course, but rather attractive she struck me as.'

'Quite.'

'I gave her the merest glance, you understand, but I should say at a venture that she has a great white soul. In fact,' said Barmy, losing his grip altogether, 'you wouldn't be far out in describing her as divine.'

'You must certainly meet her,' said the chap.

In the event this young fellow Briscoe turns out to be not Angelica's brother, but her cousin, to whom she is engaged. But the young Briscoes do not reveal that until they have put two city-slicker Dronesmen through the most frightful village vicarage torments – the Mother's Outing and the School Tea and Treat.

Then there was the other story, 'Noblesse Oblige', of Freddie Widgeon in Cannes in the south of France, and down to his last franc, and waiting outside the Carlton Hotel for the afternoon post. He had wired a friend in London for a tenner to tide him over, and he was expecting the friend's letter, containing the £10, by the afternoon post . . .

. . . when a voice at his elbow, speaking in that sort of surprised and joyful manner in which one addresses an old friend encountered in a foreign spot, said:

'Why, hullo!'

And, turning, he perceived the above-mentioned bird in the reach-me-downs as described. A tallish, thinnish chap.

'Well, well, well!' said the bird.

Freddie goggled at him. As far as memory served, he didn't know the blighter from Adam.

'Hullo,' he said, playing for time.

'Fancy running into you,' said the chap.

'Ah,' said Freddie.

'It is a long time since we met.'

'Absolutely,' said Freddie, the persp. beginning to start out a bit on the brow. Because if there's one thing that makes a man feel a chump it is this business of meeting ancient cronies and not being able to put a name to them.

'I don't suppose you see any of the old crowd now?' said the chap.

'Not many,' said Freddie.

'They scatter.'

'They do scatter.'

'I came across Smith a few weeks ago.'

'Oh, yes?'

'T.T. Smith, I mean.'

'Oh, T.T. Smith?'

'Yes. Not J.B. I hear J.B.'s gone to the Malay States. T.T.'s in some sort of agency business. Rather prosperous.'

'That's good.'

'You seem to be doing pretty well, yourself.'

'Oh, fairly.'

'Well, I'm not surprised,' said the chap. 'One always knew you would, even at school.'

The word, Freddie tells me, was like a lifebelt. He grabbed at it. So this was a fellow he had known at school. That narrowed it down a lot. Surely now, he felt, the old brain would begin to function. Then he took another look at the chap, and the momentary exhilaration ebbed. He had not known him from Adam, and he still did not know him from Adam. The situation had thus become more awkward than ever, because the odds were that in the end this fellow was going to turn out to be someone he had shared a study with and ought to be falling on the neck of and swopping reminiscences of the time when old Boko Jervis brought the white rabbit into chapel and what not.

'Yes,' said the chap. 'Even then one could tell that you

111

were bound to go up and up. Gosh, how I used to admire you at the dear old school. You were my hero.'

'What!' yipped Freddie. He hadn't the foggiest that he had been anyone's hero at school. His career there hadn't been so dashed distinguished as all that. He had scraped into the cricket team in his last year, true: but even so he couldn't imagine any of his contemporaries looking up to him much.

'You were,' said the chap. 'I thought you a marvel.'

'No, really?' said Freddie, suffused with coy blushes. 'Well, well, well, fancy that. Have a cigarette?'

'Thanks,' said the chap. 'But what I really want is a meal. I'm right on my uppers. We aren't all like you, you see. While you've been going up and up, some of us have been going down and down. If I don't get a meal today, I don't know what I shall do.'

Freddie tells me the thing came on him as a complete surprise. You might have supposed that a wary bird like him, who has been a member of the Drones since he came down from Oxford, would have known better, but he insists that he had absolutely no suspicion that a touch was in the air till it suddenly hit him like this. And his first impulse, he says, was to mumble something at the back of his throat and slide off.

And he was just going to when a sudden surge of generous emotion swept over him. Could he let a fellow down who had not only been at school with him but who, when at school, had looked upon him as a hero? Imposs., felt Freddie. There had been six hundred and forty-seven chaps at the old school. Was he to hand the callous mitten to the only one of those six hundred and forty-seven who had admired him? Absolutely out of the q., was Freddie's verdict.

Well, the pay-off of that was that Freddie gave the chap what he thought the chap was asking for – a *mille* (French for a thousand francs) – when the chap really had meant a meal: hors d'oeuvres, soup, steak, chips and salad, cheese, coffee, liqueur and a cigar, say fifty francs, including tip, at the then rate for French money. And the whole rotten situation, Freddie discovered later, was caused by the tie that Freddie was wearing – a flamboyant, stripy one he had pinched from his uncle's tie-rack. It turned out to be the Old Bingletonians tie, and the shabby chap was an Old Bingletonian and thought Freddie was old Postlethwaite of Bingleton, whereas Freddie had been at Eton and was now down a thousand francs, as the shabby chap disappeared over the horizon.

Even in the last Blandings novel of all, posthumously named *Sunset at Blandings* – the one that Wodehouse was working on when he died, at the age of ninety-three – there is an echo of the same old 'You were my hero at school' cliché. It's the usual happy Blandings story – nice young man (he's called Jeff again), penniless, smuggled into the castle under a false name, false pretences, false everything, by the romantic Galahad, so that he, the young man, may be with the girl of his dreams; she being incarcerated at the castle for the very purpose of keeping her away from 'this impossible young man she thinks she has fallen in love with' – I quote her fierce stepmother who is also one of Galahad's many fierce sisters (he and Lord Emsworth have ten sisters now, and at last count). Then Galahad finds that another young man is coming to the castle, Claude, who had known Jeff at school, and naturally Galahad is anxious that Claude shall not give the deception away by calling Jeff by his real name. This is a snatch of dialogue between Galahad and the second young man:

'First let me get quite clear as to the relations between you and Jeff. Did I gather correctly from what you were saying when we met at Eastbourne that you and he had been at school together?'

'That's right. Wrykyn.'

'A most respectable establishment.'

'We were in the same house. Our last two years we shared a study.'

'So you were constantly in happy comradeship, now brewing tea and toasting sausages, anon out on the football field, rallying the forwards in the big game.'

'I wasn't in the football team. Jeff was.'

'Or sitting side by side in the school chapel, listening to the chaplain's short manly sermon. What I'm driving at is that, linked by a thousand memories of the dear old school, you wouldn't dream of saying or doing anything to give Jeff a jab

113

in the eye with a burned stick, thus causing him alarm and despondency and rendering his hopes and dreams null and void.'

Claude could not quite follow all the ramifications of this, but he grasped the general import and replied that he could be relied on not to do anything damaging to Jeff's hopes and dreams.

'Good,' said Gally, 'then we can proceed.'

A theme that paid Wodehouse good dividends was the fear, retained into adult life, of one's headmaster. Sacheverell Mulliner was a shy fellow. Well, let's have the opening paragraphs of that story 'The Voice From the Past':

At the ancient and historic public-school which stands a mile or two up the river from the Anglers' Rest there had recently been a change of headmasters, and our little group in the bar-parlour, naturally interested, was discussing the new appointment.

A grizzled Tankard of Stout frankly viewed it with concern.

'Benger!' he exclaimed. 'Fancy making Benger a head-master.'

'He has a fine record.'

'Yes, but, dash it, he was at school with me.'

'One lives these things down in time,' we urged.

The Tankard said we had missed his point, which was that he could remember young Scrubby Benger in an Eton collar with jam on it, getting properly cursed by the Mathematics beak for bringing white mice into the form-room.

'He was a small, fat kid with a pink face,' proceeded the Tankard. 'I met him again only last July, and he looked just the same. I can't see him as a headmaster. I thought they had to be a hundred years old and seven feet high, with eyes of flame, and long white beards. To me, a headmaster has always been a sort of blend of Epstein's Genesis and something out of the Book of Revelations.'

Mr. Mulliner smiled tolerantly.

'You left school at an early age, I imagine?'

114

'Sixteen. I had to go into my uncle's business.'

'Exactly,' said Mr. Mulliner, nodding sagely. 'You completed your school career, in other words, before the age at which a boy, coming into personal relationship with the man up top, learns to regard him as a guide, philosopher and friend. The result is that you are suffering from the well-known Headmaster Fixation or Phobia – precisely as my nephew Sacheverell did. A rather delicate youth, he was removed by his parents from Harborough College shortly after his fifteenth birthday and educated at home by a private tutor; and I have frequently heard him assert that the Rev. J.G. Smethurst, the ruling spirit of Harborough, was a man who chewed broken bottles and devoured his young.'

'I strongly suspected my headmaster of conducting human sacrifices behind the fives-courts at the time of the full moon,' said the Tankard.

'Men like yourself and my nephew Sacheverell who leave school early,' said Mr. Mulliner, 'never wholly lose these poetic boyish fancies. All their lives, the phobia persists. And sometimes this has curious results – as in the case of my nephew Sacheverell.'

Shy, timorous Sacheverell Mulliner enrols in a sort of Open University Correspondence course in Self-Confidence, the Dominant Manner, the Eye that will Open an Oyster at Sixty Paces. And, as a result, this timid fellow starts bossing everybody around, including his fiancée. And everybody, especially his fiancée, dislikes it very much. The new Sacheverell, she says, has become 'a beastly, bullying, over-bearing blighter'. The only thing that strikes fear into the dominant Mulliner's heart is the remembered voice of that same headmaster, the Rev. J.G. Smethurst, now risen to being Bishop of Bognor. Sacheverell hears that dreaded voice, in a country house, at a time when he finds, also, that he has got into the wrong bedroom, the bedroom earmarked for the bishop's slumber.

Now that it was too late, he seemed to recall having heard somebody somewhere say something about the Rev. J.G. Smethurst becoming a bishop; and even in this moment of

115

collapse he was able to feel a thrill of justifiable indignation at the shabbiness of the act. It wasn't fair for headmasters to change their names like this and take people unawares. The Rev. J.G. Smethurst might argue as much as he liked, but he couldn't get away from the fact that he had played a shady trick on the community. The man was practically going about under an *alias*.

But this was no time for abstract meditations on the question of right and wrong. He must hide . . . hide.

Yet why, you are asking, should my nephew Sacheverell wish to hide? Had he not in eight easy lessons from the Leave-It-To-Us School of Correspondence acquired complete self-confidence and an iron will? He had, but in this awful moment all that he had learned had passed from him like a dream. The years had rolled back, and he was fifteen-year-old jelly again, in the full grip of his Headmaster Phobia.

To dive under the bed was with Sacheverell Mulliner the work of a moment. And there, as the door opened, he lay, holding his breath and trying to keep his ears from rustling in the draught.

And, still on the subject of old headmasters, cast your mind back to the story 'The Inferiority Complex of Old Sippy'. Bertie Wooster's friend Oliver Sipperley was editor of a weekly Society magazine called *The Mayfair Gazette*. He was in thrall to his old headmaster, who came into the magazine's office and unloaded on the wretched editor – to be paid for, too – rotten articles he had written. Well, here the old man comes, as Bertie and Sipperley are in Sipperley's office:

A knock has sounded on the door. In fact, not so much a knock as a bang – or even a slosh. And there now entered a large, important-looking bird with penetrating eyes, a Roman nose, and high cheek-bones. Authoritative. That's the word I want. I didn't like his collar, and Jeeves would have had a thing or two to say about the sit of his trousers; but, nevertheless, he was authoritative. There was something compelling about the man. He looked like a traffic-policeman.

116

'Ah, Sipperley!' he said.

Old Sippy displayed a good deal of agitation. He had leaped from his chair, and was now standing in a constrained attitude, with a sort of pop-eyed expression on his face.

'Pray be seated, Sipperley,' said the cove. He took no notice of me. After one keen glance and a brief waggle of the nose in my direction, he had washed Bertram out of his life. 'I have brought you another little offering – ha! Look it over at your leisure, my dear fellow.'

'Yes, sir,' said Sippy.

'I think you will enjoy it. But there is just one thing. I should be glad, Sipperley, if you would give it a leetle better display, a rather more prominent position in the paper than you accorded to my "Landmarks of Old Tuscany". I am quite aware that in a weekly journal space is a desideratum, but one does not like one's efforts to be – I can only say pushed away in a back corner among advertisements of bespoke tailors and places of amusement.' He paused, and a nasty gleam came into his eyes. 'You will bear this in mind, Sipperley?'

'Yes, sir,' said Sippy.

'I am greatly obliged, my dear fellow,' said the cove, becoming genial again. 'You must forgive my mentioning it. I would be the last person to attempt to dictate the – ha! – editorial policy, but— Well, good afternoon, Sipperley. I will call for your decision at three o'clock tomorrow.'

He withdrew, leaving a gap in the atmosphere about ten feet by six. When this had closed in, I sat up.

'What was it?' I said.

I was startled to observe poor old Sippy apparently go off his onion. He raised his hands over his head, clutched his hair, wrenched it about for a while, kicked a table with great violence, and then flung himself into his chair.

'Curse him!' said Sippy. 'May he tread on a banana-skin on his way to chapel and sprain both ankles!'

'Who was he?'

'May he get frog-in-the-throat and be unable to deliver the end-of-term sermon!'

'Yes, but who was he?'

'My old headmaster, Bertie,' said Sippy.

117

'Yes, but, my dear old soul—'

'Headmaster of my old school.' He gazed at me in a distraught sort of way. 'Good Lord! Can't you understand the position?'

'Not by a jugful, laddie.'

Sippy sprang from his chair and took a turn or two up and down the carpet.

'How do you feel,' he said, 'when you meet the headmaster of your old school?'

'I never do. He's dead.'

'Well, I'll tell you how I feel. I feel as if I were in the Lower Fourth again, and had been sent up by my form-master for creating a disturbance in school. That happened once, Bertie, and the memory still lingers. I can recall as if it were yesterday knocking at old Waterbury's door and hearing him say: "Come in!" like a lion roaring at an early Christian, and going in and shuffling my feet on the mat and him looking at me and me explaining – and then, after what seemed a lifetime, bending over and receiving six of the juiciest on the old spot with a cane that bit like an adder. And whenever he comes into my office now the old wound begins to trouble me, and I just say: 'Yes, sir'' and ''No, sir'', and feel like a kid of fourteen.'

I began to grasp the posish. The whole trouble with these fellows like Sippy, who go in for writing, is that they develop the artistic temperament, and you never know when it is going to break out.

'He comes in here with his pockets full of articles on "The Old School Cloisters" and "Some Little-Known Aspects of Tacitus", and muck like that, and I haven't the nerve to refuse them. And this is supposed to be a paper devoted to the lighter interests of Society.'

'You must be firm, Sippy. Firm, old thing.'

'How can I, when the sight of him makes me feel like a piece of chewed blotting-paper? When he looks at me over that nose, my *morale* goes blue at the roots and I am back at school again. It's persecution, Bertie!'

I have given this paper the title 'Old Boy at Dulwich', and I want it pronounced carefully, with equal stress on 'Old' and

'Boy'. One of the most frequent Wodehouse techniques for making us laugh is his switching of ages. Throughout his long *floruit* period from, let's say, 1920 – his fortieth year – onwards virtually to the end of his life, aged ninety-three, his technique of switching ages is a most rewarding one. Making grown-ups behave like children and children like grown-ups. Sacheverell Mulliner and Oliver Sipperley were cases in point. But my favourite encapsulation of this is in yet another Mulliner story, 'The Bishop's Move', where two old school cronies meet at the headmaster's house of their old school. In fact one of them now *is* the headmaster, the Rev. Trevor Entwhistle, and the other is a bishop. And the bishop notices a curious thing about himself at his old school now. In the old school surroundings, forty years after his actual schooldays, he begins to feel like a schoolboy again and his feelings are 'far from unmixedly agreeable'.

Once, when rounding a corner, he came upon the captain of football in all his majesty, and there had swept over him a hideous blend of fear and shame which had made his gaitered legs wobble like jellies. The captain of football doffed his cap respectfully, and the feeling passed as quickly as it had come: but not so soon that the bishop had not recognized it. It was exactly the feeling he had been wont to have forty-odd years ago when, sneaking softly away from football practice, he had encountered one in authority.

The bishop was puzzled. It was as if some fairy had touched him with her wand, sweeping away the years and making him an inky-faced boy again. Day by day this illusion grew, the constant society of the Rev. Trevor Entwhistle doing much to foster it. For young Catsmeat Entwhistle had been the bishop's particular crony at Harchester, and he seemed to have altered his appearance since those days in no way whatsoever. The bishop had had a nasty shock when, entering the headmaster's study on the third morning of his visit, he found him sitting in the headmaster's chair with the headmaster's cap and gown on. It seemed to him that young Catsmeat, in order to indulge his distorted sense of humour, was taking the most frightful risk. Suppose the Old Man were to come in and cop him!

The bishop has a chaplain, a Mulliner of course, and the chaplain has a bottle of that great tonic 'Buck-U-Uppo', which had been formulated by another Mulliner, an inventive chemist, to be put in the bran mash of the elephants that Indian maharajahs used for tiger-hunting. A tot of Buck-U-Uppo in the elephant's morning mash, and he should stand steady in the jungle against the charge of the angriest tiger. The headmaster and bishop pillage the chaplain's bottle, start by licking the cork and end by drinking several glasses of it apiece. The result of this splendid overdose of over-strength tonic is that the two men of God, the headmaster and the bishop, feel like 'young and rather rowdy schoolboys of fifteen', and they sneak out into the school quadrangle at midnight and paint the statue of a school benefactor pink: and the silly ass bishop leaves his shovel hat, which has his name in it, on top of the statue before coming back to bed.

Wodehouse played this age transference theme joyfully in one complete novel, *Laughing Gas*. There, in Hollywood, a child film star, Joey Cooley, and a visiting English earl go, each to have a tooth out, to two dentists, partners, with surgeries next door to each other's. Under gas, the soul of fourteen-year-old Joey Cooley enters the body of twenty-five-year-old Reggie, Earl of Havershot, and *vice versa*. They both wake up with soul transplants, and it makes a very pleasant light novel.

The trigger that releases Wodehouse characters into forgetting their ages may be dentist's gas, love, jealousy, sheer high spirits or strong liquor – and I include the tonic Buck-U-Uppo as strong liquor, as strong and effective as the gin that Bertie Wooster and Jeeves each sloshed liberally into the orange juice of the timorous and teetotal Gussie Fink-Nottle, when Gussie was faced with the frightful job of presenting the prizes to the students at the end of term at the Market Snodsbury Grammar School. It's in *Right Ho, Jeeves*.

I believe that Edward Lyttelton, who was a canon of the Church, a very good cricketer and headmaster of Eton, said that he could never walk in procession up the nave of a cathedral, or church, or chapel without imagining it to be a cricket pitch and wondering whether it would take spin bowling. I must say that when I first saw this fine hall here, I thought how much better it would be for today's gathering if the authorities had offered you, in it, not a fellow reading a paper and young schoolmasters reading from the great master's works, but a complete, live, three-dimensional presentation here of Bertie Wooster's narrative of the events of that prize-giving at Market Snodsbury Grammar School, with Gussie Fink-Nottle, the tee-totaller, as tight as an owl, going through the ordeal with devastating confidence. It would only need two actors, the tight Gussie, and the man Bertie refers to as 'the bearded bloke' – the headmaster who finds himself having to deal with this strangely-behaved prize-giver. Well, perhaps there might be a small boy third actor to come up, in squeaking shoes, as G.G. Simmons, to get the Scripture prize.

Not that the atmosphere in this splendid hall is comparable with that of the Great Hall at Market Snodsbury school:

In this hall the youth of Market Snodsbury had been eating its daily lunch for a matter of five hundred years, and the flavour lingered. The air was sort of heavy and languorous, if you know what I mean, with the scent of Young England and boiled beef and carrots.

Let's jump right into the middle of the prize-giving, when G.G. Simmons squeaks on to the platform and faces the seriously squiffy Gussie Fink-Nottle:

'Well, G.G. Simmons.'
'Sir, yes, sir.'
'What do you mean – sir, yes, sir? Dashed silly thing to say. So you've won the Scripture-knowledge prize, have you?'
'Sir, yes, sir.'
'Yes,' said Gussie, 'you look just the sort of little tick who would. And yet,' he said, pausing and eyeing the child keenly, 'how are we to know that this has all been open and above board? Let me test you, G.G. Simmons. Who was What's-His-Name – the chap who begat Thingummy? Can you answer me that, Simmons?'
'Sir, no, sir.'

121

Gussie turned to the bearded bloke.

'Fishy,' he said. 'Very fishy. This boy appears to be totally lacking in Scripture knowledge.'

The bearded bloke passed a hand across his forehead.

'I can assure you, Mr. Fink-Nottle, that every care was taken to insure a correct marking and that Simmons outdistanced his competitors by a wide margin.'

'Well, if you say so,' said Gussie doubtfully. 'All right, G.G. Simmons, take your prize.'

'Sir, thank you, sir.'

'But let me tell you that there's nothing to stick on side about in winning a prize for Scripture knowledge. Bertie Wooster . . .'

I don't know when I've had a nastier shock. I had been going on the assumption that, now that they had stopped him making his speech, Gussie's fangs had been drawn, as you might say. To duck my head down and resume my edging toward the door was with me the work of a moment.

'Bertie Wooster won the Scripture-knowledge prize at a kids' school we were at together, and you know what he's like. But, of course, Bertie frankly cheated. He succeeded in scrounging that Scripture-knowledge trophy over the heads of better men by means of some of the rawest and most brazen swindling methods ever witnessed even at a school where such things were common. If that man's pockets, as he entered the examination room, were not stuffed to bursting point with lists of the Kings of Judah . . .'

I heard no more. A moment later I was out in God's air, fumbling with a fevered foot at the self-starter of the old car.

I think I could quote you twenty more stories, or occasions in stories, where age transference is the essence of a wonderful Wodehouse absurdity. The old nanny – in yet another Mulliner story, 'Portrait of a Disciplinarian' – has the same effect on her (now grown-up) erstwhile charges, whom she had disciplined in their nurseries and chastised with a hairbrush, as their old headmasters had on Sacheverell Mulliner and Oliver Sipperley. She makes the man eat boiled eggs for his tea at her house, and, as a punishment for sulking, she locks both of them, the young man and the girl, into a dark cupboard. They emerge chastened, and engaged to be married, so the story ends happily. Then there was Bingo Little's old nanny, too, spreading havoc in Bingo's married home by her memories of Bingo as a baby and small boy.

And, finally, the gorgeous story of 'The Crime Wave at Blandings'. Lord Emsworth, having been ordered by his fierce sister Constance to take away his grandson George's beloved airgun, sits in his study and contemplates the offensive weapon he has impounded and remembers the days when he, too, was young and owned an airgun:

Lord Emsworth mused on his boyhood. Happy days, happy days. He could recall the exact uncle who had given him the weapon, so similar to this one, with which Julia had shot her governess. He could recall brave, windswept mornings when he had gone prowling through the stable yard in the hope of getting a rat – and many a fine head had he secured. Odd that the passage of time should remove the desire to go and pop at things with an airgun. . . .

Or did it?

With a curious thrill that set his pince-nez rocking gently on his nose, Lord Emsworth suddenly became aware that it did not. All that the passage of time did was to remove the desire to pop temporarily – say for forty years or so. Dormant for a short while – well, call it fifty years – that desire, he perceived, still lurked unquenched. Little by little it began to stir within him now. Slowly but surely, as he sat there fondling the gun, he was once more becoming a potential popper.

At this point, the gun suddenly went off and broke the bust of Aristotle.

It was enough. The old killer instinct had awakened. Reloading with the swift efficiency of some hunter of the woods, Lord Emsworth went to the window. He was a little uncertain as to what he intended to do when he got there, except that he had a very clear determination to loose off at something. There flitted into his mind what his grandson George had said about tickling up cows, and this served to some extent to crystallize his aims. True, cows were not plentiful on the terrace of Blandings Castle. Still, one might have wandered there. You never knew with cows.

123

There were no cows. Only Rupert Baxter. The ex-secretary was in the act of throwing away a cigarette.

Most men are careless in the matter of throwing away cigarettes. The world is their ashtray. But Rupert Baxter had a tidy soul. He allowed the thing to fall to the ground like any ordinary young man, it is true, but immediately he had done so his better self awakened. He stooped to pick up the object that disfigured the smooth flagged stones, and the invitation of that beckoning trousers-seat would have been too powerful for a stronger man than Lord Emsworth to resist.

He pulled the trigger, and Rupert Baxter sprang into the air with a sharp cry. Lord Emsworth reseated himself and took up Whiffle on *The Care Of The Pig*.

And that's not the end of the affair. Soon Lady Constance herself, driven by a power beyond herself, fires the airgun. Then Beach does. And, finally, Lord Emsworth, insisting on showing his sister that his first shot was not a fluke, fires the airgun again, and again at Baxter. So they had, all three, Lord Emsworth, his sister Constance, and Beach the butler, gone back in time to the age of young grandson George. George presumably got his airgun back and also got the good news that his threatened holiday tutor had jumped on his motor-cycle and gone out of his life for ever. Add airguns to the list of triggers for age-transference.

Dr Sir Pelham Wodehouse, Old Alleynian, was up to this sort of thing still at the age of ninety-three. Verily an old boy.

Postscript

1. Wodehouse's Money Received for Literary Work *notebook turned up eventually and was donated to Dulwich College Library, along with the typescript of his letters to Bill Townend which he and Townend used as material for the book* Performing Flea.

8
Mistakes, Misprints and Moustaches

The next three pieces appeared in the big catalogue made for the Wodehouse Centennial Exhibition at The Pierpont Morgan Library in New York in 1981.

'Clarence, what year was that terrible argument between young Gregory Parsloe and Lord Burper? When Parsloe stole the old chap's glasses and sold them at a shop in the Edgware Road? '96? I should have said later than that. Perhaps you're right though.'

Lady Constance cried out.

'Galahad! You're not going to print stories like that about our nearest neighbour?'

'Certainly I am. It's the best story in my book. . . .'

Wait a minute. There's something wrong there, surely. I thought Parsloe had pinched Lord Burper's *false teeth*, and had *pawned* them in the Edgware Road. But the book here says 'glasses' and 'sold'. And later on Galahad refers to the great story of Parsloe and the snowballs. *Snowballs?* No, no. It was the story of Parsloe and the *prawns* which broke butler Beach into a most unbutlerine roar of laughter when he read it in his deck chair near the laurel bush outside the back door of the castle. It was in Gally's Reminiscences, that dreaded *succès de scandale* that was never published. The autograph manuscript was eaten up in her sty by the Empress of Blandings. The horrible Percy Pilbeam had hidden it under the straw there, not knowing that the building was to be the new bijou residence of Lord Emsworth's prize-winning pig. 'False teeth', 'pawned', and 'prawns' are certainly the readings in Wodehouse's *Summer Lightning* (published 1929 by Herbert Jenkins, later Barrie and

Jenkins, later Hutchinson, London, and as *Fish Preferred* by Doubleday, Doran, New York).

The book in front of me at the moment is P.G. Wodehouse's *Summer Lightning*, adapted by Tony Augarde for the Oxford University Press in its Alpha General Fiction series of good books simplified, for foreign students learning English, into a basic vocabulary of fifteen hundred words. And in those fifteen hundred was no room, obviously, for 'false teeth', 'pawn', or 'prawn'.

Some years ago a competitor on the BBC-TV 'Mastermind' programme had offered 'P.G. Wodehouse's books' as his special subject. The BBC asked me to give them twenty or more questions to ask him, with the answers. Now, what if one of my questions had been 'Give one of the stories about Sir Gregory Parsloe that Galahad Threepwood put into his never-published Reminiscences', and what if the expert had answered, 'Lord Burper's glasses that Parsloe had sold in the Edgware Road' or 'The story of the snowballs'? Magnus Magnussen would have looked at his card and said, 'I can't give you that. It says here 'prawns', not 'snowballs', and it was Lord Burper's false teeth, not glasses, and Parsloe didn't sell them, he pawned them, in the Edgware Road.' Wouldn't the competitor have had a genuine grievance against the BBC, and the BBC a genuine grievance against me, and I against the Oxford University Press?

The very pricey market these days for first editions and original manuscripts and typescripts of Wodehouse's works may be partially explained by the fact that there are so many known variants of them now legitimately in print that the *ipsissima verba* are that much the more precious. Some bookworms must soon establish a canon, agreed on by all Wodehouse publishers, and then make a variorum volume.

Wodehouse himself re-ran certain stories. For instance, in the hard-to-find original *My Man Jeeves* there are tales told by and about Reggie Pepper which in *Carry on Jeeves*, *The Jeeves Omnibus* and *The World of Jeeves* are told, with minor changes, by and about Bertie Wooster. Then that early novel, *The Prince and Betty* (the British Library has this, incidentally, in Esperanto as well as English), appeared first in America, published in February 1912 by W.J. Watt and Company. The main character in this is Rupert Smith, an American from Harvard. He animates a sleepy New York magazine, *Peaceful Moments*, and turns it into a crusading, anti-slum-landlord force for good. In the English version, published in May 1912 by Mills and Boon, there is no New York sequence, no *Peaceful Moments*. There is still a Prince of Mervo (a Mediterranean island), and still a Betty Silver, whom he eventually wins, but in England, not America. Then, three years later, *Psmith Journalist* was published, by Adam and Charles Black, in London (but never in America). In *Psmith Journalist* Englishman Rupert Smith, who calls himself Psmith, of Eton, Sedleigh, and Cambridge University, comes to New York and takes over, and animates, the magazine *Cosy Moments* and turns it into a crusading etc, etc, as in the American version of *The Prince and Betty*. Autophagous cannibalism? Abuse of copyright? Author's bounty? Book-worms and bibliographers, fettle your footnotes!

Wodehouse allowed his own ending of *Much Obliged, Jeeves* (1971) to be changed (by Peter Schwed of Simon and Schuster, I believe) in the American edition, renamed *Jeeves and the Tie That Binds*. We have recently seen Jeeves's life story run completely off the Wodehouse rails in C. Northcote Parkinson's *Jeeves*. In that merry molehill of myth Jeeves ends up as landlord of, and sole storyteller in, the Anglers' Rest public house on the Shropshire estate of the Earl of Yaxley (*né* Bertram Wooster) and his Countess (*née* Roberta Wickham). You mustn't believe a word of it. I have myself, in adapting two Wooster/Jeeves novels for BBC radio, changed the Rev. 'Stinker' Pinker from an all-England rugby footballer into a Pegasus association footballer. And, more heinous, I have given dear Aunt Dahlia oaths and repartee that are not in the sacred texts. But those were words, winged and never in print. I could plead for mitigation of punishment, if any, on that score, I think.

We bookworms (for, adaptation jobs apart, I count myself a Wodehouse bookworm) must keep the lifelines clear back to the original sources. A small point. When the single-volume *Mike* (1912) was, in 1953, split into two books, *Mike at Wrykyn* and *Mike and Psmith*, Wodehouse's English publisher updated the names of the real-life star all-England cricketers in it. C.B. Fry had been a great maker of centuries in test matches before 1912, for instance. In the 1953 reprint he became David Sheppard, who, at that date, was the cricketer every schoolboy would have wished to be; playing for Cambridge, Sussex, and England (twenty-two test matches), and he was to be England's captain the next year, 1954. At the time I am writing this, Sheppard is the Anglican Bishop of Liverpool. What English schoolboy of today sees the cricket cap under the mitre?

I give you an even smaller point – a point pointed out to me by Wodehouse's, and my, friend Alec Waugh. In *The Inimitable Jeeves* (1923) there is a story 'The Delayed Exit of Claude and Eustace'. Bertie's twin cousins Claude and Eustace, in London when they should have been heading for jobs that were waiting for them in South Africa, were thrusting their unwelcome young attentions on Bertie's beautiful actress friend, Marion Wardour. At Jeeves's suggestion, Miss Wardour told the boys she was heading for South Africa herself, to take up a theatrical engagement, but would be travelling overland to Madeira to join the ship there. So Claude and Eustace both, but separately, asked Jeeves to book them passages (at Bertie's expense) for South Africa on the boat sailing tomorrow from Southampton. Little did either know that the other would be on board. Little did either know that Jeeves had booked them into the same double cabin. Little did either know that Miss Wardour had no intention of joining them, or the ship, at Madeira. The slip, that persists in the autograph edition of *The Inimitable Jeeves*, but which Wodehouse corrected for *The Jeeves Omnibus* (1931) and *The World of Jeeves* (1967), is that you couldn't travel overland to Madeira, since it is an island. 'Overland' becomes 'by another boat' in the two volumes of the collected Bertie/Jeeves stories.

Then we must reckon for the one-shotter shortened versions of novels that Wodehouse often sold for pre-book publication in magazines. The story, told in 18,000 words in one issue of, say, *The Ladies' Home Journal*, appeared next week at 65,000-word length in hardback on the bookstalls. Wodehouse did his own cutting. I haven't closely compared texts, an 18,000-word one-shotter against the full novel. But if he meant false teeth, pawned and prawns, he would have said so. The length was constricted to 18,000, but the Wodehouse vocabulary wasn't filleted down to 1,500 words.

I have just received my May/June issue of the current (1980)

Saturday Evening Post. In it there is a re-run of the 'Jeeves Takes Charge' story that they first ran sixty-four years earlier, in 1916. I am more than a little disturbed. I find, first, an illustration of Bertie with a monocle and an ear-to-ear red moustache. Did Wodehouse ever specify a monocle for Bertie? I do not think the 'Spot of Art' story is conclusive. About moustaches I am on surer ground. Twice Bertie grew moustaches, in defiance of Jeeves's disapproval, and both times they were small, like David Niven's. In one case Jeeves said it looked like a stain of mulligatawny soup on the upper lip. In both cases the moustaches were forfeit at the end of the story or novel. Well, illustrations to Wodehouse stories and decorations for dust jackets of Wodehouse books can claim – or anyway they enjoy – a licence. The Empress of Blandings is still frequently – indeed, on the cover of the Oxford University Press 1,500-word-vocabulary *Summer Lightning* – pictured as a pink-and-white porker. She is, and was specified twice in the texts as a Black Berkshire.

But Bertie's moustache and monocle are not my chief complaint against the 1980 re-run of 'Jeeves Takes Charge'. In its second paragraph Bertie is telling us how he came to be spending a week at Easeby, his Uncle Willoughby's place in Shropshire. He says: 'I generally did this in the summer, *for the old boy liked to have me round and, being down in his will for a substantial chunk of the right stuff, I always obliged him.* . . .'

'Jeeves Takes Charge', which relates Jeeves's arrival from the agency, is the first story in terms of fictional chronology. In the happy half-century and more of real time and of multiplication of Bertie/Jeeves books, no explanation is ever given for Bertie's never-failing pecuniosity, solvency, easy circumstances. Call it anything but 'oofiness'. 'Oofy' Prosser is the rich man of the Drones: certainly Bertie is not in the Oofy class. Bertie once refers to himself as 'stagnant with the stuff' and never has to borrow a fiver 'till the end of the month' as so many of his friends at the Drones do. He is never poverty-stricken. He is never employed. His income is undoubtedly unearned. Where then did the money come from?

According to the extra twenty-seven words (my italics, above) now injected in that part of 'Jeeves Takes Charge' Mark 2, a sizeable chunk of his capital would have come from his

Uncle Willoughby – his late Uncle Willoughby. We never hear of him, or Easeby, again in the last sixty-plus years of Wodehouse's prolific output.

Later in the re-run story in the *Post* the financial point is again touched on. It reads: '. . . as I was more or less dependent on Uncle Willoughby I couldn't very well marry without his approval. . . .' This amplifies the suggestion that Bertie relied on Uncle Willoughby at death to set him up for life. But in all the texts of the collected stories the sentence reads: '. . . as *at that time* I was more or less dependent on Uncle Willoughby', etc, etc . . . The May/June 1980 *Post* does not have that important 'at that time'. Why? We had known that at that time Bertie was getting an allowance from his uncle. We assumed that he became self-financing somehow later and we had amused ourselves theorising about the 'how' of somehow. The *Post* today clearly doesn't like loose ends and has solved the problem for us. Is it our duty to accept this post-mortem solution? I think not. We bookworms must surely keep our noses clean . . . keep them stuck into the primary sources. And now – only now – I find that the *Post* version *is* the primary source. Wodehouse himself altered it in re-publication.

It is difficult enough in a corpus of seventy or more books of Wodehouse fiction, and in a succession of new editions of Wodehouse in English in England and America, to spot variants from the originals. We wallow in a blissful world of formidable aunts, prize pigs, fizzy girls, endless house parties, goof golfers, hammock weather all summer long in England, dyspeptic American millionaires, jobless younger sons, portly and porty butlers, delightfully fiendish children, small dogs that nip ankles, Scotch gardeners, bossy fiancées (how many did Bertie have? I make it at least a dozen, one at a time), bishops buoyant with Buck-U-Uppo, and crusty magistrates, on the bench or retired, rich with the fines of decades in their bank balances. But the price of our contentment must be constant vigilance – to enjoy, if we will, the thought of young Parsloe selling Lord Burper's glasses in the Edgware Road, taking it with a knowing pinch of salt, knowing the true, the original, the vintage P.G. Wodehouse text. It was Lord Burper's *false teeth* – Lord Emsworth vouched for that: he had seen them in a small cigar box – and Parsloe had *pawned* them.

There is one further source of unholy writ which bookworms should study, the misprint due to faulty typesetting and faulty proofreading. In my copy (first edition, 1971, Barrie and Jenkins) of *Much Obliged, Jeeves* I find Boko Littleworth for Boko Fittleworth, Worpledon for Worplesdon, county for country, Steeple Bumpleigh for Woollam Chersey, and Arnold Abney for Aubrey Upjohn (as Bertie's headmaster at preparatory school). And why Bertie's old Communist 'man' Brinkley has changed his name to Bingley is never explained. *We* can see why: it's because to have Brinkley the ex-valet now living near Aunt Dahlia's place, Brinkley Court, would jar. But old (aged ninety) Wodehouse should have been helped over that hurdle by an alert editor somewhere, if not by his own ingenuity.

Then, last horror, Jeeves, on page 191, quotes a line and a half of 'Lucretius, sir, 99–55 BC', and misses out an essential '*quod*'. (These errors also appear in the American edition, entitled *Jeeves and the Tie That Binds*. Shame on both publishers!)

Well, let Wodehouse himself have the last words, in felicitous verse:

PRINTER'S ERROR

As o'er my latest book I pored,
   Enjoying it immensely,
I suddenly exclaimed 'Good Lord!'
   And gripped the volume tensely.
'Golly!' I cried. I writhed in pain.
'They've done it on me once again!'
   And furrows creased my brow.
I'd written (which I thought quite good)
'Ruth, ripening into womanhood,
Was now a girl who knocked men flat
And frequently got whistled at',
And some vile, careless, casual gook
Had spoiled the best thing in the book
   By printing 'not'
   (Yes, 'not', great Scott!)
When I had written 'now'.

On murder in the first degree
  The Law, I knew, is rigid:
Its attitude, if A kills B,
  To A is always frigid.
It counts it not a trivial slip
If on behalf of authorship
You liquidate compositors.
This kind of conduct it abhors
  And seldom will allow.
Nevertheless, I deemed it best
And in the public interest
To buy a gun, to oil it well,
Inserting what is called a shell,
  And go and pot
  With sudden shot
    This printer who had printed 'not'
    When I had written 'now'.

I tracked the bounder to his den
  Through private information:
I said, 'Good afternoon', and then
  Explained the situation:
'I'm not a fussy man,' I said.
'I smile when you put "rid" for "red"
And "bad" for "bed" and "hoad" for "head"
  And "bolge" instead of "bough".
When "wone" appears in lieu of "wine"
Or if you alter "Cohn" to "Schine",
  I never make a row.
I know how easy errors are.
But this time you have gone too far
By printing "not" when you knew what
  I really wrote was "now".
Prepare,' I said, 'to meet your God
Or, as you'd say, your Goo or Bod,
  Or possibly your Gow.'

A few weeks later into court
  I came to stand my trial.
The Judge was quite a decent sort.

132

He said, 'Well, cocky, I'll
Be passing sentence in a jiff,
And so, my poor unhappy stiff,
If you have anything to say,
Now is the moment. Fire away.
  You have?'
    I said, 'And how!
Me lud, the facts I don't dispute.
I did, I own it freely, shoot
This printer through the collar stud.
What else could I have done, me lud?
  He'd printed "not" . . .'
    The Judge said, '*What!*
    When you had written "now"?
God bless my soul! Gadzooks!' said he.
'The blighters did that once to me.
  A dirty trick, I trow.
I hereby quash and override
The jury's verdict. Gosh!' he cried.
'Give me your hand. Yes, I insist,
You splendid fellow! Case dismissed.'
  (Cheers, and a Voice 'Wow-wow!')

A statue stands against the sky,
  Lifelike and rather pretty.
'Twas recently erected by
  The P.E.N. committee.
And many a passer-by is stirred,
For on the plinth, if that's the word,
In golden letters you may read
'This is the man who did the deed.
  His hand set to the plough,
He did not sheathe the sword, but got
A gun at great expense and shot
The human blot who'd printed "not"
  When he had written "now".
He acted with no thought of self,
Not for advancement, not for pelf,
But just because it made him hot
To think the man had printed "not"
  When he had written "now".'[1]

133

Postscript

1.   I am glad to have had this opportunity to show an example of Plum's light verse. Boys in the Classical Scholarship streams at the public schools were expected once or twice a week to knead passages from English poets into Greek and Latin in the metres and languages of the best periods of Athens and Rome. Four years of this certainly provided an anthology of English verse that one remembered almost by heart.

The habit of versification tends to last. Armine Wodehouse, Plum's elder brother, a classical scholar, won the Newdigate Poetry Prize at Oxford, wrote and published good poetry afterwards and would have liked to make poetry his life work if it had paid a living wage. Young Plum wrote much expert light verse, professionally in Punch and other periodicals, and, as lyrics, for a succession of highly rewarding stage musicals. He widened the vocabulary and smile of the stage song, and was much admired in his day by the up-and-coming young – Gershwin, Hart, Rogers, Hammerstein and Dietz.

9

Spats, Weather and Gentlemen's Gentlemen

'One way of writing successful novels is mine – making the thing practically a fairy story and ignoring real life altogether.' So wrote Wodehouse in a letter to his friend Bill Townend in 1934.

I have heard it said, and seen it in print, that on a moonless night in 1942, during the Second World War, the German Secret Service dropped a spy on to Dartmoor in Devonshire; he was wearing spats and was soon marched off with gyves on his wrists. The theory is that the decision-makers at German Secret Service headquarters were, to a man, overcredulous readers of P.G. Wodehouse and thought that spats were still the proper wear for a young Englishman, not only in Mayfair but anywhere south of Scotland.

If so, they were at least a quarter of a century out in their reckoning. In the First World War a German spy in spats might have passed unnoticed in England, or, say, might not instantly have been nabbed as an impostor. But Wodehouse was not being translated into German then, and anyway, it was not till spats had virtually disappeared off the feet of the young men in England that Wodehouse wrote about them. He gave the title *Young Men in Spats* to a collection of Drones Club short stories as late as 1936. I was a very clothes-conscious young man in London then, and I don't think I would have known where to buy spats if I had wanted them for a fancy dress party.

The German ex-Kaiser – the all-Highest until the defeat of Germany in 1918 – in post-war exile in Holland had discovered the works of Wodehouse, could read them in English, loved them and used to read them aloud, in English, to the officers of his loyal but reduced staff. They were not as good at English, or at Wodehouse, as their master, who not only kept them to (seated) attention for the length of a Wodehouse short story, but, when he had read a passage which he judged specially funny, read it again for his own pleasure and, he thought, theirs.

There is no evidence that Hitler, Germany's All-Highest in the Second World War, knew his Wodehouse scriptures. But his official interpreter, Dr Paul Schmidt, was a devotee, and the word may have seeped round the Chancellery that the young upper-class Englishman wore spats and a monocle, had a valet, butter-coloured hair, no chin, and no job, and threw crusty bread rolls and sugar lumps from table to table in his club dining room.

To me, an Englishman, one of the great charms and great unrealities of the Wodehouse books is his depiction of English weather. His own preferred season in England was autumn – a walk in the park with his Pekes on a still, grey November afternoon was what he liked best of all. But in his books England seems to enjoy perpetual high summer: sunshine by day, velvety warmth at night.

I am looking particularly at the Blandings Castle books, partly because I am just surfacing from my *n*th re-reading of the whole Blandings canon, partly because it spans, as near as dammit, sixty publishing years – *Something Fresh* (1915) to *Sunset at Blandings* (1977). In fact there is a nip in the air at the beginning of *Something Fresh*. As Ashe Marson and Joan Valentine (he as a valet to an American millionaire, she as lady's maid to the millionaire's daughter) are trundled up to the castle from Market Blandings station in the uncovered horse-drawn cart reserved for servants and luggage, the cold east evening wind turns Ashe into 'a mere chunk of frozen misery'. And when he arrives and is taken to meet 'Mr Beach', the butler, in his pantry, he is given a welcoming whisky toddy. There is a fire in the grate and a kettle simmering on the hob.

In all the subsequent books, did Beach ever dispense hot drinks to his callers? Never, surely. It is port that Galahad came for, port that American Penny Donaldson demanded, port that Beach himself drank as a rule after he had served the good-night beverages in the drawing room and had locked all the outer doors for the night. Never again a fire in the grate, or a hob, or a kettle. In that first Blandings book it is early spring. Wodehouse refers to the house party, in honour of Freddie Threepwood's engagement to the millionaire's daughter, as occurring between the shooting and hunting seasons – which only shows that the young (well, in his early thirties) Wodehouse was not a shooting or hunting man. But in all the books to come the season is hay-harvest summer. Lord Emsworth goes down to the lake every morning to swim before breakfast, and at night to the Empress's sty just to listen to her breathing in her surfeited sleep. Lord Emsworth's resident younger brother Galahad and Lord Ickenham on visits assume that there will be a hammock under the big cedar for their morning cerebrations. In one book Galahad races his disliked sister Julia to the hammock after breakfast. It sounds as though the hammock is there all day and all night in summer. Tea is served on the lawn (a procession of two footmen carrying the essentials, followed by Beach to add authority) and after-dinner coffee on the terrace or in an arbour. And, further afield, three miles from the castle, the Emsworth Arms public house is serving teas and drinks on the lawn that runs down to the river. The snakeless meadows between are basking in summer, real summer: hammock weather, barring a few thunderstorms to drive quarrelling young couples into woodland shelters and each other's arms.

I can think of only three Wodehouse short stories set in winter, and I am sure that research would prove that all three had been written to magazine editor's requests for seasonal stuff for their Christmas numbers. In 'The Knightly Quest of Mervyn', Mr Mulliner's cousin's son Mervyn is challenged by his adored object to prove his adoration by getting her some strawberries. The season, winter, is required for the story, but the weather gets no mention until, while he was going for a meditative walk through the messuages and pleasances of his uncle's place, Blotsam Castle, 'the east wind went through his plus fours like a javelin.' The cold wind drove Mervyn into his uncle's hothouses, where he found ripe strawberries growing in abundance. And so. . . . Then there was the 'Jeeves and the Yuletide Spirit' story, with Bertie temporarily in love with the deplorable and adorable Bobbie Wickham, and much cold-weather by-play with hot-water bottles. Then 'The

Ordeal of Young Tuppy' – that needed a match of village rugby football, essentially a winter game.

So . . . real summer? Not the way it happens in England. Wodehouse has got it all romantic and all wrong. England has rotten weather in summer. Winter is worse, but we expect that. For some reason we expect, year after year, that the summer will live up to its name, will produce even a quarter of the hot days that Wodehouse's stories postulate. We talk, these days, in wonder about the long, hot summer of (was it?) 1976, when we got a bushel or two of sour little black grapes off the vine on the south-facing wall (good for adding to the apples for jams, jellies, and tarts); when there was no rain for the whole of the Wimbledon fortnight; when there were five days of cricket in one or two of the five-day Test Matches. And I remember – and tell of it too often – fireflies in our garden in Surrey in 1947. I had never seen fireflies in England before, and have never since. Yes, in those two egregious summers there were mornings (eleven-thirty to one o'clock) when you could read your P.G. Wodehouse in a hammock under a tree without catching a chill, afternoons when you knew you ought to have watered the dahlias that morning before the sun got at them, when the dog sought shade and slept upside down, evenings when loving couples could be heard warmly embracing beyond the fence on the heath. But never months-long summers such as Wodehouse gives us. I wonder how many foreigners have, from reading Wodehouse, come to England in summer without the necessary overcoats, warm underwear, and umbrellas.

Jobless young men with valets? I have never moved around in the best English social circles. I suppose there are still occasional young men in England who are totally unemployed, want to remain so, and, like Bertie Wooster, are happy to spend the afternoon at the club flipping playing cards into a top hat. Bertie and his Drones Club friends, from Oofy Prosser to Freddie Widgeon, did nothing, on inherited money or allowances doled out by uncles, and did it very well. It suited Wodehouse for his books to have them footloose.

Jeeves is Bertie's valet, cook, chauffeur, friend and adviser. And he is a joy. But you note that very few of Bertie's friends at the Drones have 'men'. Oofy, yes. Harold Pendlebury-Davenport, yes. And Archibald Mulliner – the one who lived in Albany and imitated so well a hen laying an egg – yes, he had Meadowes, who was a long-standing member of The League for The Dawn of Freedom and who helped his master to turn Socialist and go and try getting bread into the martyred proletariat in Bottleton East, far from Mayfair. It was Archibald himself who got martyred that evening – also a fortnight's imprisonment. Happily there was no indication that Meadowes discontinued his service just because his master, temporary Comrade Mulliner, was a jailbird. Nor did it stop Aurelia Cammarleigh from loving her wayward swain and eventually, we suppose, marrying him. (One of Meadowes's jobs for his young master had been to go into the park and carve AM/AC in a heart on the trunk of a tree.)

I wonder how many members of the Drones had spent nights, or weeks, in prison cells. Bertie Wooster was in jug more than once. On the nights of the Oxford and Cambridge boat race and rugger match, you might think, reading Wodehouse, that London's West End seethed every year with young gentlemen in top hats, tail coats, and white ties, either trying to find a policeman so as to steal his helmet (the forward push is essential before the upward lift) or, having so tried and failed, being marched off to chokey, to face the magistrate next morning. I may say that for my first two years at Oxford I looked for trouble and excitement round Piccadilly Circus on Boat Race night and the night of the rugger match, and nothing stirred, nobody seethed, the Criterion bar was only sparsely populated, Romano's and the Empire Grill silent and sedate and no policemen walked helmetless or anxious. Had they ever, even in Wodehouse's young days?

Bertie and Jeeves were, when at full strength, creatures of the 1920s and after. *Something Fresh*, published during the First World War, was of an earlier era. In that book practically all the members of the house party at Blandings had brought valet or maid. Freddie Threepwood had a valet. So did Lord Emsworth. (Lord E. for the last time. If ever a man needed a valet, it was Lord E., much more than he needed a secretary.) In post-war books Uncle Fred, Lord Ickenham, had no valet, Pongo no valet, Galahad no valet – even rich, self-indulgent old bachelor Sir Gregory Parsloe-Parsloe, Bart., had no valet. But Bertie continues with his faithful Jeeves (except for occasional breaks) to the end of the road. Hands up, anybody, in England or America, who has had a gentleman's personal gentleman, or a friend who has had one, since World War I – a man to cook and valet and drive the car and read to you when you're sleepless (as did Ashe Marson, valet to dyspeptic Mr Peters in *Something Fresh*), a man who comes with you when you go to visit family or friends, in hotels, on yachts, indeed on round-the-world cruises. I see no hands, and rest my case.

Show me a clergyman now who has a butler – in Wodehouse almost every man of the cloth above the rank of curate has one. Where today (I ask you) do house parties drift into weeks and fortnights? How many homes have knives-and-boots boys or page-boys in blue and buttony uniforms? Where can, or could, justices of the peace in England repose on a settee in their own homes and sentence a suspected miscreant to a fortnight's imprisonment without trial, without lawyers, and without argument? Lord Emsworth thinks he can, and clearly he has been a J.P. for many years and should know the ropes. Sir Watkyn Bassett, in his retirement from London magistracy, is almost as peremptory as Lord Emsworth as a J.P. in his Worcestershire home. Where in England since World War I did a country public house, or *any* public house, have its doors open to casual drinkers all day and most of the night? The Emsworth Arms (G. Ovens, proprietor) in Market Blandings knows no rules of opening and closing times. Many a weary traveller to the castle from London steps, in mid-afternoon, across from the railway station to the Emsworth Arms for a strengthening pint or courage-giving second pint of the home brew before facing the walk to the castle or the drive there in Jno. Robinson's station taxi.

Home brew? Yes, there are still public houses, owned by their landlords, not by breweries, where you can get home-brewed beer. Few now, and far between. But find me a village concert. Find me a steam train. Wodehouse has trains puffing and whistling in the slips at Paddington or Waterloo station long after England's railways have gone diesel and electric.

10
Happy Valley Fields, Home from Many Homes

I have always wondered why Wodehouse called it Mitching Hill in the 1936 short story 'Uncle Fred Flits By'. He had, eleven years before, established Valley Fields in *Sam the Sudden* (1925) and *Big Money* (1931); and when, in the novel *Uncle Fred in the Springtime* (1939), Uncle Fred harks back nostalgically to the events of 'Uncle Fred Flits By', he three times refers to the scene of his misbehaviour as Valley Fields. Mitching Hill, forsooth! 'Uncle Fred Flits By' is, and must be taken as, set in Valley Fields, which, in its turn is, of course – and I quote Wodehouse's preface, written when he was ninety-plus, to a new edition of *Sam the Sudden* – 'a thin disguise for the Dulwich where so many of my happiest hours have been spent. . . . I hope that in the thirty-three years since I have seen it Valley Fields has not ceased to be a "fragrant backwater" (so described by Major Flood-Smith of Castlewood). Though I did read somewhere about a firm of builders wanting to put up a block of flats in Broxted Road, where I once lived in the first house on the left as you come up from the station. Gad, sir, if anyone had tried to do that in my time, I'd have horsewhipped them on the steps of their club, if they had a club.'

And in 1948 he wrote, in a letter from New York, 'Awful, the bomb damage in Dulwich. But what pains me most – oddly – is to hear that The Alleyn's Head has been destroyed. I used to have bread and cheese and beer in the taproom there whenever I went to see a match.'

After he had left school and was a junior trainee in the Hong Kong and Shanghai Bank in the City of London, there was a period when Wodehouse (like Mike Jackson, a slightly auto-biographical character in *Psmith in the City*) had digs near his old school. And, as a more and more eminent Old Boy, he often came down to watch school football and cricket matches. He

141

sometimes wrote accounts of the school matches in the *Alleynian*, of which he had himself been a joint editor.

He had loved his school, his schooldays, and Dulwich itself. Say what you like about Wodehouse the chronicler of dukes, earls, and occasionally mere baronets, of Mayfair idlers at the Drones Club, of huge country castles and mansions, Wodehouse the man, as Wodehouse the boy, had his heart in the right place, and that place was Valley Fields.

'In the course of a long life I have flitted about a bit,' he wrote in the *Sam the Sudden* preface; 'I have had homes in Mayfair, in Park Avenue, New York, in Beverly Hills, California, and other posh localities, but I have always been a suburbanite at heart, and it is when I get a plot calling for a suburban setting that I really roll up my sleeves and give of my best.'

I shall never again, alas, read a Wodehouse novel for the first time. But in the late 1950s and through the 1960s, at first readings I had accurate presentiments, when a Mayfairish plot became too rich with butlers, earls, debs, and cocktails, that we would soon find ourselves, 'like swimmers into cleanness leaping' (to pinch a poetic bit from Rupert Brooke), in Valley Fields.

'I fancy one gets there by omnibuses and things,' says Pongo's Uncle Fred after lunch in Pongo's flat in Albany, when the old goat proposes to take his nephew to visit the home of his ancestors. And they did. Lord Ickenham loved it, 'stopping at intervals like a pointing dog and saying that it must have been just about here that he plugged the gardener in the trouser-seat with his bow and arrow and that over there he had been sick after his first cigar, and he now paused in front of a villa which for some unknown reason called itself The Cedars.' It is difficult to stop quoting from that gorgeous story. Suffice it to say that a nasty young spring breeze and downpour of rain drove these two interlopers to shelter in the windy porch of The Cedars, and soon Uncle Fred was introducing himself to the lone maidservant as the vet come, with his deaf-and-dumb assistant (Pongo), to clip the claws of the parrot he had seen through the front parlour windows. 'Tap your teeth with a pencil', said his uncle to Pongo when instructing him on how to behave as a deaf-and-dumb assistant veterinary surgeon, 'and try to smell of iodoform.'

Perhaps Wodehouse felt at the time that Uncle Fred and Pongo had gone too far in fooling the (pleasant but peasant) lower-middle-class citizens of the suburb, and had therefore dubbed it Mitching Hill lest beloved Valley Fields feel the slight. Certainly the venue was Valley Fields for Uncle Fred in memory, and for Wodehouse from the start. And, yes, one does still get there by omnibuses and things. The Number 3 from Piccadilly Circus goes all the way to the corner of Croxleigh Road. The train from Victoria (to West Dulwich station), which cost the Earl of Hoddesdon (*Big Money*) a shilling and a penny first-class, now has no class distinctions and, at the time of writing, costs you £1 or more. It is also quicker than the bus, if less interesting. Berry Conway in the same book could sprint from The Nook in Mulberry Grove to the station in about eighty-three seconds. I am sure young Wodehouse, whose £80-a-year salary at the bank would have been docked for repeated late arrival in the mornings, timed the sprint from 'the first house on the left in Broxted Road' (or would it have been 'last house on the right' as he hurtled down *to* the station?).

Berry Conway, otherwise a West End clubman, lived in Valley Fields, with Mrs Hannah Wisdom, his housekeeper and old nanny, because that was all he could afford. His friend Lord Biskerton (The Biscuit), son of the Earl of Hoddesdon, above, came down there to live because he wanted to disappear from his creditors and his fiancée for a spell. And The Biscuit's father, the indigent sixth Earl, came down to find his son.

'How is the guv'nor? Pretty fit and insolvent? Still stealing the cat's milk and nosing about in the streets for cigar ends?'

'His health and finances are in much the same state as usual.'

'Poor old chap!' said The Biscuit sympathetically . . .

The sixth Earl was foolish enough to come to Valley Fields wearing a grey top hat. What Valley Fields thought of toffs in grey toppers you must read for yourself.

Mulberry Grove, Ogilvy Street, Burberry Road, Roxborough Road, Mafeking Road, and their detached and semi-d. villas – The Cedars, San Rafael, Mon Repos, Peacehaven, Castlewood, The Nook – these and many more housed many nice people in peace. Well, comparative peace. Claire Lippett in *Sam the Sudden* had a revolver; and *The Ice in the Bedroom*, which, after *Sam the Sudden* and *Big Money*, dwells most lovingly on Valley Fields, brings Leila Yorke, best-selling romantic novelist, to that Elysian suburb, equipped for obscure reasons with a shotgun and ammunition, which stand her in good stead in a confrontation with those ageless crooks, the Molloys and Chimp Twist, that disturbs the peace like anything.

The presiding spirit of the place is Mr Cornelius of The Nook, house-agent and historian of Valley Fields, with long, white druidical beard, pet rabbits, and vast wealth that he keeps secret from his wife (he doesn't want her to move him away from the suburb that he loves and, probably, make him go to the opera and play polo). Mr Cornelius in *The Ice in the Bedroom* (1961) is not a day older than he was in *Sam the Sudden*, thirty-five publishing years ago; and to support his love for his 'native land', Valley Fields, he is still quoting those twelve lines from Walter Scott ('Breathes there a man with soul so dead' and so on). Though not their own, their native land – so far as is known – Valley Fields had a magnetic attraction for many other Wodehouse characters. Ex-butler Keggs – if it's the same Keggs every time, he has buttled for many masters, in England and America – owns a number of Valley Fields villas, and Mr Cornelius rents them for him. Maudie Stubbs, niece of Sebastian Beach, butler of Blandings Castle (Maudie Montrose, barmaid of the Criterion that was, Lady Parsloe-Parsloe of Matchingham Hall that's to be), had a 'neat little house' in Valley Fields. Gertrude Butterwick's father lives in West Dulwich (same thing). An old nanny in *Bachelors Anonymous* lives in Valley Fields. Lord Tilbury was twice de-bagged in Valley Fields. The secretary, later wife, of Cedric Mulliner, dapper Mayfair snob, lived there. The Rev. Aubrey Jerningham, author of 'Is There a Hell?' lives there, the new vicar. And that's not all. I hope I've made my point.

Wodehouse never did come back to his beloved suburb. But it stayed plentifully and lovingly in his memory and his books for another thirty-odd years. I would gladly subscribe something of the cost if someone put up a notice somewhere in acknowledgement, such as

144

YOU ARE NOW ENTERING
[*OR* LEAVING]
THE AREA OF DULWICH, LONDON SE 19,
WHICH SIR PELHAM WODEHOUSE,
ONCE A SCHOOLBOY HERE,
GLORIFIED AS 'VALLEY FIELDS'
IN MANY NOVELS AND STORIES. [1]

Postscript

1.   A member of the American contingent of the P.G. Wodehouse Society
which came over to England at the end of July 1989, and were wined,
dined and lodged at Dulwich College, told me that he was going to lobby
for some such notice to be erected in West Dulwich. I haven't heard where
he went to press his worthy case, nor whether he made any progress.

11
Apprentice Years

The following appeared in Encounter, *the July/August issue of 1985. It discusses a recent find of holograph material from Plum's life before the First World War. Since then three letters he wrote while still a schoolboy at Dulwich have been sold at auction (to James Heineman). These are so far the earliest strictly holograph Wodehouse items known. We continue to hope that the letters he wrote as a boy to his parents in Hong Kong may surface. But I can offer one item, reproduced from holograph — some 'poertory' he wrote at the age of five. When he was twenty-five, he had*

Oh ah that Soryful day
When on the battd field the pets did.
lay in sorryful disgrace.
With red blud
Streaming fast
There life was.
pasing fast
And in the.
camp there lay
Thousands of dead
Men.
      PJ Wodehouse

this is a bit of poertory I Made up

published seven books and was contributing many stories to the Captain,
*he gave this item to the magazine's editorial gossip department, and you'll
find it, as I did, in the bound volume of the* Captain *for 1907. I claim
credit (nobody has given it to me) for the find, and I put it on page two of
the* Penguin Wodehouse Companion *that I edited. Here it is again.
I sometimes wonder whether this was written and sent in for a competition
in some* Tiny Tots *magazine of the mid-eighteen eighties. Less
fatiguable ferrets than I might like to search the British Library shelves at
Colindale or elsewhere.*

P.G. Wodehouse's *The Man Upstairs*, a collection of his earliest
post-public-school short stories, was published by Methuen in
January 1914. The last story in the book, 'In Alcala', first
appeared in the *London Magazine* in December 1911. Neither
that story, nor the book, was ever published in America, though
most of the remaining eighteen stories had appeared in
American magazines, and many of them in the *Strand* magazine
in England. Most of the stories had been written when
Wodehouse was living in New York on the cheap, and teaching
himself to write, when necessary, in American idioms.
  'In Alcala' is a remarkable literary relic. It is sentimental or,
as we might say today, soppy. Never, as a later rule, did
Wodehouse use sentimentality except to mock it (eg Madeline
Bassett; eg 'Honeysuckle Cottage'). 'In Alcala' is basically
autobiographical. Its hero, Rutherford Maxwell, a young
Englishman on the staff of the New Asiatic Bank in New York,
is trying in the evenings to write himself out of servitude and
poverty. 'When I'm in the 20-cents-a-word class, I'll write only
once a month – the rest travelling,' he boasts to Peggy Norton.
She is the heroine of 'In Alcala', a charming American chorus-
girl, who speaks a racy and attractive New York patois which,
accurate or not, was certainly daring for a young English
author trying to sell to American editors. And the story is
unique in the Wodehouse canon in that the heroine has been,
and apparently still is, the mistress of a man she doesn't love, a
star actor. She rejects Rutherford Maxwell's ardent proposal of
marriage. He has just written, with her occasional help, a play
which, with the said actor in it, has had a wonderful first night
reception on Broadway. And on his way home in a taxi-cab (a

'car' would have meant a street-car) from the subsequent supper party, he had 'showered kisses on Peggy's upturned face' (a cliché that Wodehouse plays for laughs in many later books). No, although Peggy, wearing a picture hat, sitting on his writing-table and ruffling or smoothing his hair, has loved him and made him love her, she sends him back to the girl whose photograph is on his mantelpiece: the girl he had left behind him in Worcestershire, Alice Halliday. (An Eve Halliday, no relation, is the heroine of *Leave It To Psmith*, 1923.) Sob, sob.

Rutherford Maxwell has the cheapest possible accommodation in Alcala, a ground-floor 'hall-bedroom'. Elsewhere, up a few floors, Peggy shares a room, cheap, but not so cheap as Rutherford Maxwell's, with another girl from the theatre. For 'Alcala' read the Hotel Earle in Greenwich Village, where Wodehouse stayed whenever he was in New York between 1909 and 1913. 'Rutherford Maxwell' is fiction for Pelham Grenville Wodehouse. The latter looked good in print on the covers of magazines and under the titles of his stories on the inside pages. But it was slimmed to P.G. Wodehouse when the editorial fashion changed, and it remained at that. It was Plum to his friends, Plummie to his family. In 'In Alcala' Peggy very soon says that Rutherford Maxwell won't do in America. 'Gee! That's going some, isn't it? Wants amputation, a name like that . . .' So she calls him George.

There is no record of young (well, twenty-seven in 1908) bachelor Wodehouse having an amorous encounter with an American chorus-girl. Between the Wars, and a happily married man, yes, perhaps. Wodehouse's great friend and collaborator in the theatre, Guy Bolton, was a fount of stories, probable and improbable, which he told excellently in conversation, less excellently in print. Bolton had a story, which he called 'Plum's Wild Oat', and published in a New York magazine. In the 1920s, the days of their pecunious glory as a musical-comedy team – book, dialogue and lyrics – he and Wodehouse were travelling round America with a Number 2 company of one of their Broadway shows: a week here and a week there, and a long train journey on Sundays through the night to where they opened on Monday. The company would reserve two or more whole coaches, and there was apt to be, in spite of Prohibition, a festive party on the move for all on the Sunday evening. Double-decker aisles of sleeping-berths, curtained off, men and women mixed, formed a section of each coach, their aisles leading to the seating accommodation and dining-cars. One late Sunday evening the party, making a great deal of noise, was romping through the sleeping-car, and Plum's bald head looked out from the curtains of an upper berth, saying, 'Hush! She's asleep!' 'A charming girl in the chorus, it was,' said Bolton. But, being a gentleman, he couldn't remember her name.

I heard Bolton tell this story with two different endings. In the first, Plum's dear wife Ethel found a jeweller's receipt for a diamond bracelet in one of Plum's pockets and extracted a confession from him. In the other (which I prefer) Ethel met him and the party at Grand Central Station at the end of the tour, and he kissed her on the cheek instead of the lips. With typical feminine second sight she said, 'Plummie, you've been having an *affaire!*' And silly Plummie, who meant to say, 'Don't be absurd, Bunny!', said, 'Who told you?'

I have gone into some detail of what was known, and what might have been added by Empsonian inference from one of the early short stories, of a period (1906–15) of P.G. Wodehouse's young life not otherwise much documented. He was writing fairly often to his school friend, would-be artist, would-be writer, Bill Townend, but those letters, from the period 1899 to 1920, had not survived and *Performing Flea*, the book they published in 1953, was concocted from Wodehouse's letters from 1920 to 1952 . . . with many cuts, additions, and editings. He had given up his straight-from-school job at the Hong Kong and Shanghai Bank in London years ago. His English public-school novels and short stories could be put behind him. Though Mike Jackson and Psmith were still to emerge from his typewriter, there was no market in America for stories about cricket and footer, schoolroom rags, study frowsts with tea and sausages and no girls in sight anywhere. Not bad stuff, that, he thought later, but apprentice work, bringing in guineas while he was getting a toe-hold on his craft. In New York he had sold, or an agent had sold for him, two short stories in a single day to magazines for prices that made what English magazines paid him look paltry. He was going to write for dollars now, and so much the better if he could sell the stuff for guineas as well.

Now some new light is thrown on Wodehouse's life, thinking, and writing in his New York years before the First World War, and in the early months of his marriage to English Ethel. At Sotheby's in New York recently, two Wodehouse lots were sold:

(1) Thirty-eight holograph letters, signed: two holograph postcards, signed: and one small snapshot, of Wodehouse in a squash court, signed. Their dates ran from September 1909 to June 1915. The recipient of all these was Wodehouse's English friend, Leslie Havergal Bradshaw, who was working on the editorial side of a New York magazine, *Success*.

(2) Three notebooks with, in all, more than six hundred holograph jottings, in pencil mostly, from 1906 onwards: ideas for plots and verses, beginnings of stage lyrics, jokes, dry-runs of dialogue, good American phrases and slang, good remarks overheard, anecdotes, storiettes (as he called them) and, in the last notebook, working scenarios for *The White Feather, Sunshine and Chickens* (this title was changed to *Love Among the Chickens*; and Wodehouse, at least for Bradshaw, acquired the nickname 'Chickens') and *A Gentleman of Leisure*.

The Letters Lot was sold to Dr Ronald Levine, a gynae-cologist and Wodehouse collector in Johannesburg. The Notebooks went to Edward (now Sir Edward) Cazalet. Cazalet's mother was Leonora, a daughter from a previous marriage of Wodehouse's wife Ethel. Wodehouse adopted Leonora and changed her surname to Wodehouse. Ethel Wodehouse (Lady Wodehouse) died in October last on Long Island, where they had had a house since 1955. She was just short of her hundredth birthday, due for 22 May 1985. The Sotheby hammer prices in dollars for those lots represented respectively a fat and a very fat four figures in sterling. Both Edward Cazalet and Ronald Levine kindly supplied me with photocopies of what they bought, and I am grateful to them for allowing me to quote from this material.

Wodehouse's first letters to Leslie Bradshaw, in 1910, address him as 'Dear Bradshaw' and are signed, 'Yours ever P.G. Wodehouse'. They are still on surname terms two years later. Then Wodehouse took to signing himself, 'Yours ever PGW ("Chickens")'. By September 1912 'Bradshaw' had become 'Brad', and 'Chickens' lasted to the end of the correspondence in January 1915. Wodehouse's novel *Psmith in the City* is dedicated to Bradshaw. Bradshaw's novel *The Right Sort* is dedicated 'To P.G. Wodehouse, the right sort'. There was a pen-portrait of Wodehouse by Bradshaw in the *Captain* of March 1909.

Bradshaw was himself trying to get established as a writer, specialising in public-school stories for the same English market in which Wodehouse had made a name and was to make a bigger name when Mike Jackson and Psmith met at Sedleigh (Mike having been removed from Wrykyn, Psmith from Eton). Bradshaw had offered Wodehouse help in selling his boys' books in America, but Wodehouse wanted none of that. In a letter dated simply 'Tuesday', probably written in the autumn of 1909, he said to Bradshaw:

Thanks awfully for your letter. It's ripping of you wanting to give me a leg-up, but I'm afraid it wouldn't do. So far from wanting my boys' books published this side, I want to start here with a clean sheet as a writer of grown-up stories. The *Captain* books are all right in their way, but the point of view is too immature. They would kill any chances of doing anything big . . . I want to butt into the big league . . . I don't want people saying I was better than Andrew Home when I want them to think I'm better than O. Henry. The school stories have served their turn, and it would hurt my chances of success to have them bobbing up when I'm trying to do bigger work. I have given up boys' stories absolutely.

With the gift of the notebooks, Wodehouse wrote:

Use any public-school stuff you like in accompanying notebooks, but don't swipe me other notes!

The letters are mostly addressed from New York. But some, according to Wodehouse's movements, came from Bellport on

Long Island, from London (the Constitutional Club, which he liked because nobody knew him there) and from Emsworth House, Hampshire. This was a boys' prep-school where Wodehouse's 'slacker' friend – and sometimes enemy – Westbrook (part model for Ukridge) was an assistant master. Wodehouse at periods rented a room above a stable there, played cricket and football with the boys, and worked. He later rented, and later still bought, for £300, a house named Threepwood near the school. Threepwood, Warblington, Bosham, Bognor, Fittleworth, Rogate – Hampshire and Sussex names proved useful for the Emsworth family of Blandings, for two bishops, and for other characters in later books.

You find much the same pattern in the letters to Bradshaw as in the letters to Bill Townend. In the early years Wodehouse gives Bradshaw a good deal of advice about the manuscripts Bradshaw sends to him for professional comment. In the later years the letters are more, and mostly, about Wodehouse's own literary agonies and exultations: his acceptances and rejections by magazine editors, his fees, finances, and literary agents.

Sept. 1909. 'Have just sold a 5000-word story to *Collier's* for 300 dollars! Feeling pretty good in consequence.'

30 March 1910. He congratulates Bradshaw on 'Tommy Castleton's Case' and on an article, 'The American Boy', in the *Captain* (Vol. 23) that month. On the subject 'What the American boy is reading' Bradshaw had written, 'There are few private secondary schools, and none corresponding to the English "public-school", and naturally there are not many school stories and none of the kind written by P.G. Wodehouse, R.S. Warren Bell, Fred Swainson etc. . . . There is no magazine like the *Captain*. . . .'

Thursday, probably summer 1910. Wodehouse is trying by guile to place a story, 'Peaches', in Bradshaw's magazine *Success*. 'Tell Merwin [the Editor] he should buy now while I am going cheap. Like buying your coals early in the summer. When the summer after next comes, and PGW stories are selling at $1000 apiece, they'll have theirs all ready, bought cheap before the rise, because honestly if I am getting 5 cents a word now, when I've just started, isn't it a cinch that I shall be getting more when "Jimmy" [*The Intrusion of Jimmy*, its English title *A Gentleman of Leisure*] has had its run (and it has already sold

152

more than 7,000 before publication) and the play is on [In the dramatisation of the novel Douglas Fairbanks Sr., at the start of his career, played the hero, Jimmy Pitt. The play was rewritten, and renamed *A Thief for the Night* in 1913 when John Barrymore, at the start of *his* career, played Jimmy] and probably another novel published? . . .'

5 May 1910. 'Two more stories sold to the *Strand* . . . that makes six they have taken altogether. I've just discovered a hole in my trousers. These are life's tragedies.'

Monday? 1910. Again a ruse. 'Are you game to put in a little sneaky work for me? Show the enclosed story to Brubaker [at *Success*] and say you've got to send it back to me tomorrow as I'm going to send it off to *Collier's*, not offering it to Brubaker. If he says "Not much good", bow out gracefully. If he says "Hot Stuff!" say casually Wodehouse wants $600 for it and will keep it by him till he gets it.'

Wodehouse had just sold a baseball story to *Collier's* for $300 – probably 'The Pitcher and the Plutocrat', which he changed into 'The Goal-Keeper and the Plutocrat', published in the *Strand* in January 1912.

January 1911. 'My next Black's book is the serial I wrote for *Chums*.' This serial, written to a commission, was titled *The Luck Stone* and its author was given as 'Basil Windham'. Wodehouse says somewhere that Bill Townend had given him the plot. He gave Townend some of the loot from *Chums*. *The Luck Stone* was a blood-and-thunder/maharajah's jewel/*Moonstone*/*Sign of Four* story set improbably in an English public school. In fact Black's didn't publish it as a book, and their records do not tell why. *The Luck Stone* has never been re-published. Wodehouse tried other, more credible stories on *Chums*, but they were all rejected. Wodehouse's royalties on his school books from Black's in 1910 had come to £60.

10 Feb. 1911. Wodehouse, at Emsworth, had heard that Bradshaw's 'mater' was thinking of leaving New York and living in England. Apparently Bradshaw lived with his mother and supported her. Wodehouse says he'll try to get Bradshaw a job with Newnes or Pearson's in London.

2 March 1911. 'I wrote a story in three days. The *Strand* have taken it. When I have time to Americanise it, I'll send it along to you [to help him sell it in New York].'

153

3 April 1911. From Constitutional Club, London 'I'm sailing back to NY Saturday next in the Lusitania. It will be ripping being back. . . . If you, by some marvel, sell the serial [presumably *The Prince and Betty*], will you send me a wireless to the ship . . . just the price. I.e. the single word "two" will mean "Sold serial for $2000". . . .'

3 May 1911. Hotel Earle. 'Dear B, got to pop down town & whack up some money from my bankah!'

Saturday? 1911. 'No luck yet. Three stories rejected in three days, including a new one, by *McClure's*.'

26 Jan. 1912. From Mount Anville [where that?], *Emsworth, Hants.* 'Good news. Black will publish your story in the autumn and will pay you 10%. Same terms as I got for *The Pothunters*. Very glad. Pity we couldn't get serialisation, though. Will you do this – go to Moyle's – see Hensl (Moyle's away) and find out what places my "Dinner of Herbs" and "Ruth in Exile" have been to and whether they are out now. If you can manage to get them away (on pretence of reading them) & see if you cd. place them somewhere? . . . . I have an idea Moyle lost heart & shelved them. . . .'

21 May 1912. 'I had a friendly letter from Douglas Fairbanks yesterday in answer to mine of July last! American hustle!'

9 Sept. 1912. 'I'm coming over on the Olympic in October . . . going to take a trip to San Francisco – get some local colour. I made 27 in 7 minutes for the Authors at Lord's before being stumped. . . . Last Saty I got 50 for our village & took 7 wickets. We had to run everything out. It nearly killed me. With boundaries I should have made a century. . . .'

22 Nov. 1912. His trip to America has been cancelled. '*Brother Alfred* may come on quite soon [it did, at the Savoy, for a fortnight only: 'Ghastly frost!']. I'm busy dramatizing *The Little Nugget*. Here's a photograph of me in my squash-rackets costume. A condensed version of *The Nugget* appeared in the *Captain* as a 3-part serial. Nobody else would take it.'

6 May 1913. From Hotel Algonquin, New York. 'This new place suits me far better than the Earle. Owing to Fairbanks and others recommending me, the management can't do enough for me. . . . Grossmith made me write and re-write *Brother Alfred* till all the punch was lost, and it ran to empty houses. I never saw such notices – all thoroughly well deserved. . . . I think

Cohan and Harris will put on *The Little Nugget* in the fall. But it won't be plain sailing. The character of the crook ran away with the play so that it killed Fairbanks's part . . . i.e. a lot of re-writing will have to be done, as the crook will now be starred.'

1 Sept. 1914. Wodehouse thinks the *Saturday Evening Post* will take a story he has sent in. His agent is now Mrs Wilkening. She has sold *The Man Upstairs*, nineteen stories, to Famous Players, movie people. 'If they pay $1000 per story, this will put me in shape to treat editors like so many tripe-hounds. . . . My ambition is to inaugurate a regular reign of terror. Meanwhile I simply can't get another idea for a short story. . . . About editors and agents . . . my real trouble is that I don't really like these people. . . . Life is infernally monotonous: work, feed, bed. In between stories it's rotten. That's why I have always enjoyed Emsworth. There was never a day without something breaking loose, if it was only the dog rolling, or one of the kids breaking a window. . . . I dined with Bob Davis last night [Davis was editor of a whole stable of 'pulp' magazines in New York. Wodehouse sold him stories for these, and he found Davis very fertile with suggestions for plots]. Picked him up at his office. He was too tired to say a word hardly. Dined, talked spasmodically for about an hour, and then he turned me out, as he had a lot of manuscripts to read. It was New York all over. I never get any sense of repose with these devils. They either exhaust me with their excess of vitality or else are practically logs. . . .'

1 Oct. 1914. Hotel Astor, New York. 'Dear Brad, excuse delay in answering letter. Been busy getting married . . . to Ethel Milton. Yours ever, Chickens.' This was written the day after the wedding. Ethel Newton-Rowley was a lovely young English widow whom Wodehouse had met in New York on 3 August, the day before England went to war with Germany. In this letter he had got his bride's name wrong, as he did, at first, on the marriage certificate.

10 Oct. 1914. From Bellport, Long Island. 'Married life really is the greatest institution that ever was. When I look back and think of the rotten time I have been having all my life, compared with this, it makes me sick. And when I think that I was once actually opposed to your idea of getting married. I am amazed at myself. My latest and final announcement on the

155

Brad-Olive situation is Get married at once and don't care a blow about anyone [Bradshaw's 'mater' had been opposed to his marrying Olive], because it is borne in on me very strongly that this business of marriage is so exclusively one's own business that it is ridiculous to let even one's mother have a say in it. The only point to be considered is finance. Do you feel that you can undertake the contract from a financial point of view? The idea of my talking prudence is pretty thick, seeing that I have at this moment $70 in the bank! But I am hoping for more eftsoons and right speedily. . . . Speaking as an old married man (ten days!) I think the main question about marriage is not so much whether you are in love with each other as whether you have the essential points in common which enable you to live with each other without getting on each other's nerves. I know you and Olive have. . . . I can only argue, of course, taking a line through my own case. All I know is that for the first time in my life I am absolutely happy. It is a curious thing about it that the anxieties seem to add to the happiness. The knowledge that it was up to one to support someone else has a stimulating effect. . . . Ethel sends her love. She liked you tremendously. She says you must come down when you can manage it, but says not until she has got a maid. However, that only means a day or two. Apparently maids are plentiful in these parts after the middle of this month.' [Bradshaw married Olive.]

19 Oct. 1914. Bellport. 'I have about $425 in the bank, besides my London savings. Living here is cheap. If I come to New York, I must get back early. A night here alone would give Ethel the willies! Dramatisation of *Little Nugget* dragging its feet. Still no maid.'

24 Oct. 1914. 'Ethel has come out very strong with three fine plots! I am working on them now. If she can keep this up, the maintenance of the home is a cinch! I never appreciated married life so much as last night. I came home, tired and hungry, after having walked out from Patchogue and having had nothing to eat for hours, and there was a fine dinner and a blazing fire, and E. fussing over me, and all sorts of good things. It was perfectly ripping. . . . We are still without a maid, but I have developed a wonderful liking for washing dishes. I find it stimulates thought and is generally soothing. So I am going to take on that department till we get a maid. We have two kittens

156

and a puppy now. The puppy kept us awake the night before last from 2.30 onwards.'

20 Jan. 1915. 'I found Reynolds [Paul Reynolds, Wodehouse's new literary agent in America] a very good sort indeed. He was pleasantly different from Seth and Mrs Wilkening and didn't make one windy promise of selling my stuff for millions. . . . He is a man of a certain position, thank goodness. What I mean is that he belongs to decent clubs, where he presumably doesn't get tight, and that is a great thing. One always felt about Seth that at any moment he might disappear into nowhere with a lot of one's money and never appear again. Reynolds seems to be one of the aristocrats of the profession. The first man we met in the club was Scribner, and his attitude towards Reynolds was a sort of respectful chumminess. Horrid thought: was it a "property" Scribner, a pal of Reynolds simply engaged to pretend to be Scribner so as to impress me! . . . Have you ever read *The Guest of Quesnay* by Booth Tarkington? It is one of the best books I have read recently. I thought of writing to congratulate him, but prudence intervened. I want to crib his heroine, and it is imperative that, if denounced, I shall be able to say, "I never read any *Guest of Quesnay*. Who is this Booth Tarkington of whom you speak??". . . Mrs Westbrook wrote to say she had a big deal on with the movie rights of my stories, and a few days ago cabled me to suggest prices as a basis for her to work on, so it really looks as if there were something doing, though I don't want to be too sanguine after the Wilkening fiasco.' Wodehouse's friend Westbrook, assistant master at Emsworth House prep-school, which was a model for the prep-school in *The Little Nugget*, had married Ella King-Hall, sister of the headmaster. She had written the music for *The Bandit's Daughter*, a musical sketch by Wodehouse and West-brook: not successful. She had for some time been working as a literary agent, for Wodehouse and others.

3 June 1915. Bellport, Long Island. Wodehouse has sold a story to the *Saturday Evening Post* for $500. This puts him in the 10-cents-a-word class. They have a car. Ethel is a very good driver. Dulwich reports a magnificent football season last year. They have a 'freak wing ¾, who was 6ft and 11½ stone at the age of 14. He has scored lots of tries in all the school matches and has two more years. Mizzi has 4 kittens.'

157

25 June 1915. 'I am re-writing *Brother Alfred* for Lawrence Grossmith for a musical play in the fall. Jerome Kern is doing the music. Douglas Fairbanks is a good sort. . . .'

For his purpose of writing English boys' school stories, Bradshaw would have found most nourishment in the first and earliest of the three notebooks Wodehouse gave him. There are several long musings, with recognisable Dulwich names in them, about school affairs. In his own public-school stories and novels – about Wrykyn, Sedleigh, Ripton, Eckleton and St Austin's – Wodehouse made his headmasters minor characters but major powers: more spoken about than speaking, men of quality and authority with butlers at their doors: and distant from the dust and heat of inter-house and inter-school games rivalries and in-house raggings. In his prime, in the Mulliner stories (eg 'The Bishop's Move' and 'The Voice from the Past', and the Jeeves story 'The Inferiority of Old Sippy'), the headmasters are comic heavies. In an item in Notebook Number 1, Wodehouse broods on Gilkes, the 'Old Man' of his years as a boy at Dulwich College.

For School Stories – Write one round a headmaster like Gilkes, who tries to rule by kindness. When he catches anybody breaking rules v. flagrantly, he makes him a school prefect. The chap, thus getting more liberty, thinks the Old Man a fool & becomes worse than ever. Might make hero of story head of the school, whose best laid schemes are thwarted by this tendency of O.M.'s. Show his growing despair.

In re Gilkes: – he does not in the least understand the moral blindness and callousness of boys. Thus he thinks that by apologising to a boy, he will touch his heart and make him repent and turn over a new leaf. Not a bit of it. Boy thinks he has scored off Old Man, tells everybody he has made him apologise to him, thinks him a damned weak fool, & runs amok. *Boys respect strength, nothing but strength.* They may dislike it, but they respect it. A school is like a child. The mother who alternately spoils and storms at a child makes it unmanageable. Same with headmaster & school. Gilkes goes on apologising to everyone, even when he is in the right, & then when they get out of hand he makes them worse by stopping a concert or field day or, worse still, by saying he has stopped it, & then giving way at the last moment. As an example of Gilkes' folly, the other day he was arguing with Lawrion about something, & L. actually said: 'I disagree with you entirely & I do not wish to hear a word more!' He was saved from sudden death by the entrance of Hope who wished to discuss something with the Old Man. Later the O.M. met Lawrion, & putting a hand on his shoulder said, 'Well, L., I hope you have got over your temper!' Naturally a story like that gets about, & chaps lose their respect for him.

Another point in which G. failed was this. After an exceptionally good athletic year, as Dulwich had when Northcote was footer captain, there comes a relapse, & the school, all its best men having left, gets beaten in matches. Then school gets restless and out of hand. That is the time to tighten the reins. He loosened them.

Nearly all the prefects have had their caps taken away & given back. The value of prefect's cap has sunk lower than ever before.

And

The Classical Sixth Form is really the criterion of the school. In my time we were all big & all colours & could have played the rest of the school at anything. There was consequently no disorder. Now, in 1905, the Sixth was actually unable to turn out a footer team of 15 men, & playing only 8, got beaten by the Science Sixth. No wonder the School is disorderly.

The third notebook contains early scenarios or episodes for novels that are recognisable as *The Gold Bat* (published 1904), *Love Among The Chickens* (1906), *The White Feather* – it was to have been *The Honour of the House* – (1907), and *A Gentlemen of Leisure* – discarded titles, *The Amateur* and *The Black Sheep* – (1910). There is also a group of notes of what was to have been a stage farce entitled *The Bishop*. There is quite a lot of preliminary scribbling when Wodehouse was trying to clarify a plot for what became 'The Good Angel'. That was the earliest Wodehouse story in which a butler plays a strong part, and the first of several uses of

159

Keggs as a butler's name. 'The Good Angel' starts, you may remember:

Any man under thirty years of age who tells you he is not afraid of an English butler lies. Outwardly he may be brave – aggressive even, perhaps to the extent of calling the great man 'Here!' or 'Hi!'. But in his heart, when he meets that cold, blue, introspective eye, he quakes. . . .

And here in the notebook is a first scribble:

Open. 'Any young man says not afraid butler lies. One called a butler "Here you!" once. But he was never the same man again. Yet many a butler has a heart of gold.'

One plot, perhaps rightly, never got beyond the single page at the end of Notebook 3:

Strict Training
X., young ass with legacy comes up from country town and becomes a bounder. Y, a chorus girl, shows partiality for him, practically cuts him out with another c.g.; X very flattered. Tries to kiss her. She knocks him out. Sends Z, husky stolid chap, to train him. (Mem: She is going to marry Z if he makes a man of X.) She says in her note that it takes eight days to get a new idea into Z's head & that his one idea now is to train X. Describe how Z shadows X, makes him run in Park early in morning, take cold baths, & go to bed early etc. X tries to get rid of Z (how?). Finally comes to Y, & says he is in good condition & is quitting for home. Thanks her & asks why she took the trouble. She says she is his fiancée's sister.

Of the other hundreds of items, in all three notebooks, very few have emerged recognisably (to me) in the Wodehouse published works. A good deal of Wodehouse ephemera has appeared in print but has not yet been identified and re-published. His *The Luck Stone* contained a cheery Indian boy at an English public school, a ragger named Ram. But Ram came, surely, from F. Anstey's 'Baboo Jabberjee' in *Punch*. There are no practice swings in these notebooks at Ram's orotund, book-learned mishmashing of English. In the *Globe,* a London evening paper, Wodehouse's 'By the Way' column – a dozen or so short snippets and a set of verses – was a distant and comparatively pallid forerunner of Beachcomber's 'By the Way' in the *Daily Express.* Some of the items in these notebooks may have gone into that. Wodehouse and Townend did 'Answers to Correspondents' in *Tit-Bits* for a period in 1908. These have never been brought to book. Wodehouse wrote, under a variety of names, 'extras' for the elegant monthly New York magazine, *Vanity Fair,* besides being its theatre critic. He contributed anonymous bits and pieces, verse and prose, to *Punch* for a decade from 1902 onwards. These have not yet been dredged and collected for re-publication. We may yet discover that Wodehouse worked up, and made into guinea-earning *obiter scripta,* more than a handful of these pencil-jottings. That was certainly their purpose in the beginning. At random, then:

He was the sort of person who would take every egg out of a nest and excuse himself on the ground that he was preventing (in the future) cruelty to worms.

You haven't got a mind. You run along on a cheap substitute of putty and mud.

It is a terrible thing to wake suddenly to the knowledge that one is not a genius.

Two months later he appeared with many apologies and a beard.

Pringle's grandmother died when that youth was still unable to speak. To this cause may be attributed the fact that he never taught her to suck eggs.

Of a baby's smile: a slit appeared in the baby's face.

Of a man who was too much addicted to the pleasures of the table: His exit (from life) was hastened by his entrées.

161

Americanisms: She talked a blue streak. Get a wiggle on (i.e. buck up). Scared stiff. A peach of a pencil. He's not worth two bits. He makes me tired.

For a nonsense poem: Policeman was also a burglar, at last arrested himself and got promotion and penal servitude simultaneously.

For frightful pathos: Blind man writes stories, his one amusement. His wife pretends they are accepted, though they are invariably refused, and reads them out to him as though from magazines.

For a poem: 'The Soft-hearted Heavyweight'. [Perhaps this man was remembered for Ukridge's champion, Battling Billson?]

Quotes from or about people . . . his friend Westbrook, his elder brother Armine, Conan Doyle, Cosmo Hamilton, W.S. Gilbert, Gilkes, Margie ('says if you ever want a free ride, hunt about at the bottom of a cab with a match at the end of a ride, then go indoors saying you have lost a sovereign in the cab and are going for more matches, telling cabby to wait. When you come back, c. will have departed'):

'Looks like a sinful butler,' said by Mrs Belloc Lowndes of Humphry Ward, 1905.

Instead of saying 'All was jolly, jollity and song,' JEG says 'All was j.j. & s.' [Perhaps that was the seed for a later flowering, in Bertie Wooster's burble, of cliché phrases cut down to their first letters, as 'I sank into a c. and passed an agitated h. over the b.' in *The Code of the Woosters*.]

Oliver Rae re Seymour Hicks bullying his wife who adores him. 'Women like being bullied. At least they don't exactly like it, but they like the man who does it.' [Later an asterisk against the name Hicks gets a gloss:] Later bulletin (1906). This is a lie. He doesn't. PGW.

For Punch? 'The Bank Opera.' Hero's song:

> *She wore a hat of novel style.*
> *Her eyes were azure stars.*
> *And, with a soft bewitching smile*
> *She spoke to me through bars.*
> *Ah, yes, she spoke to me and oh!*
> *I felt I'd perish for her,*
> *But duty bade me answer 'No*
> *Effects. Refer to drawer.'*

Chorus:　*To duty's call he bowed and so*
　　　　Referred her to the drawer.

Mem for Windsor or Punch. Barry Painful article: – the man who took up as his profession the extinction of bores. He was a man of vast information, & if anybody had a friend staying with them who persisted in collaring the conversation, on any subject, the man was sent for & by means of his superior information crushed him (e.g. the Switzerland and foreign travel bore: the children's story bore etc). Mem. Might make this a long story. A sort of Dr Watson friend to tell the story, & the tale to begin by person calling in the expert for advice, as he has a man staying with him who is a combination of all the sorts of bore known.

Curious characteristic of the female mind, the love of *teasing*. Men never do it. E.g. MEL and EHML. Joan on the other hand does not do it. Why?

Gags, nifties, captions, one-liners . . . there are hundreds more where those came from. One reads a professional humorist's notebooks at one's peril – the peril of thinking, 'Good Lord, did Wodehouse think that funny?' Actually, no. But he saw capabilities in it, as Lancelot Brown could see in a nobleman's estate a capability for landscaping: as an oyster, perhaps, feeling a piece of grit in his shell, works on it till it becomes a pearl.

Three more entries, for variety:

163

Impressions of visit to Laurence Housman. I had expected to find him drooping and yearning over a lily. Brisk, cheerful man with a pleasant smile: total absence of poetic pose: caricatures his friends, and rags about it with them: Miss H. rather soulful; the room unpapered, but distempered in cream colour: candles: benedictine & chartreuse: whisky: L.H. says, when I ask him to dilute it, that he hates to see anything drowned, whether it's cats or whisky: not enough chairs: L.H. expressed an opinion that a couple can do very well with two comfortable chairs and a settee, but they mustn't give an At Home. 'Poetry', says L.H. 'is the language of the brain': e.g. some poems you can't bear to hear read to you, because the sound of the voice seems an intrusion. He can always work better in London than the country, because in the country he feels too well to do anything but be a mere animal: he wants to feel rather ill to work. [Didn't brother Alfred Housman say that poetry came to him more easily if he had a slight indigestion?]

Mems about Conan Doyle.

(*a*) Sent *Micah Clarke* to James Payne, & got back J. P.'s usual illegible letter. At last managed to decipher the first sentence. It ran 'How can you, how *can* you waste your wits and your time writing historical novels?' 'Nice & encouraging that, wasn't it?' says C.D. 'Just for a start, y'know.'

(*b*) Was sent in his early days a picture of two girls & a boy in a yacht by *Cassell's* to write story to. Thinks that was the lowest depth to which he has ever sunk.

(*c*) 'A man who does anything worth reading at 21 is going to make his name. You write better at 30 than at 21, & better at 40 than at 30.'

(*d*) 'The life of an author is divided into 2 parts. During the first he goes to the publishers. During the 2nd they come to him. Then he begins to get a bit of his own back.'

(*e*) 'If you can write so as to please schoolboys, you will do well. There is no better critic (within limits) than a schoolboy.'

(*f*) 'A man who can manage a cricket team on tour & see that they don't think the match is next week & don't lose their cricket-bags & don't let their wives get ill the day before a match is fit to govern a colony.'

(*g*) 'The success of a book is a gamble. Reviews of the ordinary sort don't help it much. Of course if a critic says it's the very finest book that has appeared for the last ½ century, then people may be influenced by it. But if he simply says it's good work, nothing comes of it.'

(*h*) When I told him that if I liked a book, I liked to buy it & keep it, he said, 'Ah, but you're a young literary man. The public aren't all young literary men. I wish they were.'

And:

Jim Deane's description of a corpse in S. Africa.

(*a*) Corpse of a black boy killed by other black boys of Remount Dept: age 14: lying in the sun 2 days: all swollen: throat cut from ear to ear: body stark naked & covered with black blood: arms stretched back where someone had knelt on them, & legs straight out, having been sat on while boy was being killed. Motive for murder probably because he cheated his pals at gambling. It was a Saturday night, when they get their pay.

(*b*) a corpse looks like clay: grey cheekbones: nostrils dried up: eyes half closed: limbs stiff & pointing in all directions.

12
Diary

This is a diary page I contributed to the London Review of Books *in the autumn of 1984.*

I have had recently to cut the 65,000-word P.G. Wodehouse novel *Quick Service*, published in 1940, down to about 25,000 words for a BBC Radio 'Book at Bedtime'. Ten periods of fourteen minutes, nine of them to start with a minute or so of re-cap of earlier chapters, and all except the last to end, preferably, at a gasp-moment which will encourage listeners to switch on again tomorrow night.

I have done several such jobs for BBC Radio on Wodehouse novels. I have not found him easy to abridge. His plots are very tightly laced. A snatch of dialogue or narrative on page twenty may be a plant for a twist in the story on page 220. *Quick Service* is one of the best Wodehouse light novels. Joss Weatherby, the brash, buzzing, bouncy hero (how, in Wodehouse, with that name could he be anything but the hero?) and Sally Fairmile (find me a Sally in all the ninety-plus Wodehouse books who is not the heroine, or at least on the side of the angels) are headed for the last-page fade-out towards the altar. It's painful to cut a word of Joss's bright, amorous fencing. He's the sort of Wodehouse hero his elders call 'a darn sight too fresh': the sort who, in love at first sight, grabs the heroine to kiss her, and gets his shins kicked. But Sally is soon shocked to find she likes it, engaged though she may have become last night to Lord Holbeton, who has perfect manners, an outsize Adam's apple and a rather good tenor voice. He sings 'Trees'.

Can we do without Lord Holbeton and thus save ourselves a few thousand words across the board? No, he is twined into the plot in a dozen places. Well, what about Chibnall the butler, engaged to Vera, barmaid at the Rose and Crown? Surely we shall be able to confine Chibnall to his butlerine duties and

166

omit vapid Vera altogether? No, not a chance. If Vera doesn't report that J.B. Duff's moustache is false – Chibnall had come into her bar unexpectedly and seen her stroking it and jumped to the wrong, jealous conclusions – no, the plot is far too intricate for such deep cuts. Well, what about J.B. Duff's dyspepsia? From long study of Wodehouse I know that the middle-aged unmarried man's dyspepsia is going to be cured, later if not sooner, by the advice and medicaments of that kindly, unattached, middle-aged woman: and love will take the place of heart-burn in the party of the first part. You've got to let Duff keep his dyspepsia.

The breakfasts must stay. It's mouth-watering to read, and it would be really sad to cut, a Wodehouse country-house English breakfast: 'silver dishes warmed by little flames, smiling from the sideboard', scrambled eggs, sausages, bacon, fish and kedgeree. And, in this case, a large, pristine ham is waiting to be sliced. One of Duff & Trotter's Paramount hams. What a challenge to today's slim fibrous breakfasts!

Following Wodehouse and, I imagine, paying the Wodehouse estate handsome tribute for the name, there *is* now a Duff & Trotter, in SW8 and the London telephone book. I understand they cater (food, wine and waiters) for the sort of parties that get a mention from 'Jennifer' and the *Tatler*. 'Jeeves of Belgravia' is now an established name for cleaning and valeting services in London. There is a Drones restaurant at Number 1, Pont Street. And now *Punch* has, or recently had, an 'Oofy Prosser's City Column'. Who else in the fiction of this century has provided names for such a handful – a catering firm, a valeting service, a restaurant and a City column? What next?

In *Quick Service*, in his courtship of Sally, Joss compares her to an exquisite Tanagra figurine. Much of Wodehouse's humour is word-play with cliché and jargon: the clash of pulpit prose with racecourse slang, Shakespeare with music hall. Wodehouse knew that 'exquisite Tanagra figurine' was a cliché, but I bet that he, and Joss and Sally, thought that a Tanagra figurine *was* exquisite. I know better now. The passage in *Quick Service* made me realise that I had never to my knowledge seen a

Tanagra figurine, nor did I know where Tanagra was –
assuming that it was a place, not a sculptor.

So I went to the British Museum: up the main stairs and then
sharp to the right. A trove of small terracotta figures was dug up
by archaeologists in 1873 in a village, Tanagra, in Boeotia,
north of Athens. The BM has three showcases for Boeotian
terracottas, two of them being for items from the Tanagra dig.
Dates 300–200 BC. The figures are not much disfigured by age,
and a number of them retain traces of the colours that were
painted on them more than 2,000 years ago. Gods, demi-gods,
heroes, goddesses, satyrs, animals, small groups. But none at
all seemed to me to rate the word 'exquisite', which is part of the
cliché. In fact, amateur work, I'd say: some of the figures could
have been shaped by children puddling clay, as toys. They are
between three and twelve inches in height. Not even attractive.
In fact, if Joss Weatherby had seen the BM's Tanagra
figurines, he wouldn't have compared his loved one to any of
them. Had Sally seen them, she might have gone back to
kicking Joss's shins for his intended compliment.

How, then, had the phrase 'exquisite Tanagra figurine' come
into the language with sufficient mileage to make it a cliché? I
went to the London Library and looked up Tanagra in the
Subject Index. I was referred to a pamphlet – a print-off of an
address given by Quentin Bell, 'formerly Professor of the
History and Theory of Art in the University of Sussex', in May
1976: his fifth Gwilym James Memorial Lecture at the
University of Southampton. I recommend the pamphlet, titled
'A Demotic Art'. It told me, learnedly and amusingly, just what
I wanted to know about the 'coroplasts of Boeotia'. (The
nearest my Shorter Oxford Dictionary comes to 'coroplast' is
'coroplasty', a word used in eye-surgery, 'an operation for
forming an artificial pupil'. Professor Bell's word must come
via the ancient Greek for 'a modeller of small figures', which I
found in my Liddell & Scott lexicon.

These small terracotta figures have been found, as easy-
to-make dolls and grave-offerings, all round the Mediterranean, and some in the Crimea. Christianity diminished the
demand for them. It was not till the big find at Tanagra in 1873
that they became fashionable possessions for collectors:
Tanagra figurines suddenly became the rage. They were

claimed to be 'the most charming works of Hellenistic civilisation'. Prices soared. 'Tanagra, once trash, had become Art, or acquired the status of High Art,' says Professor Bell. By 1877 the Greek government had to put guards round the Tanagra excavation site. Theft, fraud, forgery and clumsy restoration were rampant. Bodiless heads were stuck on to headless bodies, eyebrows and lips touched up with new paint. There arose a factory for forgeries at Myrina, second only to Tanagra as a productive dig. The British Consul in the Piraeus warned travellers and collectors against the most barefaced local restorers – Xacousti, Lambros and Rousopolis were names to remember, he said.

Then the market broke: partly because forgeries had swamped it, but largely because Greek art of the last centuries before Christ was no longer regarded as the all-time absolute of beauty. Professor Bell remembered that in his youth Boeotian coroplasts were being sold, cheap and in quantity, like Christmas tree decorations, at a little Mediterranean coastal village called St Tropez, which was so far off the map then that he and his friends were able to swim naked in the sea there.

Professor Bell's pamphlet answered my question. The phrase 'exquisite Tanagra figurine' became current in the short period when fashion dictated that the figurines *were* exquisite, in the 1870s, '80s and '90s. Then fashion and taste (and prices) turned away from the glory that was Greece, and the bottom fell out of the market for Boeotian coroplasts, whether made two years ago or two millennia. But the cliché lives on.

On the blisteringly hot last Friday of the Wimbledon fortnight (semi-finals of the Men's Singles on the centre court) we were shuffling along in the queue on the road towards the gate. Suddenly the calm was broken by running figures, a man, perhaps a bag-snatcher, pursued by a policeman. The miscreant sprinted across the road and turned in at a gate towards the Golf Club. The young cop in pursuit was going well, and the last I saw of the chase was the cop throwing his helmet into the shrubbery the other side of the fence. I hope that, thus disencumbered, he caught his man.

There was a don at Corpus Christi College, Oxford, named

169

Grundy, of whom good stories were told, in imitation of his voice and self-glorification of his exploits. Grundy may well have been a tutor at Corpus, in Ancient History, to Wodehouse's elder brother Armine. Armine became a theosophist and for a period was in charge of the young Krishnamurti who, he believed, was a new Messiah.

Well, yes, Grundy. . . I never met Grundy when I was at Oxford. He may have died before that, leaving a fragrant memory in the Grundy stories. One of them (and I won't try to cope with the voice effect) was of a Varsity rugger match in which he had performed in the year dot. It went this way. 'It was the Inter-University Match, and Cambridge that year had a very fast wing-three-quarter, very fast. The scores in the last minute were ten points to us, nine to Cambridge. Then this Cambridge winger broke clean away from a scrimmage, clean away, and raced for our line. Our captain came up to me and said, "Grundy, catch that man." My word, what a crash we came!'

Policemen's helmets were trophies in several of the Bertie/Jeeves novels and stories. I fell to wondering, as we shuffled on, what Bertie would have done that afternoon had he been in my place in the queue at Wimbledon. He had a strict code about pinching policemen's helmets – a game that roused graduate members of the Drones Club to their best efforts. The code of the Woosters was strict and Bertie had been arrested more than once for sticking to it. A policemen's helmet is only a fair trophy if it has been removed from the very head of the officer. Bertie would not have left the queue and gone to the shrubbery to pinch the cop's lid. Unsporting.

I hope the cop, having got his man, retrieved his helmet safely.

A collector recently bought, for £175, a short typed letter from Wodehouse to a Mr Slater, dated 2 July 1953. Mr Slater had asked Wodehouse where Market Blandings was, the station for the castle, with Jno. Robinson's taxi waiting to rattle you up to the home of the Earls of Emsworth. Wodehouse wrote:

I have never revealed the fact before, but Market Blandings

is Marlborough. I passed through it years ago on a motoring tour and was much impressed by it. It seemed to me just the town which ought to be two miles away from Blandings Castle . . .

This late-revealed statement will put the cat among the pigeons in the tight little world of Wodehouse topographical scholarship. In this context the names of two retired soldiers, Colonel Norman Murphy in Cumbria, and Colonel Michael Cobb in Devon, spring to the lips.

Marlborough is now on the metaphysical overlay map of Wodehouse's Merry England. Back to your plotting-boards, colonels!

13
A Personal Treasure Hunt

At least a decade before Plum's death, shrewd collectors and dealers in England and America had established a quiet market in his first editions, inscribed copies, play-scripts and so on. Today, for items that were then traded in single figures of pounds or dollars, you may have to add two noughts. And so on up. But the market is still quiet. An expert may have a shrewd idea of what another expert possesses, whether he is trying, or going, to sell or trade it and what the likely asking price may be. Major collectors, on the advice of their insurance companies, if for no other reason, do not shout their wares, nor the whereabouts of them.

I know of two major Wodehouse collections, or archives, one in England, one in America. I was allowed access to the English one and hope to see the American one eventually.

Puppies for sale – Mother pedigree collie. Father comes from a good neighbourhood . . .

This is in Plum's handwriting, on the top sheet of one of those bound piles of tear-off scrap paper, encased in leather for the study desk ('ideal Christmas gift for the busy man'). I take it the words were a draft of an advertisement to go in the Long Island weeklies: that the 'Mother' was the Wodehouse's beloved Minnie, the 'good neighbourhood' Remsenburg and the Hamptons, and the 'Father' . . . well, that meant 'Sorry, we don't know who he was, but, coming from round here, he would have been of good pedigree too, though not, probably, a collie.'

The bound notepad was on Plum's desk in the study of that house in Basket Neck Lane, Remsenburg, Long Island, New York State, where he and Ethel had lived for the last fifteen years of his life. (It, and much else, was brought back to England when Plum died, in 1975, at the age of ninety-three – Sir Pelham Grenville Wodehouse, newly gazetted Knight of the British Empire 'for services to English literature'.)

We are in a large, comfortable house far from beaten tracks and with views over woodlands and pastures. At the end of a corridor there is, on the wall, an engraved slate plaque:

Archive
P.G. WODEHOUSE
1881–1975

The 'P.G. WODEHOUSE' is in facsimile of Plum's signature.

Blown-up to near double crown-poster size, a cheerful photograph of Plum, in slacks, in the Long Island sun, in his young eighties, hangs below the plaque.

Turn right and you are in a space about half the cubic capacity of a squash court, if you imagine the court with its roof lowered to the height of the service-line on the front wall. This space contains, in two even narrower corridors and an inner sanctum, about 1,300 feet of bookshelves, two big armchairs and a desk. There is a cabinet behind the door. Its contents include the insignia of Plum's KBE; the Warwickshire County Cricket Club's tie, which they gave him in honour of the cricketer Jeeves, killed in the First World War, from whom Plum took the name for Bertie Wooster's master; a pipe; a silver case for calling-cards, and some cards, one of them giving the Garrick Club as Plum's address. He had resigned from the Garrick as politely and as soon as possible ('all those hearty lawyers').

Such wall-space as is left unshelved in the archive has photographs, thickly serried and framed, of Plum at all stages, from boyhood to his ninety-third birthday: in groups – the three brothers in 1885 and 1895, the four of them in 1902 and 1912, with his parents, with Ethel, with family, with friends; Plum with pipe, with dogs, in rugger shorts and cricket whites at Dulwich, in plus-fours, in dressing gown (Boxing Day, 1941, in Tost Internment Camp in Silesia), at Remsenburg. Also head (cloth-capped) and shoulders, Plum, the last alphabetically (John Buchan to P.G. Wodehouse) in a framed set of cigarette cards of the twenty top English writers in 1937. That up there is a photograph of Plum talking to Alan Ayckbourn and Andrew Lloyd-Webber at Remsenburg when they were roughing out plans for a musical based on *The Code of the Woosters*. (It was not

173

a success when it went on in a West-End Theatre in due course.) And this is a photograph of Ethel in her mid-nineties at the party at The Morgan Library in New York on 15 October 1981, the exact centenary of Plum's birth and the opening day of the exhibition of Wodehousiana that the Library staged. The same extensive material came over to London and made a similar exhibition at the National Theatre on the South Bank in 1982. One addition at the National was the seated waxen image of Plum from Madame Tussaud's. Image? Well, although Tussaud's had sent over to America a man to measure Plum's ninety-year-old features with calipers, the result looked more like Plum's friend Guy Bolton than Plum himself. The body itself was too small. It was Guy-size, not Plum-size.

One of the photographs on the walls that I hadn't seen before is of the Hong Kong and Shanghai Bank's Rugby XV 1900–01, with Plum in the front row, in shorts, seated, and the President of the Bank, Sir E. Cameron, KCMG, standing at the side, in City dress and the high-rise bowler hat of the period. The President has a huge white moustache such as his soon-to-escape employee later gave to the Duke of Dunstable.

The only sad photograph on the wall is that one taken of Plum in a dressing gown at Tost, in the Commandant's office in the internment camp that had once been a lunatic asylum. Plum is looking thin and cold. But, if he was hungry too at that moment, that may have been temporarily eased soon. He has in his right hand a tin of beans that has just arrived in a food parcel from Ethel, herself in Lille in France then, probably not too well fed either. Plum lost three stone in nine months of internment, and said he felt fine at the end of it. But he had been almost permanently hungry on his way to this state of lissom good health. One of the treasures of the archive is the diary he had kept from Day 1, 27 June 1940, of his internment. Under the date line 26 August he wrote:

At Liège [where the new internees had been incarcerated uncomfortably for a few days on their way to Tost] Parson and I used to stride up and down agreeing that this was all a wonderful, spiritual experience and was making us all unselfish. Today I met him grumbling because the other rooms always seemed to get more potatoes than his.

174

Knowing the frequency of Plum's references – in parody of parsonic Victorian novels, I think – to Lady Bountifuls (and Stiffy Byng in a rosy preview of herself when married to the sainted and beloved oaf, the Rev. 'Stinker' Pinker – if he ever had preferment to a vicarage) taking 'soup to the poor', I love this from Plum's camp diary:

August 12th [in a deserted, and filthy, Belgian Army barracks]. For the first time I fetch soup in a bucket from cookhouse. Frightful sense of responsibility. Suppose I dropped it!

Much of the material for the five talks which he was encouraged, by the German authorities, to give to still-neutral America from Berlin after his release from Tost, was taken ready-made from this diary.

In his ample spare time in internment, and in Germany after his release, Plum had been working on the novel that became *Money in the Bank*. Among the items on the shelves of the archive is a gold turnip watch in a special case. After his release from Tost, Plum, with Ethel and Wonder the Peke – these two had been allowed to come from France to join him in Germany – had been guests, in the country, of the Bodenhausens, friends of a German, Raven Barnekow, whom the Wodehouses had known well in Hollywood. Plum, walking one day in the mud and reeds of a pond in the grounds, had found beneath his foot a hard encrusted object that turned out to be this watch, lost for many years. The Bodenhausens had it polished up and they gave it to Plum as a memorial keepsake. If you remember, *Money in the Bank* had a cache of diamonds, a dowry for his niece, hidden, and then forgotten, in the bank of a pond by the addle-pated Lord Uffenham. I think you'd find that the dates make it not only possible but likely that the chance find of that watch on the brink of the Bodenhausens' pond gave Plum the plot-twist, and title, for the novel. (I have recently read that Alan Turing – the mathematical genius who was largely responsible for breaking the German Enigma code – had, at the beginning of the war, bought ingots of silver with his mother's and his own capital, and had buried these and then forgotten where. Turing was very far from being addle-pated.)

175

I had long suspected that somewhere in Plum's life, or surroundings, or possessions, was, or had been, a mantelpiece figurine of the Infant Samuel at Prayer. As early as 1912, in a story 'Pots o' Money', published in the *Strand Magazine*, and later in the collection *The Man Upstairs* (1914), an angry man throws a loaf of bread at a young singer, misses him and breaks a plaster statuette of the Infant Samuel on top of the piano. Again, in *The Code of the Woosters* (1938), at Totleigh Towers, Bertie's Aunt Dahlia, having learnt that her host, Sir Watkyn Bassett, is trying to get her peerless chef Anatole on to his payroll and into his kitchen, is looking seethingly for something in Bertie's bedroom 'to break as a relief to her surging emotions!' Bertie 'courteously drew her attention to a terra-cotta figure of the Infant Samuel at Prayer on the mantelpiece'. Aunt Dahlia 'thanked him briefly and hurled it against the opposite wall'. Well, here is the ornament (if it can be called ornamental) that begot the mentions in Plum's texts: three inches of curly-headed white plaster innocence, in a nightgown, his hands in the Dürer position of prayer, kneeling on a low stool or hassock, with ten bare little toes peeping from the drapery behind. Ugh! Wonderfully vulnerable and breakable: excellently suitable for an angry aunt, in the house of a hated host, to sweep off a mantelpiece. Here, in the archive, on a shelf, it is, three dimensional and intact.

Other portable properties on that shelf are two heavy copper book-ends (or perhaps door-stoppers) representing a dachshund puppy chewing the binding of a book; a porcelain cow-creamer with the animal's left horn broken – perhaps modern Dutch? Uncle Tom Travers and Sir Watkyn Bassett would know; a small glass cocktail shaker with silver lid which, properly filled with gin, vermouth and ice, would make two big, strong, dry martinis such as Plum and Ethel liked before their supper (6 pm: their Polish cook drove herself off at 6.15 sharp) in Remsenburg; and a wooden tobacco jar. Under its top is screwed a round of what looks like hardened white chalk ('AZTEC US Pat. Off.'), and, cut into its outer ring, 'WHEN COLOR FADES ADD COLD WATER'. I take it that this in its day was a method of keeping the tobacco in its jar moist. But I don't know what the moisture-retaining gimmick was. In my day (tobacco jar with College crest on mantelpiece) we put bits of orange peel in to moisten the contents. Any suggestions on how Plum's earlier, American method worked?

There is an excellent forty-one-page typescript inventory, or *Catalogue Raisonné* of the archive by the professional archivist, Kristin Thompson, that gives the categories of the books she has sorted and shelved, and of the contents of the thirty box files of letters and documents; letters to Plum, letters from Plum – hundreds of each; letters about Plum; letters from and to members of Plum's family.

'A soldier has fallen asleep on my shoulder, and I must come to some arrangement with him . . .'

This is the ending of a long handwritten letter to Denis Mackail from Leonora Cazalet, daughter of Ethel by a previous marriage, and adopted 'Wodehouse' by Plum. She had been sitting wedged in a troop train somewhere in England in 1942, shortly before her utterly unexpected death in hospital in her thirties. Plum had had high hopes for Leonora as a writer, and, if he ever saw this letter, he must have been delighted, as I was, by the understatement of the second half of the sentence quoted from it. Many of Leonora's letters, to 'Plummie' and others, are in the archive, in addition to the many of Plummie's to her – 'Snorky' as she was known in the family.

Being personal and selfish, picking and choosing, I find, framed, a letter I myself wrote, to *The Times* in June 1980. Knowing James Heineman, rabid collector of Wodehouse material and Trustee of the The Pierpont Morgan Library in New York, and knowing his and the Library's plans for the Wodehouse centenary (they call it centennial in America) exhibition, I had asked, in this letter to *The Times*, if anybody knew the whereabouts of interesting Wodehousiana that would suit this exhibition. And I instanced the original artwork of the Low portrait of Plum in that series in the *New Statesman* in the 1930s. (We still can't locate it, in 1990.) I asked about the original of the lyric that Plum wrote for the song 'Bill' that was one of the hits of *Showboat*. It hasn't turned up yet, either. I also asked about the striped golf umbrella, the first and only trophy Plum had won at golf 'in a hotel tournament at Aiken, South Carolina, where, hitting them squarely on the meat for once, I went through a field of some of the fattest retired business men in America like a devouring flame'.

177

I had put that item into my suggestions because I had recently been reading it in the introduction Plum had written to a collected edition of his golf stories. It came fresh into my typewriter and the letter to *The Times*. But the umbrella was found, and it is there, in the archive, leaning up against the wall in a corner, alongside an old wood-shafted putter which had somehow survived extra decades of use as a walking stick. There is, too, on the nearby shelf, a proper walking stick, showing multiple tooth-marks of dogs who had been allowed to carry it and wrestle for it and chew it. With the walking stick is a dreadful old grey Trilby hat, without a lining or even the leather sweat-band inside.

When I accepted to write, for Messrs Herbert Jenkins, the book eventually titled *Wodehouse at Work*, Plum mentioned two old friends of his in England who might be able to give me background material: Bill Townend and Denis Mackail. 'Who in hell is Richard Usborne?' wrote Townend to Plum in a letter dated 21 May 1952. But after Derek Grimsdick of Herbert Jenkins introduced us and gave us lunch, Townend was enormously helpful to me in letters. (He was rather deaf and he seldom came to London.)

I duly sought audience with Mackail in his flat at Burton Court, which he shared with a very old and friendly Pekinese. It must have been shortly after Christmas, because I remember Mackail gave me Christmas cake (cake was a rare treat – all its ingredients were rationed in those days) for tea. And I fleeted his time pertinaceously with a string of questions. Mackail was one of only two people I ever met who had heard Plum's voice delivering one of the five talks on the German short-wave to America at about 4.30 am English time.

Not all Mackail's letters to Plum have survived. All Plum's letters to Mackail – 110 of them – are safely in the archive. There is much interesting gossip – writer to writer – about mutual friends and acquaintances, about their books, about plays, about actors and actresses. (All theatre critics, especially Bernard Shaw and Max Beerbohm, get Plum's thumbs-down.) And yes, A.A. Milne.

Plum and Milne had been on terms of less-than-bosom friendship before the war, but Plum had always enjoyed – and

178

continued to enjoy – Milne's books and plays. In 1933 Milne
had inscribed his book *Four Days Wonder*:

> To Plum
> As welcome as the dews that wake
> Each morn the drooping salpiglossis,
> As soothing as a pound of steak
> On battered eye or bruised proboscis,
> As warm as in a shower of sleet
> The comfort of a 'lifted' brolly
> So, to the undersigned, so sweet
> Your liking for his Four Days folly.
>
> A.A.M.

But Plum was always conscious of a streak of jealousy in Milne.
And, when Plum was in the pillory for those broadcasts he
made, in all innocence and stupidity, from Berlin in 1941,
Milne wrote a clever, nasty, snide letter about his 'old friend' to
the *Daily Telegraph*. Plum eventually came to understand the
impulse behind the vulgar philippic that William (later Sir
William, 'Cassandra' of the *Daily Mirror*) Connor spat at him in
BBC radio prime time – it had been a put-up, political
counter-propaganda job, though none the less nauseating for
that. And he and Connor became 'Plum' and 'Bill' after the
war. But Plum was not so accommodating about Milne. In his
post-war novel *The Mating Season*, and a golf story, 'Rodney has
a Relapse' (*Nothing Serious*), Plum mocks Milne's Christopher
Robin stuff hilariously. But in his letters, to Mackail and indeed
Townend, he expressed himself less than charitably about the
'old friend' who had been so quick to heave a brick at him in the
stocks.

The boxes of letters and documents are piled neatly on
shelves in the inner sanctum of the archive. You enter it up
some steps, and with bowed head (as Plum's 'Mustard' Pott at
Blandings, counting £10 notes that he had won off Lord Bosham
at 'Persian Monarchs'). The ceiling of this little bothy is only
5ft. 4ins. from its floor, and there are lights in it which would be
the first to stun the unwary. Sit down in the big armchair, and
you will be within reach of books in the shelves on either side:
books, his own, that he had inscribed, books inscribed or

dedicated to him by other authors. Also his re-bound *Bartlett's Quotations* (1891, 9th edition). Ten quotations in it are marked in pencil, and I recognised four – three from Shakespeare and one from Coleridge – recurrent in Plum's Wooster/Jeeves novels and stories. One other that he has marked is from Tennyson's 'Princess':

> A rosebud set with little wilful thorns
> And sweet as English air could make her, she . . .

Doesn't that nicely sum up Plum's hell-raising young heroines – Bobbie, Corky, Stiffy, even Lottie, though Lottie was Hoboken Irish, wasn't she?

And here's the *The Complete Works* of Shakespeare (Shakespeare Head Press, 1934) which Plum had taken with him – his only book – when he packed to follow the German sergeant. They were off to the van which waited to take Le Touquet's British enemy aliens to rally, with suitcases, at the Commandant's place in the town. I expected to find this Shakespeare full of markings. Plum has said that he read it from cover to cover in Tost, and the whole corpus every two or three years since. But this book is curiously *un*marked. He kept a diary of dates in it at the back, subtitled 'One Man's War', from 'Arrival at Loos Prison July 21st 1940 9 pm' '1st week, 2nd week' and so on, to 'Released June 21st 1941'. It reminds one of the charts one used to keep at boarding school – so many days to the end of term, each day crossed off, 'a day's march nearer home'. The cover of Plum's Shakespeare is rather tattered, and the first eighteen pages of prelims are missing, perhaps used as cigarette papers. But it doesn't feel as though Plum had read this particular volume through much. He had marked the Sonnets. If X is a mark of excellence in his opinion, then he marks as excellent each of four of the Sonnets: 'When forty winters shall besiege thy brow', 'When I consider everything that grows', 'To me, fair friend, you never can be old' and 'Let me not to the marriage of true minds'. He gives XX to three: 'Shall I compare thee to a summer's day?', 'When to the sessions of sweet silent thought' and 'Full many a glorious morning have I seen'. Bertie Wooster botches this last memorably, but I can't remember where.

180

There is a large collection of Townend's letters to Plum in the archive. (*Performing Flea* is Plum's letters – parts of them – to Townend.) Plum and Bill Townend had been at Dulwich together and shared a study. And Plum had written often and at length advising the hard-working but unsuccessful novelist and short-story writer Bill about his career. Not mentioned in *Performing Flea*, but to Townend's eternal and outspoken gratitude – for instance in his letters to me – Plum was always smuggling money to Bill. 'Smuggling', because Ethel was in charge of the Wodehouse finances and overt payments to Bill from the joint Wodehouse account would have provoked strong curtain-lectures.

Bill's letters to Plum did not cease when Bill and his Rene died in the early 1960s. In 1968 or '69 a medium wrote to Plum to say that she was getting messages for him, via someone named 'Uvani', from his old friend 'on the other side'. Should she transcribe the messages and send them on? Plum had said 'Yes', and the messages arrived. Cheerful letters: Bill and Rene were blissfully happy, well and young. No more toil, worry or illness. 'Rene looks wonderful and says that I do too. We have a house with a lovely garden.' 'Yes, old friends do meet again,' 'Yes, dogs and other pets find their old owners.' On smoking – 'the wish to smoke would not be likely to remain, but while you want to smoke you can have all the sensations of doing so.' 'There is swimming, and concerts to go to with marvellous music!' 'Dear old Plum, when you come, you will find your devolvement into a state of great happiness to be easy and quick. You have been so kind and cheerful – a giver of joy in your life and writing. You will go on writing here if you want to. There are many of us waiting to enjoy what you write. You will revel in this "life". You will not be bothered by that horrible arthritis of yours. You were so kind to Rene and me – we long to have you and Ethel – give her our love – with us again.' 'I believe if there are any questions you want answered, I might be able to tell you what you want to know.'

In the aggregate these 'letters' seem more than clever fakes. I wonder what Plum thought of them. He had become interested in spiritualism at a period when Conan Doyle, his hero, whom he read hungrily, had once interviewed and played cricket with several times, was advocating it as a subject worthy of faith and research. There are more than fifty books in the shelves marked *Religion, Philosophy, Spiritualism* in the archive. It may be relevant to remember that Plum's admired older brother Armine became a theosophist.

In a book, *The Wisdom of the Gods*, by H. Dennis Bradley (1925), there are descriptions of three of Bradley's séances at which Plum had been a guest – two of them with Leonora – in 1923, '24 and '25. At the third the actress Fay Compton and her husband Leon Quartermaine had been fellow séantists. No very significant messages came for Plum or Leonora, but the fact that he went three times is interesting. Fay Compton had been starring in London in Barrie's play, *Mary Rose*, a heart-stopper, full of psychic, ghostly meaning and effects.

Eight or nine feet of shelf space in the archive are given to books dedicated in print or inscribed by hand to Plum by author friends and admirers. Agatha Christie's *By the Pricking of my Thumbs* (1968) is inscribed 'To P.G. Wodehouse with reverence, admiration and many long years of deeply enjoyed writing. No one like you!' Her *Halloween Party*, the year after, is dedicated 'To P.G. Wodehouse, whose books and stories have brightened my life for many years. Also, to show my pleasure in his having been kind enough to tell me how much he enjoys my books.' Leslie Charteris's *Getaway* (1932) is dedicated 'To P.G. Wodehouse who had time to say a word for the Saint stories when he could have written them so much better himself.'

Books inscribed include five from Anthony Powell, three from Evelyn Waugh – one of the War Trilogy 'For P.G. Wodehouse, D. Litt., the head of my profession, from Evelyn Waugh 1961'. Two of Bill Townend's books are inscribed 'To P.G.W. from W.T.', a third, in jest, 'To P.G. Wodehouse from G. Bernard Shaw'. Tom Sharpe inscribed his *Porterhouse Blue* (1974) 'To Plum, in appreciation of all the help you have given me'. Leo Rosten inscribed his *The Return of H*Y*M*A*N K*A*P*L*A*N* (1959) 'To Plum and Ethel with love from Leo Rosten and Zimi' and Rosten's earlier *Captain Newman M.D.* (1956) is inscribed 'For the P.G. Wodehouses, because he is, dash it all, but I mean, don't you know, old chap, a most wonderful writer and surely the funniest of our time'. Ogden Nash inscribed his *Marriage Lines* (1964) 'For the winner, and still the champion, with many years of admiration and gratitude'. Compton Mackenzie's *Poor Relations* (1919) is inscribed 'With blessings to you, dear Plummie'. Robert Graves wrote in his *Operation Author* (1969) 'To P.G. Wodehouse, with a lifetime of thanks'. Hilaire Belloc inscribed his *The Postmaster General* (1932) 'To P.G. Wodehouse. *Faber fabro*' (craftsman to craftsman).

Robert Birley had been a Wodehouse fan long before he went to Eton as a junior master. He told Plum in a letter that he had then been admitted instantly into Provost Monty James's friendship by producing a buried and obscure quotation from Wodehouse into a conversation. When Birley returned to Eton as headmaster, and by that time an expert on precious *incunabula*, he used to do a lot of his thinking and worrying in the College library, often in the small hours. He wrote, and published in pamphlet form, a list of what he considered the one hundred manuscripts and printed books of greatest importance in the Eton Libraries, and of course he included its Gutenberg Bible, Number 17. This had been given to the school by John Fuller of Rosehill (died 1831), 'the last Member to be imprisoned by the House of Commons for defying the Speaker'. When he sent a copy of the pamphlet to Plum in 1970, Birley's inscription was 'Mr. P.G. Wodehouse, from the author, a devoted admirer of his works, with special reference to No. 17'.

The tale that thereby hangs is this. In Birley's learned half-page annotation on the provenance and importance of this great incunable – the first book printed from movable type – he had added 'To the recorded 48 copies of the Gutenberg Bible should be added one in the library of Blandings Castle in Shropshire.' In the first Blandings book, *Something Fresh* (1915), you may remember that Lord Emsworth had a muddled museum in the castle, 'an amateur junk-shop' never again mentioned in any of the near-dozen subsequent Blandings books. The museum contained many trivia, such as 'a bullet from the field of Waterloo, one of an assignment of ten thousand shipped there for the use of tourists by a Birmingham firm'. There was also the Gutenberg Bible. A letter from Birley to 'Mr Wodehouse', accompanying a copy of the booklet, said, about this one (alleged) at Blandings Castle, 'I am very hopeful that some German professor will write to me asking what he should do to inspect the book. I shall, of course, suggest to him that he catches the 11.18 or the 2.33 train from Paddington Station for Market Blandings, having secured a room at the Emsworth Arms Hotel and making use of the services of Mr. Jno. Robinson and his station taxicab.'

In the event, the great international book-dealer, the late H.P. Kraus, took the bait. He asked Maggs, the equally prestigious book-dealer in Berkeley Square, to find out about this 'new' Gutenberg. And Maggs explained to Kraus politely that it was a joke. Birley, lecturing in New York a year or so later, was told that Mr Kraus would very much like to meet him, and he steeled himself nervously for harsh words. On the contrary, Kraus was all smiles and thought it a very good joke. In the 1960s Kraus had offered for sale, for £1 million, what he had thought was the only and last Gutenberg Bible still in private hands.

Within reach of the armchair in the sanctum are books from Plum's Remsenburg shelves in which he had marked passages or scribbled remarks in pencil. Occasionally these markings suggest that Plum had found an idea for a plot, or a plot-twist, or a shape for a new hyperbole or 'nifty'. But his scribble on the fly-leaf of his copy of H.G. Wells's *Select Conversations with an Uncle* is what looks like American stock-market quotations: 'Radio 100, B. Steel 109½, Pullman 82⅜, West[?inghouse] 148, G[eneral] M[otors] 85½, E.C.L. and Power 63¼, F.P. 64½, C.P. 234¼, Pub Serv of Jersey 79½'. From those prices it would be an interesting puzzle to work out what the year and day was when Plum had jotted this list down.

And here I need help. In his copy of J.B. Booth's *Pitcher in Paradise* (Plum's character Galahad Threepwood had stepped fully formed out of Booth's books), among the markings is one which gives 'the linnet's rough song: "*Tolic gow-gow, tolic joey-fair, tolic hickey-gee, tolic equay-quake, tuc-tuc-whizzie, equay-quake-a-week, tuc-tuc-weet*".' Now somewhere, I know, Plum puts these poignant syllables into the mouth of a character, in a novel or short story, who specialised in bird songs and bird impressions. I thought it would surely be Wilmot Mulliner in Hollywood. He knew all about the cuckoo's call, and risked his job as Nodder to Mr Schnellenhamer and Mr Levitsky by insisting that they get it right in their films. But I can't find it in that story. Where does it come, please? On a post-card.

I must read more of George Ade. He is new to me. A slim volume of his here in the archive seems to have impressed Plum, and may have sharpened his facility for manufacturing his images and hyperboles. For instance, in George Ade's *Knocking the Neighbours* (1911), a hangover that might have called for Jeeves's mixture double-strength:

> He had a temperature of 102 and his ears were hanging down. Also, during the period of coma, someone had extracted his eyes and substituted two hot doorknobs.

A fat man:

> His general contours suggested that possibly he had just swallowed a full-sized water-melon without slicing it up.

Love:

> He looked deep into her eyes and began to throb like a motor-boat.

Those could walk into a list of Plum's nuggets and no questions asked. A letter in the archive, from the same George Ade in 1937, puts Plum first in a list of humorous writers, a list that includes Harry Leon Wilson, author of *Ruggles of Red Gap*, and Damon Runyon.

A Year that the Locust. . . (1935) is a mixture of diary and essays by A.S.M. Hutchinson, who wrote that smash-hit of my boyhood, *If Winter Comes*. Plum has written on the title page of his copy a list of the characters that went into his *Cocktail Time* (1938) – 'Hero, Heroine, Uncle Fred, Sir Raymond Bastable, Oily Carlisle, Cosmo Ford, Butler, Phoebe, Nannie'. Hutchinson himself, in a three-page encomium of Plum that Plum had sidelined, wrote, under the date 2 May:

> Wodehouse Day. Read the better part of his new one, *Blandings Castle*, and went to bed with all my lines and wrinkles smoothed out . . . I wish some reviewer would

185

occasionally take the trouble to explain his art to the public . . . He gets his effects in no degree by what he writes of but solely how he writes it. His humour is never humour of situation, always it is humour of phrase. His characters are all impossible people. It is their speech that makes them more than possible – sublime. And that is genius.

Nice praise, Hutchinson. But no 'humour of situation'? Gussie at the Market Snodsbury prize-giving? Lord Ickenham at Mitching Hill in 'Uncle Fred Flits By'? The air-gunning of the Efficient Baxter? The headmaster and the bishop painting the statue in the school close? Oh, come, Hutchinson!

And yes, here's Colette. On the only occasion that I met Plum, shortly before his ninetieth birthday, I remember noting in his study shelves a surprising (to me) number of Colette's books, in French, in the old French fall-apart, soft-back style. I had forgotten to ask him then what his connection with her books had been – in French too. I remembered later that he had written to Bill Townend about her, in *Performing Flea* or the letters from which *Performing Flea* had been hewn. He was in New York, in the 1950s, and America was not buying his stuff. He was still under a cloud with editors for those 1941 broadcasts. The *Saturday Evening Post* had for years before the war regularly bought, and for highest prices, his short stories, and his novels for serialisation. Now it turned its back on his agent. The editor wouldn't even read the stories sent to him if the by-line was P.G. Wodehouse. And the sales of his books were sadly low too. Plum wrote to Townend, perhaps half seriously, that he was thinking of writing stories under a new name, and he was remembering how Willy, Colette's first husband, had run a stable of writers, including Colette, writing books that he set them, and issuing them with his own name, as author or part-author, on their spines. Plum was thinking wistfully of doing it the other way round – putting another name – or other names – on books he would himself now write in one or more different styles.

Here now in the archive are seven early books by Colette, and two of them Plum had clearly read as exercises to improve his French. Colette is by no means easy for the foreign learner. She has a very wide vocabulary, much greater than most

French popular writers. She uses unguessable technical words that you can't skip – *mots justes* that floor you – birds, flowers, moods of people, cats, dogs and weather. Plum had worked through all 217 pages of *Mes Apprentissages* and 131 pages of *Claudine à Paris*, writing in the meanings of hard words he had looked up in the dictionary, like a schoolboy. He had had lessons in French at Le Touquet and could read it easily (barring the difficult words, as in Colette) and speak it adequately if he was forced to. But he said it tired him mightily to speak it for any length of time at a stretch. On the end-papers of *Mes Apprentissages* he had pencilled a list of his characters in *The Mating Season*.

In Agatha Christie's *There Is a Tide* (1948) Plum has scribbled a few lines of dialogue which come in his posthumous and unfinished novel, published by Chatto and Windus as such and titled *Sunset at Blandings*. He had been working on it in hospital to the day he died. The bit of dialogue is:

–Helping him rally the forwards on the game . . .
–I wasn't in the rugger team
–Well, sitting side by side in the school chapel, listening to the Chaplain's short, manly sermon. Anyway, doing something together. . . ?

Remember it? Well, look it up. It's Galahad speaking to the Claude character in Chapter 8. In Plum's later typescript he had tightened up the wording, but the passage is easily recognisable.

Ah, now here's a book with the printed sticker

From the Library
of P.G. Wodehouse

but clearly it belonged to Plum's friend Guy Bolton. The book is *The Cat who Could Read Backwards* by Lilian Jackson Bronson. Written in it is a snatch of dialogue in a handwriting that I can recognise as Guy's. And I can recognise that this snatch of dialogue pencilled in is from one of the last plays he wrote, *My Darling Clementine*, about Churchill and his wife. The play had been a success here and there in the English provinces and

South Africa, but it never got to the West End, and wasn't bought for the movies.

All Plum's own books – the ones he wrote – are on the archive shelves in various editions. Well, perhaps not all. I didn't check. Probably not his very rare *By the Way Book*, of 1908. It is a selection of paragraphs and verses that Plum and his on-and-off friend Herbert Westbrook contributed for years to the 'By the Way' column in the pink London evening paper, the *Globe*. (Westbrook was largely a prototype of Ukridge. Westbrook used to steal Plum's clothes. It must have been some compensation to Plum that he was able to steal Westbrook himself for Ukridge.) James Heineman has a copy and he, with permission and with the Sceptre Press Ltd. in 1985, had a facsimile made, with the same W.K. Haselden illustrations. The original is a rarer book than the Gutenberg Bible.

Plum occasionally gave copies of his own books to strangers who had written nice letters to him, or had sent him their copies of his books to sign. Some of such are in the archive. I found two similarly inscribed by him:

> You like my little stories do yah?
> Oh, glory glory alleluia!
> P.G. Wodehouse

and almost all the books that Plum owned at the time of his death have here found safe transfer to the archive. More than 3,000 by my rough computation. Two notable sets – the complete Tolstoi (in English) in fifteen volumes, and the complete Balzac (in English) in thirteen. Twenty-one books by Barry Pain. I wish I had read more of him. Plum told me that he read everything by him and felt that he had learnt much of his craft from him. Barry Pain's 'Two', a school story, had appeared in the first number of *Chums* (1892, Plum thought, when he was eleven) and it later became a book, *Graeme and Cyril*. Plum had written to me in 1955:

> It made an enormous impression on me. It had practically no plot but the atmosphere was wonderful. I was re-reading it only the other day and it's great stuff.

Plum's copy of *Ruggles of Red Gap*, by Henry Leon Wilson, is on the shelf of books that Plum had marked. He had told me, when I was preparing *Wodehouse at Work*, that he had read *Ruggles* first, serialised in the *Saturday Evening Post*, in 1914 – the story by and of an Englishman's valet handed over to an American in payment of a poker debt. Plum had liked it very much, but he felt that Wilson had got the English valet all wrong. (Do you remember Charles Laughton in the Hollywood film of it, and his reciting of Lincoln's Gettysburg speech at the end?) For instance, he said, no English manservant would have been so docile about his transfer. Well, what about those English butlers supreme, Blizzard and Vosper, in the stories 'High Stakes' and 'Keeping in with Vosper', in Plum's *Golf Omnibus*? And Jeeves himself was subject to transfer once or twice, wasn't he? Plum told me that he thought *Ruggles of Red Gap* might have seeded the idea of Jeeves in his mind. Plum had been in New York when Jeeves first appeared in print, albeit then in only a couple of lines.

Two more items that I found in the archive: one a telegram of more than a hundred words from Gerald Ford, then President, at the White House, Washington, to Plum's widow, Ethel, when Plum died. The other is a long and amusing letter to Plum from Richard Burton after he and Elizabeth Taylor had discovered that her longtime friend Sheran (Lady) Hornby was the granddaughter of their favourite writer (see the Preface).

When the Queen Mother unveiled the plaque on the house in Mayfair where the Wodehouses had lived in the 1920s and '30s, she mentioned that Plum had dedicated his first novel, *The Pothunters* (1902), to three cousins of hers, Joan, Effie and Ernestine Bowes-Lyon. I remembered that there had been a lot of entries about these three sisters in those notebooks that Plum had kept in his apprentice years before World War I.

Plum, working in London and a very young Old Alleynian, may have been a paid tutor to – he clearly had an avuncular relationship with – this Bowes-Lyon family, and he used to scribble down in notebooks things the girls said and did. In 1902, when *The Pothunters* was published, the sisters' ages were Joan thirteen, Effie twelve and Ernestine (Teenie) ten. But the notes cover the four or five later years. Plum described to the girls' mother his own position in the family (and noted it down):

189

I occupy in your house a position equivalent to that of cold beef at lunch. If there is nobody more exciting, the cold beef is welcomed. If there is nobody new to talk to, the Lyon cubs talk to me.

Joan:

'The worst nightmare I ever had is when I dream I am being kicked by a cow. And then it always turns into Chamberlain or somebody.'

Joan buys opera glasses and spends hours at the window of the schoolroom scanning the square to see the guardsman opposite come out of his house in uniform.

Effie:

'My dear, can't I work and talk too, you ass?' (that was to Plum)

'Don't be noxious and repugnant!'

'How d'you think Adam shaved himself? There were no razors and he's always pictured clean-shaven.'

'People with red beards are always restless. They are always wanting to get away from their beards.'

'Marry a plain girl, because they are always nice. In my experience pretty girls are never nice.'

'I would marry a rich man, however much of a beast he is, simply to get a horse.'

'Wolsey was such a *smug*!'

'A gannet is a sort of other duck.'

'I like Henry VIII much better than Henry VII. H.7 was such a grasping, avaricious man. H.8 was nice and bluff. I mean to have ten husbands when I grow up.'

To Teenie after reading *Macbeth*: 'You young fry of treachery!'

Teenie:

'I've got £25 in the Bank. When I come of age, I'm going to buy a HAT!'

190

'If you're feeling very full, lean back and draw yourself up very high, and you'll find lots of room for more.'

Of a sentimental poem, 'a beastly lovery poem'.

'Oh, he's absolutely off his dot!'

'Men with moustaches are always the nicest.'

Many of Plum's contemporaries (eg A.A. Milne and Ian Hay) wrote about cute little girls of governessable age saying cute things in fractured English. *Punch* of the pre-World War I period was full of them. Plum didn't make any published use of the notes he took on the Bowes-Lyon cubs, as far as I know. But I think, and hope, that Effie, Teenie and Joan grew up to be Stiffies, Bobbies and Corkies rather than Florences, Madelines and Gertrudes.

14
A Voice from a Watery Grave

It is clear, from the many books in his library on spiritualism and kindred subjects, that Plum had a more than sketchy interest in these matters. He might have been intrigued, therefore, to read of the 'spirit' of someone who must have been a paternal great-uncle of his.

One result of the ghastly casualties in the First World War was a widening practice of do-it-yourself, experimental spiritualism in England, and doubtless in France, Germany and other countries involved. Spirits of the dead speaking to the living – it was nothing new – older than the Old Testament. The Oxford Dictionary gives 1853 for the first use of the word 'medium' as 'a person supposed to be the organ of communication from departed spirits'.

We go now to 1916, 7 December, and into a sitting room in Oxford. Two ladies were trying to work the oracle. One of them was Gertrude, a daughter (one of seven, blonde and beautiful) of A.L. Smith, then Master of Balliol. Gertrude was married to Harold Hartley, a Balliol scientist, who had, incidentally, been in the Sixth at Dulwich with Plum. Gertrude's friend and fellow séantist that day was Bessie (Lady) Gorell. Bessie Gorell fancied herself, perhaps rightly, as something of a medium.

There were various methods of evoking the spirits, all of them more likely to succeed if the lights were low and the curtains drawn. Spirits could be contacted directly through the medium, who spoke to the spirits and got messages out of them which he, or more often she, relayed in her own or facsimile voice. Or by table turning – joining fingers on a table-top in a ring and then finding that the table was rocking: once for A, twice for B and so on, till it had rocked out a message. (A quicker method was to ask only questions to be answered Yes or No. Then one knock meant Yes, two No.) Or through a wine glass upturned on a smooth table-top inside a ring of all the letters of the alphabet. The glass was expected to move round the ring and touch letters that spelt out a message. Another method was automatic writing – you held a pencil ready to write on a piece of white paper and then, if the spell was working, you found your hand and pencil moving to write a message. Or the so-called ouija-board or planchette. I seem to remember it as a heart-shaped piece of plywood with a pencil stuck in a hole at the sharp end, with small wheels to let the board travel on the paper – and again, with your hand on the board, it would, or might, spell out messages. I remember myself thinking that the ouija board that I had made in carpentry class at my prep-school might be discouraging the spirit, and I bought a proper one from Gamages. My brothers and our mother tried all the methods – more as a party game than in urgent need to know anything more vital than the horse to back for the Derby – but no spirits came up from the vasty deep for us. They did for Bessie Gorell and Gertrude Hartley on 7 December 1916. Gertrude wrote it all down afterwards, and her account turned up recently in the papers of the family. It was passed on to me by a friend of mine whose mother had been another of the seven Smith girls.

Bessie Gorrell and Gertrude Hartley had, between them, brought into play one Arthur Darbyshire, who had died the year before, 1915. He had been at Balliol in that special vintage that had gone up to the College in the last years of the nineteenth century and got blown to pieces, most of them, in the four years of trench warfare that lay in wait for them. Raymond Asquith, son of the prime minister, was killed in 1916. He had been the acknowledged guiding star of that Balliol galaxy, but Arthur Darbyshire was always spoken of with great affection as one of the brightest among the rest.

Gertrude Hartley wrote that she and Bessie had tried the wine-glass method, but the glass had pushed the letters off the table. Then Arthur Darbyshire came through, in handwriting. He said:

That slow old game! I used to like it, but not from here, thank you. I want to introduce a man I have met here. He is not very happy because after doing some fine things in his life he

193

did a mean thing at the very end. He makes himself miserable now among many who after a very ordinary life come up to the scratch at the last. He is very interested in this. He is here waiting.

(change of handwriting)

Fear led me to do a very evil thing. I cannot forgive myself: it is not what the world thought: I have missed my chance.

Now Bessie and Gertrude question the newcomer.

What is your name?	Wodehouse. I was here many years ago.
At Balliol?	No, at Exeter College.
When did you die?	I died about . . . so long ago. I think about 50 years.
Did we pass your grave this afternoon in Holywell?	I have no grave.
Did you die in battle then?	No, had I died fighting I should be happier now.
Have you been unhappy then for 50 years?	No, but since I have seen so many splendid deaths, I remember.
What is your name?	Wodehouse. James Wodehouse.
What did you do?	It did not succeed, but I would have saved myself at the expense of another. Intentions are everything. Neither of us escaped.
Escaped what?	Death.
How did you meet Darbyshire?	In the field of battle I saw him die, and since have seen him help others to die.
(We tried to comfort him)	Yes, that is what he says, to come and help, not to be stopped by things which were passed 50 years ago, but I stand by full of regret. I taught others, myself I could not teach.

(Again we tried to comfort him)	That is what he says.
What was your work here?	I taught the Word.
A clergyman?	Yes.
Where was your work?	The name has gone. It was very far away.
Were you married?	Alas.
Can we do anything for you?	I have only just begun to realise what I did. Help me by prayer, it is everything.
Tell us where you died	*(Written very faintly)* London.

The rest of the story is in Gertrude Hartley's voice, handwriting and persona.

'We discussed this case a good deal. "London" puzzled us, as he said he had no grave. My father inspected the register of Exeter Honours men, but could not find James Wodehouse. Then, today, December 15, the Bursar of Exeter sent the following particulars from the College Register.

WODEHOUSE, JAMES. 3rd son of the Hon. and Rev. Thomas Wodehouse (died 1840).

Born Newton, Kent, September 25th 1829.

Matriculated from Exeter College January 28th 1847, aged 17.

In University (rowing) Eight 1849.

BA 1851.

In Orders.

Went to Australia, was lost in the 'London' in the Bay of Biscay, Jan 11th 1866.

From an official account of the disaster:

'The *SS London*, fully rigged as well as equipped with a 200 hp engine built by Humphrey and Tennant of Deptford Green, was launched in 1864. It was designed to cut the time on the voyage between England and Australia, and on its maiden voyage did so, reaching Melbourne in sixty days instead of the clippers' minimum eighty. But it was an uncomfortable voyage, the vessel was sluggish, slow to answer to the helm and too low in the water.

'The *London* sailed from Plymouth on her second outward

voyage on Friday 5 January 1866. She carried 350 tons of railway equipment, and 200 tons of engine coal, and spare spars were stacked on deck. There were 180 passengers, including a number of clergy. As soon as she was out of sight of land six stowaways were found. This, plus sailors' superstitions about a Friday sailing, was regarded as a bad omen by the crew.

'The *London* immediately ran into severe weather. By Tuesday, in the Bay of Biscay, it was blowing a gale, and the Captain decided to return to Plymouth to refit. At 4 am on the 11th a huge green sea rose up to windward on the port side – a flood of water poured into the engine-room and at once extinguished the fires. Most of the lifeboats had been smashed or washed away. Only one was successfully launched, in it sixteen crew and three passengers, who were picked up twenty-four hours later by an Italian barque. All the remainder, 239 women and children, were drowned when the ship sank.'

Postscript

Arthur Darbyshire, according to James Wodehouse, died 'in the field of battle'. In fact he died of meningitis on Boxing Day 1915; in camp.

1916 was fifty years since the London *went down. There may well have been half-centenary articles in the press about the wreck, and these may have, consciously or unconsciously, put thoughts into Bessie Gorell's mind.*

Where, then, does this Rev James Wodehouse fit into the family tree? There was a line of Norfolk baronets starting with an Armine Wodehouse at the end of the seventeenth century. They became barons in the early nineteenth century until John, born 1826, became the Earl of Kimberley (a Norfolk village). The father of the Rev. James Wodehouse who went down with the London *was an Hon. and Rev. and thus, surely, a son of the baron. Plum's father referred to the baronial side of the family as upstarts, his own side as downstarts.*

15
Blithe Spirit

I wrote this obituary for the Sunday Times *three days after Plum died. It told, at some length, the story of the broadcasts he made to neutral America from Berlin in 1941 after being released from the internment camp. It is a story that has been told again since, with variations and additions, in Iain Sproat's* Wodehouse at War, *Frances Donaldson's official biography* P.G. Wodehouse *and my own* Penguin Wodehouse Companion. *I have omitted here several paragraphs about the whole sad, innocent business.*

Once, asked 'How do you get yourself started?', Wodehouse said 'I sit at my typewriter and curse a bit.' In his seventies, eighties and nineties the stuff came less exuberantly, but it was always farcical, fizzy, irreverent and rowdy.

He never preached. He had no message. But he backed young against old, prisoner against magistrate, nephew against aunt, chorus girl against star, curate against bishop, best-selling female novelist against precious pastels-in-prose writer or willowy poet.

He was never a satirist. He was a humorist, a merryman, a jokesmith. A stylist, too. And, incidentally, a great money-maker. The Wodehouse establishment for man, wife and daughter in a Mayfair house in 1934 included a butler, a footman, a chauffeur, a cook, two housemaids, a parlourmaid, a scullerymaid, a chauffeur and a Rolls.

His imagery was fresh, frequent and often wildly funny. And his formulas were good: the most rewarding being the constant reversion of his adults to school-age behaviour. Show a benefactor's statue to a Headmaster and visiting Bishop crony, and, rejuvenated by Buck-U-Uppo, they steal out at midnight to paint it pink. Put a boy's airgun near Lord Emsworth, his sister Connie and Beach the butler, and a force beyond their ken makes them fire it at someone's trouser seat.

What great writer wrote "She directed him to the bed, and he disappeared beneath it like a diving duck"? Who but Wodehouse, pure as the driven snow, if not purer? In his stories a bed was something to hide under, puncture the hot water bottle in or make an apple-pie of. A bedroom scene was when someone had hidden a necklace, a hot manuscript or a policeman's helmet in a drawer and someone else came in to search the place.

He was a marvellous mimic. Re-read the short story 'Honeysuckle Cottage' for the voice of the novelette. Re-read all the Jeeves and Mulliner stories about church affairs for the voice of the pulpit. Wodehouse's mental thesaurus seems to have included all Conan Doyle, school Shakespeare and Tennyson, all the humorous parts of Dickens, all W. S. Gilbert, Mark Twain and Kipling, much detective fiction and acres and acres of tushery-toshery by Victorian headmasters, prelates and sob-sisters.

The scheme of the Jeeves/Bertie story is as of the Holmes/Watson . . . triumph of The Brain narrated by The Bungler. But listen carefully to bungler Bertie's prose burble, a voice which Wodehouse largely invented and virtually patented.

> As I sat in the bath tub, soaping a meditative foot and singing, if I remember correctly, 'Pale Hands I Loved Beside the Shalimar,' it would be deceiving my public to say that I was feeling boomps-a-daisy . . .

Now read that to yourself in a Spike Milligan/Curry-and-Chips voice. The baboo joke in essence is gobbets of poetry, jargon and slang stirred together by someone who has learnt English by reading and writing, not by ear.

Kipling had his baboo-talk in *Kim*. Wodehouse had Ram, the boy from Calcutta, at an English public school in that 1908 serial he wrote for Chums, *The Luck Stone*. Frank Richards had Hurree Singh at Greyfriars. And, most recently, we have had G. V. Desai's H. Hatterr. Bertie Wooster might seem a far cry from these, but you can hear it.

Scholarly Oxford honoured Wodehouse with a Doctorate of Letters in June 1939, and, in that September's *Scrutiny*, Leavis took a swing at Wodehouse and Oxford, sarcastically calling the occasion 'something of a date in cultural history.' (In 1943 a longer *Scrutiny* article on Wodehouse said that his Ukridge was a direct crib of Coker of the Fifth at Greyfriars. In fact Ukridge pre-dated Greyfriars.)

When the Germans swept into Le Touquet on May 22nd 1940, the Wodehouses were there, in the house (flanking the 14th fairway of that golf course in 'the forest') that they had bought in 1935. Why Le Touquet? Because it was virtually English; because it was a short plane-hop to London where Wodehouse had plays running and Dulwich football and cricket matches to watch; because they could take their beloved dogs back and forth from France, without quarantine, to America, where Wodehouse had plays on Broadway and stints in Hollywood. Tax domicile in France had some advantages for a big earner in many currencies. And Ethel liked casinos.

They were over-run in their own home. After some weeks Wodehouse was told to pack a bag. With the golf-pro, the caddy-master, a barman or two, a piano tuner and other British male relics under the age of 60, 58¾-year-old Wodehouse went off, by bus and cattle-truck, via a French prison and two Belgian army barracks, to a lunatic asylum converted to an internment camp in Tost, Upper Silesia (now Poland). Civilian Prisoner Number 786 Wodehouse stayed there till his release (interrupting a game of camp cricket) in mid-June, 1941.

He had been a prisoner for 49 weeks, and there were 15 weeks to go to his 60th birthday – the age at which internees are normally released from lock-up. Word had reached Wodehouse's friends in America that conditions in the camp, shortage of food especially, were telling on Wodehouse's health. A petition, with a flock of important signatures – editors, producers, Senators – had been handed to the German Chargé d'Affaires in Washington. *Post* or *propter*, Wodehouse was offered a chance to broadcast from Berlin shortwave to America (which was not yet in the war). He was glad to, and to be able to say that he had lost 3 stone and was well. The tragedy was that he described so innocently and amusingly, in five talks, his experiences in a durance not all that vile, and that the Nazi Propaganda Department repeated his talks long wave to England. The news here then was grim, from the Atlantic, from Russia and from the Middle East. It was no time for an Englishman to be heard making light of captivity.

It was the work of a moment for English newspapers, and some of his English fellow authors, to jump on Wodehouse's neck with spiked boots. Old Boys turned his picture face to the wall in the pavilion, some librarians and even some literary critics said that his books were no longer funny, and journalists jobbed back and travestied him as having welcomed the Germans who had surrounded his Le Touquet home in 1940 with 'Enter dear old beans! Cocktails coming up!' It was easy money – 20 guineas – for Cassandra (Bill later Sir William Connor) to spit at Wodehouse on BBC radio as a playboy, traitor and quisling. (The BBC Governors hated this to a man, be it said, but Duff Cooper, Minister of Information, had demanded the broadcast and, Cassandra hinted, Churchill wouldn't have taken the BBC's 'No' for an answer.)

For every one person in England who had heard Wodehouse's essentially innocuous broadcasts, short wave or long, from Germany, ten thousand had heard Connor's sneering attack on him in prime time on BBC radio. He never came back to England. He became an American citizen in 1955. There were rumours that he would be back in London for his eightieth birthday, and talk of a big dinner for him at the Garrick. *Punch* tried to get him to come and carve his initials on their table. He said he might come if a projected Blandings Castle musical opened in London. He was much too old to come back for his knighthood.

In a 1925 Jeeves/Bertie story Bertie, in America for a long sojourn of escape from his Aunt Agatha, had said prophetically, "What I mean is . . . much as I like America I don't want to have England barred to me for the rest of my natural."

The innocent stupidity of the Berlin broadcasts does not affect the work Wodehouse left behind him: nearly a hundrd books, plus involvement in 36 plays and 24 films. In his day he was one of the great writers of words to music, and he was much admired by his successors, the American lyric-writers of the post-war musicals. He published more than 300 songs, best known being "My Bill," his words for Jerome Kern's music, from *Showboat*. But it is arguable that Wodehouse might have, in his post-war sixties, been recognised by the millions (and the Palace) for what, in his pre-war fifties, he was known to be by the thousands, and not only at Oxford . . . a giant of English letters. As it is, it has been possible for millions to get by without having to know his books and his stature.

His literary *floruit* spanned a quarter of a century, 1930–1955. But he was writing well for twenty years before that and for nearly twenty years after.